Over a decade ago, I came to know Rob Solberg. He impressed me back then with his searching heart, scholarly mind, and passion for apologetics. He has now offered a masterful work, well researched and very well-argued. Were I still a seminary professor, I would require my students to write reviews on this volume.

Dr. Stephen Drake,
Former Professor of Ministry at Southern Baptist Theological Seminary

Engaging and well-developed content on a tough topic. Rob addresses lofty theological issues with incredible accessibility and application. He reminds us to not just stay in our heads and win arguments but to love people well as we fight for what is true.

Derek Bareman
Lead Pastor, Church of the City Spring Hill

This is an excellent, balanced, scholarly refutation of the heretical teaching of Torahism. Solberg does so with a wide array of Scripture, great Christian writers across the centuries, and impeccable logic. Not only does it address and answer the challenge of this new heresy, it serves as an apologetic in the best tradition of Christian scholarship. Exceptional work. I have reviewed thousands of books in 30 years. This book deserves to be read!

Rev. David "Doc" Kirby (Retired)
Host of the "On The Bookshelf" podcast

Impressively written and researched! Aberrant theologies have existed throughout time, requiring trusted biblical guides to bring much-needed reproof. Solberg does this superbly in his book, Torahism. And, he accomplishes this task with much 'gentleness and respect' (1 Peter 3:15). Even if you are not immediately confronted with this heresy, a careful reading of Rob's book will deepen your understanding of the gospel of Jesus Christ.

Ed Smith, Ph.D.,
President, Williamson College

In the early days of my pastoral ministry, I encountered a group of people at an adult forum my church hosted. As I listened to the instructor, I realized he was denying the Lordship of Jesus Christ and instead making Jesus subservient to the Torah! After that initial encounter, I learned that scores of people from places far and wide had also fallen victim to this type of dangerous teaching. I am so encouraged that Rob has written this important book that boldly confronts this heresy, yet compassionately points the reader toward the truth of Jesus. This is a book that deserves to be read and shared with others.

Thomas S. Kelly
Pastor

I'm glad that the book has been written . . . You don't need to have a Seminary background to understand what is being said here. Solberg writes in simple language and does not use complex terminology. Each chapter is stand alone so you can look at each section that is relevant to what you're talking about and getting it from there. Of course, you could read straight through like I did, but it's not necessary. The information is really easy to find . . . It is always good to see people filling a niche in the apologetics world. A group like the one called Torahism is one that needs some responding to. I am thankful Solberg took the time to answer them and I hope that there will be further expansion on this work.

Nick Peters
Deeper Waters Apologetics

As a Jewish believer, I am asked all the time about the Hebrew Roots movement. I never had a resource to direct people to. Now I do and an excellent resource at that. This book is very thorough and not belittling of their positions but provides great answers to the challenges often raised. This is a must-read!

Andrew Rappaport
Founder/President, Striving for Eternity Ministries

Amazon Reviews from Verified Buyers

Brilliant Book (5 stars)
As someone who has a 25-year history in Torahism (or Hebrew roots as I know it as), I can say that this book is excellent. Well laid out presentation of the errors and false teaching that is spreading amongst Christians today in various degrees. I particularly enjoyed the section about the future temple worldview that many have and the clarification that we must have on the work and person of Yeshua/Jesus. I also loved the different arguments from certain passages in scripture that R. L. Solberg has presented and I had never noticed before. A well written book and a must have for those who have encountered or even are in Torahism. (Wes, U.K.)

Phenomenal book – every Christian should read it! (5 stars)
R. L. Solberg does an incredible job helping the average believer in Christ understand the truth of God's Word regarding the Torah. He uses the Bible to shed light and truth on the main controversial claims of the Hebrew Roots Movement. This book has been a great blessing to me, and I plan on buying copies for all my close friends. Also, check out his YouTube channel - he has some great videos on the same issues. (Riley Shay)

Excellent and Compelling (5 Stars)
A completely readable and accessible book refuting specific Torahist views on biblical Christianity. A necessary resource when speaking to a Torahist . . . In the many examples given in this book, when speaking to a Torahist, their views might seem plausible and even laudable, but as Mr. Solberg concisely and completely points out, are not compatible with the scriptures taken as a whole. Best thing: at no time does the tone of the book's writing denigrate or demean the Torahist. The subject is treated with exceptional kindness and not the all-too-common internet shout down, cancel and insult. This book is even helpful

to those who are not explicitly interested in Torahism because it presents the Christian faith in all its beauty, mystery and joy. (SDAKOTA)

GREAT book on an important issue! (5 stars)
Over the years I have seen non-Jewish Christians join synagogues for the cultural aspects and eventually walk away from Christianity, or at the least, become the source of contention among their Christian friends. If a Christian doesn't have a good understanding of salvation in Christ, and how it relates to the Old Testament, they can fall into believing they must keep the law of Moses. This book does a great job of explaining the issues. It's very practical and easy to understand. If you are an evangelist or apologist, you need this book. (Kick Flipper)

Readable and great scholarship (5 Stars)
I have encountered a few people who adhere to what Solberg calls "Torahism." His assessment of what it is and how to argue against it is incredible. What I appreciated about this book was that it is very readable. You don't have to have a background in theology in order to understand what he is saying. That being said, the concepts and the sophistication of the arguments he puts forward are excellent. Lastly, Solberg's tone and demeanor towards those he is opposing is one of love and respect. Multiple times he states that people with errant views are not our enemies, and we should love them. Lies, false beliefs and bad theology are the enemy that should be opposed. I would highly recommend this book to any Christian who wants to be able to defend their faith against the attacks of Torahism, and do so lovingly and respectfully. (Shereen Lashua)

A Sound, Exegetical, and Biblical Resource (5 stars)
God used R.L. Solberg to write an excellent resource to understand and Biblically refute what he has coined "Torahism." Solberg did not construct a strawman in this book. He even uses actual quotes as "sources" to allow for the Torahists to speak for themselves. Each chapter deals with an aspect of Torahism along with a Biblical comparison. Bottom line, this book is worth every penny. Even if you do not have someone in your life who is heading down the Torah compliant path, the book is an excellent study to understand the relationship of God's Law and the Gospel. (Norman Patterson, Jr.)

Reasoned defense of the faith (5 stars)
Mr. Solberg presents a well-reasoned refutation of a growing movement in Christianity. Unlike so many pundits in today's adversarial climate, he refutes ideology and not people. He gives credit where credit is due and corrects misinterpretations in Christian love. He supports his arguments by allowing scripture to interpret scripture. I look forward to any future offerings by Mr. Solberg. I highly recommend this book to those interested in the appropriate relationship a Christian should have with the Torah and our Jewish roots. (James S.)

A great exegesis of God's Word (5 stars)
In a wonderful step-by-step sound exegesis of Scripture, R.L exposes the false
and dangerously deceptive doctrine that teaches Christians are still under the
law of Moses—the Torah. Good job R.L. Solberg. Keep it up as this heresy
needs to be called out for what it is. (Private Citizen)

Very useful tool (5 stars)
This book has shown the many aspects in which the Hebrew Roots
Movement has erred while explaining various orthodox Christian doctrines
and beliefs that are sometimes difficult to express. (Jorge L. Viramontes)

Informative and Captivating! (5 stars)
This book gave me great insight into Torahism, which is something I knew
nothing about. I appreciated the explanation of this different perspective on
the Bible. Also, I enjoyed this book as a great work on the apologetics of the
Christian faith. It is well worth the read on both accounts. I was encouraged in
my own beliefs! (Amazon Customer)

Great Read (5 stars)
R.L. Solberg does a great job in diving deep into the theological errors of
Torahism, while maintaining a spirit of Christian charitableness and
thoughtfulness to those within the movement. Easy to read, many scriptural
references, I would highly recommend this book for anyone seeking to
examine or refute the errors of Torahism. (Bryan Scharf)

TORAHISM

*Are Christians Required
to Keep the Law of Moses?*

R. L. SOLBERG

WILLIAMSON
COLLEGE
PRESS

Unless otherwise noted, all cited Bible verses are from the English Standard Version (ESV) translation (Wheaton, IL: Crossway Bibles, 2016). Used by permission. All rights reserved worldwide.)

Cover Image: Ten Commandments illustration @gldburger/iStockPhoto

ISBN: 978-1-7336721-5-3 Paperback
ISBN: 978-1-7336721-7-7 Hard Cover
Edition 2.1

RLSolberg.com
Defending the Biblical Roots of Christianity (YouTube)

Williamson College Press
274 Mallory Station Road,
Franklin, Tennessee 37067
williamsoncc.edu

Table of Contents

Preface

You hold in your hands a revised and expanded second edition of a book I never thought I would write in the first place. As a theologian and Christian apologist, my area of interest was always at the intersection of science and God, atheism and faith. I was busy exploring the metaphysical and theological grounds of Christian truth claims when, one day, I stumbled into the world of Torah-observant Christianity. I say "stumbled," but there was nothing accidental about it from God's perspective. This was a divine appointment.

In the three years since *Torahism* was released, I have only fallen more in love with the biblical and historical roots of the Christian faith. And my understanding of the passions, arguments, and dangers put forward by Torah-observant Christians has grown as well. I now hear from people daily whose marriages, families, or friendships are suffering—or in some cases, were destroyed—because of Torahism.

I have also come across new and better arguments and been exposed to more reasonable positions from both Torah-observant Christians and Messianic Jews. As a result, I have developed stronger and more nuanced responses. My thinking and understanding have also evolved in a few areas. I remain convinced that Gentile Christians are not required to keep the Law of Moses. And I've developed a biblical framework that lends clarity to that position. Yet, in the pages of Scripture, I've also discovered more room for grace between Torahism and mainstream Christianity.

Whether you are a Torah-observant Christian or have someone in your life who is, I pray you find this new edition helpful. And as always, if you have a story to share or a question to ask, I would love to hear from you.

R. L. Solberg

Acknowledgments

Back when I made my living as a musician, I remember being envious of authors because they didn't need bandmates, producers, or sound engineers to create their art. I thought they could just sit all by themselves in a room and create, no collaboration required.

Boy, was I wrong.

The process of writing my first book has taught me how critical collaboration is to the discipline of writing. God has blessed me with a collection of friends and mentors who were willing to selflessly volunteer a great deal of their time to read my manuscript and share their feedback. This informal "book review panel" was made up of pastors, educators, a musician, and a lawyer; each one of them wise and godly. I want to extend a heartfelt *thank you* to my "bandmates"—Dr. Stephen Drake, Carli Smith, David "Doc" Kirby, and my parents Jon and Laura Solberg. I also want to thank Jeremy Maxfield and Dr. Paul Wilkinson for their invaluable theological and editorial input. This book would not be what it is without this group of talented people.

I also owe a debt of gratitude to pastors Derek Bareman, Steve Helm, and Tom Kelly for their support and guidance along the way. And special thanks to Stan Meyer (of Jews for Jesus Phoenix), Michael Owed, and Bruce Gore and for their kind assistance. I also need to acknowledge the incredible professors and staff at Williamson College here in Nashville for their support, especially Dr. Ed Smith, David Dillon, David McCall, Karen Hudson, and Carli Smith. They are a group of educators who represent excellence and, more importantly, embody Jesus' mandate to love God and love people.

Lastly, to my wife Debra, who not only reviewed the book and contributed several brilliant insights, she also believed in me enough to help me chase this crazy thing down. My heart is eternally yours.

Foreword

The best conversations aren't planned. The best conversations are those that happen spontaneously amongst sincere, passionate seekers wanting to learn, mature, and progress in their faith and life. R. L. Solberg has blessed us by inviting us into just such a conversation.

The relationship between the law of Moses given by God to theocratic, wandering Israel and the liberty secured and compelled through the person and work of Jesus has been a tension present since the earliest moments of the Gospel. We see Paul passionately pleading with the Galatians to seek first the Gospel of Jesus and to fulfill that law. We see the Jerusalem Council in Acts 15, when the Gospel had, surprisingly, made its way to pagan Gentiles, seek to not put any extra burdens upon these new believers other than some basic prohibitions: food offered to idols, blood, eating strangled things, sexual immorality.

Solberg's work continues the exploration of this persistent tension. What aspects of the Law have been fulfilled in Christ? What aspects of the Law are we required to follow? What liberties does the Christian have?

But be sure to catch this truth: Solberg's work is not about how to do the least work for the most grace, nor is it about how to avoid obligations, duties, and work. No, much more than that, Solberg's question is about how we who claim to be children of God best glorify, worship, and obey him. And can we glorify, worship, and obey God if we misunderstand or supplement the reconciliation God has offered, namely, the person and work of Jesus? Solberg wants to know what it means to be "godly" and "righteous" in light of the crucifixion and resurrection of Jesus.

This book is a read that flows because it originates in genuine conversations between friends and passionate believers. It is reminiscent of the ancient dialogues with questions, points, and counterpoints. Within the flow of conversation, Solberg works in historical realities to set the context of the Scriptures in question and highlights appropriate and significant theological doctrines to aid the discussion.

Solberg faithfully challenges himself, seeking to understand what's the price to pay for those seeking to be righteous through the Law and what's the price to pay for those who claim that much of the Law has been fulfilled through Jesus' work. Solberg is winsome, challenging, and introspective. He does not assume he knows, rather he sincerely asks those of a differing opinion than him to help him think through the crucial implications of certain beliefs.

I met Rob when I came to his church to talk about the possibility of teaching and equipping for apologetics. I was impressed by his passion, knowledge, and focus. But more than those, I was encouraged and convicted by a man who really wanted to know: what does it mean to be faithful? What does it mean to defend truth? What does the kingdom life look like? Solberg has continued with that same authenticity as he asks whether Christians are to keep the Law in response to the person and work of Jesus.

I invite you into Rob and his friends' conversation. I was challenged, encouraged, and taught by the insights Solberg brings to the fore. I pray that you heed his call to take seriously what it means for the Christian to live the godly life; to be like Jesus.

Paul Wilkinson, Ph.D.

To Bob & Sue

Introduction

Who is wise? He who learns from all men.

BEN ZOMA

I T ALL BEGAN WITH A SERIES OF FACEBOOK POSTS an old friend of mine, whom I'll call Bob, published just after Thanksgiving. Bob had taken a dogmatic tone and was aggressively taking Christians to task for celebrating the pagan holiday of Christmas. This struck me as odd because I'd always known Bob and his wife, whom I'll call Sue, as devout Christians. While I've debated with plenty of atheists over the alleged pagan roots of Christmas, I'd never heard this charge leveled by a fellow Christian. I decided to chime in on Bob's posts and soon discovered that I had stumbled into a mystery of, well…biblical proportions.

Over the ensuing months, I was exposed to an unfamiliar theology I have come to refer to as *Torahism*. This is an umbrella term for a loose collection of religious movements in which followers of Jesus have become "Torah-observant." They teach that even non-Jewish Christians are required to keep the Law of Moses, including the annual feasts, the kosher food laws, the Saturday Sabbath, circumcision, and so on. The theology of Torahism is held by groups you might know as the Hebrew Roots Movement or Torah-observant Christianity, and to a degree by Seventh Day Adventists and Jehovah's Witnesses.

When I first read some of Bob's posts, I sensed what he claimed was wrong, but I couldn't quite pinpoint why. He was quoting from the Bible and referencing history, and most of his facts rang true. He spoke with such passion and authority that I wanted to learn more. I had to ask myself if maybe he had a point worth considering. Is it possible some of the things I had learned about Jesus and Christianity over the years were errant? Or worse, had I built my theology, as Bob charged, on an anti-Semitic, Roman corruption dating to the early centuries after Christ that was passed down through the generations until it replaced the truth of the Christian story?

I decided to engage with Bob and Sue. They were gracious enough to stick with the conversation for quite a while and wander with me deep into Scripture and theology. Our conversation turned into perhaps the rarest literary genre known today: a productive Facebook argument. They shared videos of Hebrew Roots teachers, and I began to do my own research on the belief system. The more I learned, the more apparent it became that Torahism does not align with what the Bible teaches. The most obvious examples are found on the extreme edges of the belief system where the Trinity is rejected and Christ's divinity is challenged. But even for those Torah-observant Christians who accept the deity of Christ and confess faith in Him as the only way to salvation, there are problems. For these reasons—and many more, which we will explore in this book—I came to see Torahism as a dangerous path for current believers in Christ and a stumbling block for future believers.

As my debate with Bob and Sue played out on social media, an interesting thing happened. Strangers started contacting me privately. Friends, acquaintances, and even family members thanked me for engaging with Bob and Sue and defending Christianity. They were worried about the changes they saw but unsure how to address the issue. And that's a big part of the difficulty of Torahism. While it may instinctively seem wrong to many Christians, it is often hard to put your finger on why. The theology can be nuanced and difficult to pin down. It requires a lot of study to identify and untangle the errors on which Torahism is built. I spent months studying Scripture and investigating each new claim I encountered. Realizing what a daunting task this is and seeing how the work I had already done was helping others in my shoes, I decided to share what I had been learning.

In this book, we'll walk together through my journey, exploring Torahism's claims and arguments and working out what the Bible says about these important issues. I will tell you upfront that I learned a lot as I dug in, and I came away with a different understanding of this belief system than I expected. That may be your experience in reading this book, too.

Although there are many commonly held arguments for Torah-observant Christianity, each "flavor" of Torahism is a little different.

There is a spectrum of thought on the role biblical law ought to play in the life of the Christian, and I'm convinced there is room for honest disagreement even among orthodox Christian denominations.[1] I certainly don't have all the answers. But I believe I have uncovered enough historical, biblical, and theological evidence to make out the big picture and tell in which direction it points.

There are two ways in which I pray this book will serve the reader. First, as a resource for the Christian who encounters Torahism in their community. My goal is to help you gain a working understanding of the teachings and beliefs of Torahism and see how they compare to Scripture and mainstream Christian teaching. In addition, this book will provide ample Scriptural and historical evidence, which you may find useful to refute the arguments of our Torahist friends and help convince them of the truth of Jesus and the New Covenant.

One hundred percent of the Torahists I have read or engaged with are former Christians who walked away from the faith due to an incomplete and/or errant understanding of Christian theology. So, the second way I pray this book will be helpful is as a resource that teaches the fundamentals of the Christian faith. A proper response to Torahism requires a robust understanding of the basics of biblical theology. Pastors, teachers, and leaders in the Christian Church can help reverse the spread of heretical ideas like Torahism by promoting biblical literacy and arming believers with a solid understanding of sound Christian theology. In this post-Christian age of moral relativism, the Church must teach not only what we believe but *why* we believe it.

A Few Notes on This Book

First, Christianity is indisputably a faith rooted in Jewish history and theology. Jesus is the Jewish Messiah promised in the *Tanakh* (Hebrew Bible, aka Old Testament). He was born into a Jewish family and culture and lived His life under the Law of Moses. As Heiser wisely reminds us, "The proper context for interpreting the Bible is the context of the biblical writers—the context that produced the Bible. Every other context is alien or at least secondary."[2] Therefore, I've chosen to use many Hebrew words and names throughout this book. For example, I will

---

[1] The term "orthodox" refers to the accepted traditional beliefs to which mainstream Protestant Christianity conforms. This is the intended meaning of the term *Christianity* throughout this book. I do not present a defense of Roman Catholic theology here.

[2] Michael S. Heiser, *The Unseen Realm* (Lexham Press), p. 16.

interchangeably use the English name *Jesus* and its Hebrew equivalent *Yeshua*. Both terms refer to the same Person: Christ, the Son of God.

Yeshua is just one of many Hebrew names and terms you will encounter when engaging with Torah-observant Christians. And don't worry. I will define the Hebrew words when they first appear, and in the back of the book, you'll find a glossary should you need a refresher. The more Christians understand our faith's true biblical and historical roots—including its origins in the ancient Hebrew people—the more our faith comes alive!

Second, the term I have chosen to use in this book, *Torahism*, is not necessarily used by those who hold to this belief system. Many Torahists I've talked to simply call themselves "believers." But that term is not very helpful since every adherent of every belief system is a "believer." So I coined the term *Torahism* because this is a belief system centered on the keeping of the Torah. And I would hasten to add that the label *Torahism* is not intended in a derogatory sense. It is merely a convention for describing a belief system and its adherents. When I refer to someone as a *Torahist*, it is no different than referring to someone as a Christian, Jew, or Muslim.

Third, this book is built on a number of presuppositions—claims that I take from the outset to be true and will not argue for directly. These include the belief that God exists, that the Bible is true in all it teaches and asserts, and that both the Old and New Testaments of Scripture are divinely inspired and, therefore, our ultimate authority. I also presume that any reader interested enough to pick up this book has a general familiarity with Scripture and Christian doctrine.

Fourth, throughout this book, I will directly quote numerous Torahists with whom I have engaged. I feel it is important to present their arguments in their own words as much as possible. That said, I have cleaned up the comments received in written form for clarity and readability. In doing so, I was careful to leave their intended meaning intact.

Fifth, this book is organized into two parts. In Part One, we set the table by looking at what Torahism is and believes. In Part Two, we dive into the most common claims you are likely to encounter when engaging with Torah-keeping Christians. To help make this a user-friendly resource, you will find a summary at the end of each chapter in Part Two. There is also an index of names and topics at the end of the book.

Lastly, we must remember that Torahists are not necessarily our enemy. The aim of this book is to examine the theological differences between Christianity and Torahism. But I caution the reader against slipping into an "us versus them" mentality. Although there are some Torah-keepers who teach outright heresy and should be rejected, I've found the typical Torahist is someone who loves God and wants to worship Him in truth but has been caught up in questionable teachings. And, yes, their comments can sometimes become antagonistic and even hostile. But as much as we can, we need to interact with them in love (John 13:24-45) and defend the Christian truth claims with gentleness and respect (1 Pet 3:15). "If you love those who love you, what benefit is that to you? For even sinners love those who love them" (Luke 6:32). Scripture teaches that we should be speaking the truth in love (Eph 4:15) with words full of grace, seasoned with salt (Col 4:6). In an increasingly fractured culture, I believe Christians should be known for showing love and grace to those with whom we disagree.

This book isn't about winning an argument. Rather, it is about clearing away untruths, errors, and misconceptions to see God and His Word more clearly. We may disagree with what Torah-keepers teach, but our theological differences need not be a test of friendship. I believe it is possible to disagree with someone and still be friends. So, as we endeavor to determine whether—or to what degree—Christians are required to keep the Law of Moses, remember our fight is not with people but with ideas!

> For though we live in the world, we do not wage war as the world does. The weapons we fight with are not the weapons of the world. On the contrary, they have divine power to demolish strongholds. We demolish arguments and every pretension that sets itself up against the knowledge of God, and we take captive every thought to make it obedient to Christ. (2 Corinthians 10:3-5)

PART ONE

Setting the Table

2

What Is the Torah?

*The observant Jew has his own sense of values. Torah Judaism
is his blueprint for this life, his target for existence.*

MEIR KAHANE

ERE IN PART ONE WE WILL lay the necessary groundwork for
our examination of the claims of Torahism in Part Two.
Because the basic premise of Torahism is that believers should
be keeping Torah, we need to start with the question "What is the
Torah?" And it is surprisingly tricky to answer. We need to step into the
Hebrew understanding of the Torah before we can engage in a
meaningful way with our Torah-keeping friends. And this is a beautiful
thing. As followers of the Jewish Messiah, there's much we can learn
from our Jewish and Torah-keeping friends in this area.

The Torah is a part of the Christian Bible and, as such, part of our
faith history. It was given to Israel by Yahweh and considered the
inspired Word of God by Jesus, the apostles, and the New Testament
authors.

> For everything that was written in the past was written to teach
> us, so that through the endurance taught in the Scriptures and
> the encouragement they provide we might have hope. (Romans
> 15:4)

> All Scripture is God-breathed and is useful for teaching,
> rebuking, correcting and training in righteousness, so that the
> servant of God may be thoroughly equipped for every good
> work. (2 Timothy 4:16-17)

The Hebrew word *torah* means "teaching, doctrine, or instruction."[1] However, the words *law* and *Torah* are often used interchangeably. And as we'll see throughout this book, when the word Torah is used to mean "law" it can give a wrong impression and open the door for misinterpretation and confusion. Jewish Rabbi Adin Even-Israel warns us that,

> To translate Torah as "law" misses the mark, even though the Bible may be seen as a book containing laws and moral instruction for living. On the other hand, this aspect of instruction—the teaching—is certainly basic to Torah; without it the Torah would be just a monumental work of literature.[2]

The term *Torah* can be tricky because depending on who you're talking to, it can refer to different things. It is most commonly used to refer to the *Pentateuch*—the first five books of the Bible, also known as the *Books of Moses*. These five books form the basis of all Jewish law and practice.[3] *Torah* is also commonly used in a narrower sense to refer specifically to the *Law of Moses*—the 613 mitzvot (commandments)[4] found in the books of Exodus through Deuteronomy. This is the meaning most often used by Torah-keepers. The Mosaic Law served as the terms of the *Sinai Covenant*.[5] If Israel kept this law, she would be blessed. And if she disobeyed, she would be cursed.[6]

Additionally, because *Torah* means "instruction," it is sometimes used in a broader sense to refer to the entire Hebrew Bible, which Jews call the *Tanakh*[7] and Christians call the *Old Testament*. Although the books are in a different order, and in some cases, the verse numbers differ, the Tanakh and the Old Testament contain the same body of text.

---

[1] Isaac Rabinowitz and Warren Harvey, "Torah," in Encyclopaedia Judaica, ed. Michael Berenbaum and Fred Skolnik, 2nd ed., Vol. 20 (Detroit: Macmillan Reference USA, 2007), 39–46.
[2] Adin Even-Israel (Steinsaltz), "Torah Eternal," *Chabad*, www.chabad.org/library/article_cdo/aid/2888/jewish/Torah-Eternal.htm.
[3] MJL Staff, "What is the Torah? The Five Books of Moses in the Bible," *My Jewish Learning*, www.myjewishlearning.com/article/what-is-the-torah.
[4] Jewish tradition holds that there are 613 commands given in the Torah. However, that number differs depending on who is doing the defining and counting.
[5] The covenant (contract) Yahweh made with Israel at Mount Sinai. Because God used Moses to mediate this covenant, it is also called the *Mosaic Covenant*.
[6] See Deuteronomy 28 for the blessings and curses.
[7] *Tanakh* is an acronym made up of the first Hebrew letter of each of the Hebrew Bible's three traditional subdivisions: *Ta* is for Torah, which means "Teaching" and includes the Five Books of Moses. *Na* is for Nevi'im, which means "Prophets," and *Kh* is for Ketuvim, which means "Writings." Thus, the word is sometimes written with alternating capital letters: TaNaKh.

Lastly, in its broadest sense, *Torah* has been used to refer to the whole body of Jewish law and teachings, which includes the Hebrew Bible plus the wider body of Jewish civil and ceremonial law known as the *Talmud*.[8] As Helyer says, "The Torah outlines a way of life for the people of Israel and is nearly synonymous with Judaism."[9]

Thus, if we were to ask whether the word *Torah* refers to the Law of Moses, the Pentateuch, the Tanakh, the Talmud, or all Jewish Law, an acceptable answer would be "yes." Because of this ambiguity, things get tricky when engaging with our Torah-observant friends. It is easy to find ourselves talking past one another, so the journey into Torahism requires our close attention. We need to be especially careful with our terminology. Therefore, let's clearly distinguish between the terms *Torah* and *Mosaic Law*. This book will endeavor to use the word *Torah* to refer to the first five books of the Bible, and *Law of Moses* (or *Mosaic Law*) to refer to the set of commandments given by Yahweh to Israel at Mount Sinai. It is this set of commands that Torahism teaches is binding on all Christians today.

Many Torah-keepers resist this distinction and are adamant that the Torah and the Mosaic Law are one and the same. As we'll see in the coming chapters, when Torahism teaches that all Christians are to "keep Torah," it means we should be keeping the Law of Moses. However, Scripture supports our distinction. For example, Paul says the Law of Moses wasn't given until 430 years after Abraham (Gal 3:17). The Law of Moses is distinct from the Torah. In fact, the Mosaic Law is part of the larger story of the Torah. And the Torah, in turn, is part of the larger story of Scripture. And the overarching storyline of Scripture (including both the Law and the Torah) is one of God leading His people into a right relationship with Himself through *Yeshua HaMashiach* (Jesus the Messiah).[10]

Since *Torah* is commonly translated as "law" in the Bible, Christians often associate it with burdensome regulations and restrictions. In Judaism, however, *Torah* does not carry that negative connotation. Instead, it refers to God's teaching, guidance, and instruction in a positive and beautiful sense. It is our loving Creator teaching us how to

[8] Talmud (literally, "study") is the "textual record of generations of rabbinic debate about law, philosophy, and biblical interpretation, compiled between the 3rd and 8th centuries." (Sefaria.org)
[9] Larry R. Helyer, "How Does the Bible Relate to Judaism?" *Apologetics Study Bible*, ed. Ted Cabal, (Holman Bible Publishers, 2007), p. 1758.
[10] The literal translation of the Hebrew word *Mashiach* is "the anointed one," which refers to a ritual of consecrating a king or high priest by pouring holy anointing oil on his head. In the NT, the word "Christ" means the same thing. Thus, "Jesus Christ" is the English equivalent of the Hebrew name and title "Yeshua HaMahsiach," Jesus the Messiah.

live. Tverberg notes, "It was a joy and privilege to teach others how to live life by God's instructions. This was the goal of every rabbi, including Jesus."[11] And as we'll see in Part Two, while all Christians are still under the authority of the Torah as Scripture, we are not all bound by the Laws of Moses.

We can all agree that the Torah, however we define it, is rooted in the inspired Word of God. It comes from the pages of Holy Scripture, it was given to mankind[12] by God Himself, and His Word and His Law are perfect.

---

[11] Lois Tverberg, "What Paul Says about Fulfilling the Law (part 2 of 3)," *Our Rabbi Jesus*.

[12] I will often use the terms "mankind" and "man" in a gender-neutral way to refer to the human race.

3

What Is Torahism?

You have led in your steadfast love the people
whom you have redeemed; you have guided them
by your strength to your holy abode.

EXODUS 15:13

T ORAHISM IS AN UMBRELLA TERM for the theology underlying
a diverse body of modern religious movements whose focus is
on Christ-followers "keeping Torah." You may know it by a
different name: Hebrew Roots Movement, Torah-observant
Christianity, Pronomian Christianity, Messianic Christianity, or simply
Messianics. Torahism, in one form or another, is taught by a wide variety
of teachers and organizations, including but not limited to:

- 119 Ministries (David Wilber and others)
- A Rood Awakening (Michael Rood)
- Corner Fringe (Daniel Jospeh, Joshua Antilla)
- Growing in Messiah (Caleb Hegg)
- Kingdom in Context (Sean Griffin)
- Parable of the Vineyard (Adam Fink)
- Passion For Truth (Jim Staley)
- Philia Ministries (James & Lea Dinonno)
- New2Torah (Zach Bauer)
- The Pronomian (Scott McKenzie)
- Torah Institute (Lew White)
- Torah Life Ministries (Paul Nison)
- Torah Resource (Tim Hegg)
- Triumph in Truth (G. Stevens Simmons)
- Unlearn the Lies (Lex Meyer)

The theology of Torahism is expressed in various ways, but the common thread is a belief that all followers of Yeshua, whether Jew or Gentile, are obligated to keep Torah. And again, by "Torah" they mean the set of commands given by Yahweh to Israel at Mount Sinai as recorded in the Scripture. And interestingly, Torah-keepers have just a handful of commands in mind. Their theology is primarily concerned with four aspects of the Law: the weekly Sabbath, kosher food, feasts, and circumcision.

Torahists do not challenge mainstream Christianity on moral laws having to do with issues like murder, stealing, or adultery. Christians agree these laws are still in effect. In fact, mainstream Christian theology holds that none of the Mosaic commands regarding right and wrong, loving God, or loving people have changed. Unlike the Sabbath, the kosher food laws, the feasts, and circumcision, Yahweh's moral commands have existed since the very beginning. But, as we will discover in Part Two, this is not true of the "big four" of Torahism. God did not always require those commands. Rather, they were given at a specific time to a particular people for a specific reason.

Torahism also does not lobby for the civil or social Mosaic laws on issues such as property, inheritance, marriage, divorce, the death penalty, and so on. They will typically concede that these laws were specific to the theocratic nation of ancient Israel and, as such, cannot be carried out by God's People today. (And, yes, this does introduce the idea of "cherry-picking" from the Torah. We will get to that in the coming chapters.)

As Torah-observant Christianity has grown, it has been forced by Scripture to normalize on several important issues, salvation being primary. Only a handful of Torahists openly continue to teach that keeping Torah is a matter of salvation. Most categorize it as a matter of obedience, teaching that, once saved, keeping the Law is how we rightly live out our faith. At the same time, they believe keeping the Mosaic commands is required of all Christ-followers, and those who do not "keep Torah" are openly living in sin.

If you're thinking Torahism sounds similar to Judaism, you're right. Observant Jews (and Messianic Jews) also keep the Torah. The primary difference between Judaism and Torahism is that Torahism recognizes Jesus as the Messiah promised in the Hebrew Bible and Judaism does not. Torahists do not claim to practice a form of Judaism. Rather their stated goal is to return to the Jewish roots of the Christian faith. Thus, Torahism can be seen as a sort of middle position between Judaism and Christianity.

However, Torahism is not a position that arose historically or in chronological order. It is not as if Judaism evolved into Torahism, which then evolved into Christianity. Rather Torahism is a movement occurring solely among Gentile Christians. In fact, every Torah-keeper I've come across has two things in common: they are Gentile (not of Jewish ethnicity) and they come from a Christian background. Torahists are Gentile Christians who believe mainstream Christianity wrongly left the Law of Moses behind when Yeshua arrived. As they see it, they are "correcting course" by returning to the keeping of the Law.

Nothing New

Torahism can be traced back to the time of the Apostles when the Judaizers first advocated for it. As we will discuss in coming chapters, this was the very issue debated at the Jerusalem Council in 50 CE (Acts 15:1-29), and it has surfaced many times in history. In the early centuries of the faith, Jewish Christian sects such as the Ebionites, Nazarenes, and Elkasites shared similar beliefs. Like modern Torahism, these groups were dedicated to keeping the whole Torah as enlightened by the *halacha* (teachings) of Rabbi Yeshua.[1] They also emphasized the restoration of the "true faith," which they believed the Jewish groups of Second Temple times had lost.[2] Some even rejected the concept of Jesus as the Son of God.[3]

In the fourth century, the bishop Epiphanius described the Nazarenes in terms that can be directly applied to modern-day Torahism.

They disagree with Jews because they have come to faith in Christ; but since they are still fettered by the Law—circumcision, the Sabbath, and the rest—they are not in accord with the Christians.[4]

The early sects of Torah-observant Christians appear to have died out around the fifth century, and the theology remained largely underground until the 19th century. Modern-day Torahism grew like a small branch out of the Second Great Awakening (c. 1790-1840). Through the Millerite Movement (1830's) came Seventh Day Adventists, founded in 1863 by Hiram Edson and Ellen G. White.

[1] Dr. James Tabor, "Nazarenes and Ebionites," *The Jewish Roman World of Jesus.*
[2] Ibid.
[3] Samuel Krauss, "Nazarenes," *Jewish Encyclopedia.*
[4] Epiphanius of Salamis, *Panarion* 29.7.4, (~375 CE).

About a decade later, the Jehovah's Witnesses movement developed among the followers of Charles Taze Russell (1870's). The beliefs of these two sects—including their views on Saturday Sabbath and the "pagan" holidays of Christmas and Easter—were picked up and expounded on by other sects. The first notable presentation of the theology of Torahism came from Herbert W. Armstrong, who founded the Worldwide Church of God (WCG) in 1933. Decades later, WCG abandoned its Torah-keeping theology as heresy and changed its name to Grace Communion International. However, some of its members held to their Torah-centric beliefs and founded the United Church of God in 1995.

Rabbi Tovia Singer (an orthodox Jew) believes the Torah-keeping Christian movement was significantly impacted by post-Holocaust theology.[5] Such horrific evil and suffering on such a large scale forced Christian theology to grapple with, among many other issues, the reality of anti-Semitism. Perhaps there is something to the idea that such evil committed by a country that had been so staunchly Christian for 1,500 years motivated some in Christendom to swing the pendulum back the other way, to seek to honor and acknowledge the Hebrew roots of the faith. And those in the Torah-keeping movement have taken a good idea too far.

Spectrum of Beliefs

There is a wide range of beliefs across the continuum shown below, and the differences between them are not always easy to identify. Because of this grey area, I believe we should extend a generous portion of grace as we engage with others.

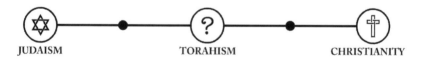

On the right end of the spectrum is what we will call mainstream Christianity, which teaches that Jesus is both God incarnate and Messiah and that salvation comes by grace through faith in Him. This is the biblical position held by mainstream Christianity and Messianic Judaism (Jews who have come to faith in Yeshua). Messianic Jews continue to celebrate the richness of their Jewish heritage along with the joy and

---

[5] He shared these thoughts during a personal conversation on May 23, 2022.

freedom of life in Christ. As we'll see throughout this book, there is much that Gentile Christians can learn about the true Hebrew roots of our faith from our Messianic Jewish friends.

On the left end of the spectrum is Judaism, which rejects the New Testament as Scripture and denies the divinity and messiahship of Jesus. The middle position, Torahism, is the focus of this book. Many Torah-keepers still consider themselves Christians and believe salvation comes through faith in Christ alone. And while many claim that keeping the Law is not required for salvation, as we will see, their teachings seem to indicate otherwise.

Summary of Beliefs

It should be noted that Torahism is not a monolithic belief system. It is a religious view held by various sects and beliefs can and do vary between those groups. There is no central church body or set of doctrines. At least not yet. If left unchecked, some believe that Torahism will eventually evolve into its own distinct denomination. There is already a Hebrew Roots kid's summer camp,[6] and Hebrew Roots translations of the Bible have begun to hit the market.[7] Additionally, the brand of Torahism that calls itself "Pronomian Christianity"[8] has issued an official statement intended to "serve as an overarching standard of agreement for future Pronomian conferences and to help network existing Pronomians with each other."[9]

A lack of central doctrine means that each time we engage with a Torahist, we're likely to hear a slightly different flavor of the theology. So, I've assembled a collection of general beliefs, which includes actual words and phrases that Torah-observant friends have shared with me. The statement below was curated from multiple sources, so not every Torah-keeper will agree with every point. But it is a general outline of the fundamental claims of Torahism.

> Yahweh gave us His Law through Moses and declared it is eternal and will never change. No one can add to or take away from its commands. Nothing in the Bible says the Mosaic Law has ended. In fact, Yeshua taught that not one jot or title would pass from the Law until heaven and earth pass away. Therefore,

---

[6] Camp Yeshua in Lawton, Oklahoma.
[7] For example, the *Hebraic Roots Bible* produced by the Congregation of Yahweh (coyhwh.org).
[8] The word "pronomian" comes from the Greek prefix *pro*, meaning "in favor or support of," *nomos*, the law.
[9] See rockhillstatement.com.

all Christians, whether Jew or Gentile, are "under" or "subject to" all of the laws that Yahweh gave at Sinai.

Christians don't keep that Law today because their theology was corrupted in the early centuries after Christ. Rampant anti-Semitism motivated early Christian leaders, including the Roman emperor Constantine, to create a false theology intended to separate believers in Yeshua from the Torah. He and others of his era conspired to remove the "Jewishness" from the faith. As a result, the theology inherited by Christians today is false and was built on a corrupt and racist ideology.

Torah-observant Christianity is growing in popularity because literacy rates and access to the Bible have skyrocketed over the past couple of centuries. This has allowed us to read the truth for ourselves rather than blindly believing what the church teaches. We have come to recognize this historical corruption and are responding to it by throwing out the false Greco-Roman teachings of the Christian church and returning to what the Bible *really* teaches. Namely, that Yeshua, as Mashiach, did not change the standard of godly obedience. Rather, He affirmed both the weightier and lesser matters of the Law for those who have put their faith in Him.

As for the future, the Mosaic Law will grow in its supremacy and beauty as the end of days draws near. The book of Revelation teaches that those who hold fast to Yeshua and the Law of Moses will be rewarded in the end.

There is a sense in which Torahism can be viewed as a noble cause undertaken by brave people. It isn't easy to walk away from the beliefs you grew up with and once held dear. Especially when your friends and family still hold to those beliefs. I find it admirable that Torah-keepers are so committed to their convictions that they are willing to make dramatic changes in their lives. But of course, the wisdom of any commitment is ultimately measured by the accuracy of its foundational convictions. And this is where we find Torahism running into trouble.

Classifying Torahism's Beliefs

There is disagreement on exactly where the theology of Torahism falls on the continuum of Christian beliefs between orthodoxy and heresy. The hierarchy of importance of Christian beliefs is often visualized as a series of concentric circles. For our purposes, let's label them as follows.

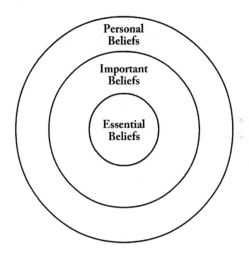

Where does the theology of Torahism fall on this chart? *Essential Beliefs* are the minimum required set of beliefs necessary to Christianity. An example of a necessary belief would be that salvation comes by grace through faith (Eph 2:8-9). There are no mandatory rituals, ceremonies, or special words that bring salvation.

Exactly which beliefs should be placed in the center ring is a matter of tremendous theological complexity and beyond the scope of this book. We can, perhaps, agree on a few essential beliefs, such as *God exists* and *Jesus is Lord*. But I will leave it up to the reader to determine the specific beliefs they believe should be labeled "essential." For our purposes, it is enough to acknowledge that there is a center ring.

The second ring, *Important Beliefs*, includes convictions about secondary, non-salvific issues. Here we can affirm a range of positions as falling within biblical parameters where honest disagreement can exist between Christians. For example, infant baptism or believer's baptism? Calvinism or Arminianism? Premillennialism or amillennialism? These are not unimportant issues. Some may even be considered matters of heresy. But they are secondary in the sense that there is room for disagreement among believers. We can expect Heaven is full of

Calvinists, Arminians, Roman Catholics, Lutherans, Eastern Orthodox, Baptists, Pentecostals, Methodists, and so on. I believe we will discover Torahists in Heaven, as well.

God allows His people a wide swath of grace in which to live out their faith. Which brings to mind an anonymous quote that greatly comforts me: *When God put a calling on your life, He already factored in your stupidity.* Mercifully, the divine purposes of God do not hinge on the ability of His creatures to execute their duties flawlessly. I believe the same holds true of salvation. Our salvation in Jesus does not hinge on our ability to fully understand or rightly define biblical doctrine but rather on the authenticity of our faith. Which is not to say that we shouldn't try to get things right. We should! My point is this. Mankind may set boundaries on how much heresy will get one kicked out of the Church, but how much heresy will get a genuine believer kicked out of Heaven? I have a sneaking suspicion that man's boundaries are not God's boundaries. This is why I am not quick to dismiss Torahism as an outright heresy.

The third ring, *Personal Beliefs*, refers to those matters of personal conscience which we are free in Christ to decide for ourselves. Theologians call these issues *adiaphora*, a Greek word that literally means "without difference." It refers to doctrines or practices that are neither commanded nor forbidden in the Bible. This is the level at which I believe the teachings of Torahism should be placed. As we will look at in the coming chapters, the Mosaic traditions are not commanded of all Christians in Scripture, nor have they been forbidden for anyone. Thus, for Christ-followers, they can be categorized as "permitted but not required."

However, Torahism does not allow itself to be classified in the outer ring of *Personal Beliefs*. Rather, most Torahists prefer to place their theology at the secondary level of *Important Beliefs*. And the minority who believe salvation comes through keeping the Torah would put themselves in the center ring of *Essential Belief*. But of course, that view of salvation is patently unbiblical and a deadly heresy.

The majority of Torah-keepers admit that keeping the Law of Moses is not a prerequisite for salvation, but they view it as a matter of proper, biblical obedience. And here is where things get tricky. Teaching that Torah-keeping is *required* of all Christ-followers, even as a matter of obedience, has consequences. It means *not* keeping Torah is sinful and lawless behavior. Thus, Christians who do not observe the weekly Shabbat, eat kosher, keep the feasts, etc., are "living in sin." This suggests

Torahists do not view their theology as a matter of secondary beliefs. Christians can disagree—even vehemently—on issues such as baptism, free will, and eschatology without assigning their opponent the status of operating in sinful disobedience. The same cannot be said of Torahism. So perhaps the appropriate place to put Torah-keeping on the chart above is in a sort of grey area between the *essential* and *important* rings.

The Dangers of Torahism

Why does it matter? Why do you feel the need to attack someone else's belief system, especially when they believe in the same God and read the same Bible that you do? Shouldn't we all just get along? I hear these questions often and they are fair game. My answer? Torahism is dangerous. Before I offer three specific reasons why, let me put a human face on it.

I received an email from a woman named Elizabeth even as I was putting the finishing touches on the second edition of this book. She did a beautiful job of describing—from an insider perspective—the insidious way that Torahism works its way into a relationship and makes one feel turned around and confused. Her experience is echoed in many other messages I receive. If you're dealing with Torahism in your life, it will likely resonate with you at some level.

Hello, Mr. Solberg,

I recently watched your teaching "What Is Wrong with the Hebrew Roots Movement?" Lately, I have been on a mission to discover the truth of what the Bible truly teaches in regards to what we are to obey as commandments as believers today. I have been a Bible-believing Christian all my life. I was not introduced to Torah observance until 2019. Even then, I did not truly know what it was.

I met a man, who I began dating, that claimed to be Torah observant and part of the Hebrew Roots Movement. I did not know what that was or what it meant at the time. However, I was familiar with Sabbath observance and the belief of refraining from pagan holidays, so I was open to new perspectives.

Long story short, he turned out to be very emotionally, psychologically, and mentally abusive. He was also unfaithful to me, even in our time of marriage, and struggled with many demons. While he was knowledgeable of scripture, this knowledge was used as a tool of personal pride and self-exaltation. This is common in the Torah observant community as a whole. They act as if their beliefs have catapulted them to a more elite level of Christianity, and therefore look down on believers who disagree with their view of scripture. I often felt this way in my relationship and all throughout my marriage. Scripture was used as a weapon to make me feel inferior to my husband. I was never "allowed" to disagree with the Torah observant viewpoint he held.

I began to consider myself Torah observant as well. I listened to my husband's views of scripture adopted from popular YouTube channels like MTOI, Parable of the Vineyard, 119 Ministries, and Kingdom in Context. He never read or studied scripture with me. He would simply reiterate points from these channels to me that, again, I wasn't allowed to disagree with. I began to adopt these beliefs as my own over time, as some of the points seemed valid. For example, it seemed like a good thing to refrain from animals that God did not create to be eaten. So I changed my lifestyle to only eating "clean" foods, keeping the ordinances of the Sabbath, observing the feast days, etc.

It felt very burdensome. However, I just thought that I needed to afflict my flesh and let go of the things in my life that were "idols" so I could find joy in the ways of truly following the commandments of God. It wasn't long before my now ex-husband's Torah observance became deeper and more radical.

He began using only the Hebrew names for Jesus and the Father, Yahshua and Yahuah, saying that any other names are pagan. He began to preach to me that Jesus is not God but a created being, meaning the trinity was a pagan deception. He began to believe that we were not in the new covenant, but still in the old covenant. Lastly, he went down the path of denying that Paul is a true apostle and denying his writings in the New Testament.

I refused to even consider that the Word of God was not true, infallible, and divinely inspired. The reaction to this refusal was not pleasant and resulted in many angry episodes. Studying scripture began to feel tiring, as I began this new life of trying to obey every single old covenant commandment according to the precise letter of the Law. So, I simply allowed myself to become brainwashed by many of the things my ex-husband believed.

Since my divorce, I have only come across more and more radical beliefs from the Torah observant community. Some even state that Jesus was not born of a virgin. I now have denounced this movement and am trying to separate myself. However, some of these beliefs still linger with me and I struggle to part with them in fear that I am disobeying commandments and separating myself further from God. I have been trying to figure out what I truly believe the Bible teaches. I want to undo the brainwashing and know that what I believe is what I believe because the Bible says so. Were all foods truly made clean? Is it unnecessary to keep the Sabbath and the biblical feasts? If so, why did Paul observe the Sabbath and feasts in the New Testament? Will we be keeping the feasts and the Sabbath in the Kingdom? Is it okay to observe these things, as we can learn a lot from them, even if it is not necessarily required anymore?

I apologize for the lengthy email. However, I would love your help and insight to answering some of these questions. I am open to any form of communication if you are able and willing to help. No matter what the outcome, I greatly appreciate your time and attention. Thank you for reading!

Warmly,
Lizzie S.

Lizzie's story powerfully illustrates the confusion and damage Torahism can cause. The questions she raised are common, and we will look at each in turn in the coming chapters. Her story also demonstrates the three reasons I believe Torahism is a dangerous theology.

1. Torahism is Unbiblical

I get it. The idea of Christians keeping the Law of Moses can sound appealing, even beautiful. It can be seen as connecting us to our spiritual roots in ancient Israel and providing a framework to live out our faith today. This is what draws people into Torahism. But the bottom line is that Torah-observant Christianity is unbiblical. Scripture does not teach the Mosaic Law is binding on all Christians today. In fact, that Law was not given to the entire world but only to the ancient nation of Israel (Ex

19:1-6). It served as the terms of the Sinai Covenant, which has become obsolete (Heb 8:13). The Mosaic Law was given to guide the Israelites until Christ came (Gal 3:24-25). Many of its' commands were shadows of the Real Thing: Yeshua (Col 2:16-17; Heb 10:1). And as we will see, many of its commands have been fulfilled and are no longer in effect. This is what we will unpack throughout the rest of this book. Torahist teachers claim their theology is biblical, and I'm sure many of them genuinely believe that. But the proof is in the pudding. And in the end, as we will see, the Bible teaches that followers of Jesus, Gentiles in particular, are not obligated to keep the Mosaic Law as a matter of salvation or righteousness.

This brings up one of the primary challenges in recognizing and resisting this false belief system. If a Christian sect wanted to teach, for example, that adultery was lawful, we could cite plenty of Scripture that directly contradicts them. Demonstrating that adultery is unbiblical would be pretty straightforward. But with Torahism, there is no specific verse in the Bible that says, "Christians are *not* required to keep the Law of Moses." At the same, no verse explicitly says, "Christians *are* required to keep the Law of Moses." The relationship of Christians to the Law is far more nuanced than that, and rightly understanding it requires us to dig into the Word. This requirement for basic biblical literacy and Christian theology can trip up believers and allow Torahism to sound biblical.

God wants us to eat His Word, so to speak, to ingest it every day. We spend time with God so He can feed us His truth. And the more we get to know the truth of the Word, the easier it is to spot counterfeit teaching, which is what we find in Torahism. If you are reading this book as a teacher of Torah-observant Christianity, I urge you to soberly reconsider your position. There are many ways to acknowledge and honor the true Jewish roots of the Christian faith without, as the apostle Peter said, "putting God to the test by placing a yoke on the neck of the disciples that neither our fathers nor we have been able to bear" (Acts 15:10).

2. Torahism is Divisive

The second big danger is that Torahism causes division in the body of Christ. It damages marriages, friendships, families, and even churches in two ways. First, Torah-observant Christians often make matters of keeping the Law of Moses a test of faith. They view these Mosaic traditions as *required* of all Christians, not optional. Therefore, many

Torahists look down on Christians who don't keep the Saturday Sabbath or the kosher food laws, or who celebrate Easter or Christmas as living in sin. For example, in my debate with Hebrew Roots teacher David Wilber, he took the position that Christians who do not keep the Saturday Sabbath are living in sin and deserve the death penalty prescribed in the Torah.[10]

But here's the thing. Even though many Torah-observant believers profess that salvation comes through faith in Christ alone, I've come across very few willing to take a peacemaking attitude that we can agree to disagree on the issue of the Mosaic Law and still be brothers and sisters in Christ. The overwhelming majority of Torah-observant Christians I have interacted with take a prideful and judgmental attitude toward Christians who don't "keep Torah." You will find examples of this attitude in the many quotes cited in the chapters that follow and in the comments sections of my social media platforms.

The second way Torahism causes division is when the average Christian senses something is wrong with the idea of Torah-observant Christianity, but they have a hard time articulating exactly why. So the mainstream Christian and the Torah-observant Christian often end up talking past one another, quarreling without resolution. During my public conversations with Bob and Sue, I was contacted privately by two different people (a sibling and a friend of the couple) to thank me for confronting their views. The Torah-observant couple was causing so much turmoil and division that their friends and family were at their wit's end and didn't know what to do.

I also had a woman from Minneapolis reach out to me because her husband planned to leave the family and move to the Middle East. He no longer identified as a Christian and believed it was his duty as a believer to make the three annual pilgrimages to Jerusalem required in the Torah. I met with him and we talked for almost two hours. Despite being a Gentile who was never commanded to keep Shabbat, He was quite upset that he was being "forced" by mainstream Christianity to worship God on Sunday. This man was respectful and intelligent and knew his Bible. But he was unwilling or unable to even consider that keeping the Mosaic traditions might not be required of Gentile Christians under the New Covenant. He remained committed to leaving his wife and kids in service to Torahism.

---

[10] Although he readily admitted that the death penalty required in the Torah cannot be carried out today. The debate "Are Christians Required to Keep Sabbath?" took place live on May 2, 2022, on the "Faith Unaltered" YouTube Channel.

The danger is real. Here are other comments I've received.

I've been raised in the Hebrew Roots Movement my entire life and since being married and moving away from my Hebrew Roots parents, I've been feeling a tug at my heart to question my beliefs. In your video . . . you said it causes division between Christians and Torah keepers. I would go even further to say that there's also a lot of division within the movement. No one can agree, everyone fights about interpretations of the law, falling outs and congregations falling apart are common. I could go on and on about all the issues I've seen first-hand, but for now I'll just say thank you!! This is a difficult time for my husband and I, and my family has no idea that I'm considering leaving the movement. Any prayers would be appreciated. (Kathleen G.)

My son married a girl recently that her family had been strongly involved in the Hebrew roots movement. So I am researching for myself. I do not believe in the movement myself, nor does my son. But, we have to get along with the in-laws. (Tim S.)

My elder brother just sent me this link [to a Hebrew Roots article]. Is this what your book on Torahism is about and do you deal with this subject? I want to learn more in case my brother is going down a wrong path. By the way, I've been a pastor for over 32 years and have an M.Div. Please, any help you can offer is greatly appreciated. (Matthew S.)

With one of my best friends falling into the Hebrew Roots Movement (I partially blame 119 Ministries), I have been struggling to find answers to the questions he raises. Thank you so much for your biblical and logical teaching in your book and on YouTube. (Riley S.)

I have been looking into the Hebrew roots for two years since my daughter-in-law has taken my son and grandchildren down this path. It is starting to get really scary now. I believe she is teaching our grands that because we don't do as they do, we do not love or believe in Jesus. I am sad. They have a mindset that they are enlightened and we are deceived. Any way to help? (Brenda O.)

My son has fallen under this false gospel. I can't seem to reach him because he rejects a lot of what Paul teaches. They do not interpret the scripture clearly as you well pointed out. They pick and choose to random scripture to build a false doctrine. He's all in with the Torah family with his wife and five children. The dietary restrictions, the feasts and festivals, the Sabbath the harsh comments about Christians who see the scripture for what it really says. Have you got any words of wisdom for me? (Russell W.)

A Christian author and scholar from Spain also contacted me about this movement. He and I ended up chatting via video, and he explained how Hebrew Roots teachings are growing in Spain, especially among the Gypsy population. (Many gypsies identify themselves with the ten lost tribes of Israel.) He told me that several prominent Christian leaders in Spain had recently stepped down from their positions in the church to pursue some form of Torahism.

I am also part of a Hebrew Roots help group on Facebook, and a regular topic of conversation is the crumbling of marriages due to the teachings of Torahism. Many who have joined are married to a rigid Torahist and looking for advice on how to save their marriage. Thankfully Torahism is nowhere near as big as other Christian cults like Mormonism or Jehovah's Witnesses. At least not yet. One of the reasons I do what I do is to help make sure Torahism never gets that big.

That said, no belief system should be judged by those who abuse it, including Torahism. And to be fair, there is no Torah-observant tenet that *requires* its adherents to cause division in their families and communities. But there is a virulent strain of distrust—sometimes even outright rebellion—against the mainstream Christian church in many Torah-observant communities. Romans 14 addresses the in-fighting in the Roman church on the issue of kosher food. Paul admonished the Jewish and Gentile believers that,

> the kingdom of God is not a matter of eating and drinking but of righteousness and peace and joy in the Holy Spirit . . . so then let us pursue what makes for peace and for mutual upbuilding. (Romans 14:17, 19).

When we look at the common fruits of Torahism, we find the opposite of what Paul taught. Rather than peace and mutual upbuilding,

Torahism is prone to cause disunity in the body of Christ. And it has done needless damage to families, friendships, and churches.

3. Torahism Undermines the Work of Jesus

The third and perhaps most significant danger is that the theological concept at the heart of Torahism undermines both the Gospel of Jesus and the sufficiency of His work in making us right with God. It is not just that by pointing Christians toward Moses, our focus is taken off Jesus. That much is true, of course. By emphasizing a works-based, law-focused lifestyle, Hebrew Roots' teachings deemphasize the "abundance of grace and the free gift of righteousness" (Rom 5:17) that is ours through Jesus. But the danger is even bigger that what it does to our focus. The core theology of Torahism contradicts and undermines the accomplishments of Jesus through His life, death, and resurrection.

Look at it this way: if Torahism is correct and the Law of Moses remains fully in effect even on Gentiles, what did Yeshua's work accomplish? What was the point of His death and resurrection? Throughout the rest of this book, we will investigate the many passages in Scripture that reveal how the teachings of Torahism are incompatible with the work of Jesus.

The Difficulties of Engaging with Torahism

Two issues make the teachings of Torahism difficult to identify and challenge. First, rather than sitting in outright opposition to Christianity, Torah-keeping often varies by a matter of degrees. Some of its positions are diametrically opposed to mainstream Christian teaching and easy to recognize. But a lot of what it says is accurate and aligns with the Bible.

The difficulties live in the many small inaccuracies. These seemingly minor teachings can be challenging to spot. And they are insidious because they start with a small error—typically an interpretation based on an errant presupposition—and before you know it, they have given birth to full-blown false teaching. As any marksman can tell you, if the barrel of your gun is off by a fraction of an inch while aiming, your bullet will miss your intended target downrange by several feet. And that's what happens with the theology of Torahism. What seems at first glance to be a valid point often ends up missing the mark by a mile when worked out to its logical conclusion.

The second difficulty is that the average Torah-keeper loves God, knows their Bible, and is well versed in theological arguments. This makes sense, considering the typical path that leads someone into Torahism. Every Torahist I have engaged with began as a Christian who wanted to worship God in truth. Many studied Scripture and were attentive enough to understand and discuss doctrine. Others came across teachers that resonated with their desire to know the "real" truth. At some point along the way, they were introduced to theological and historical ideas they deemed credible enough to consider.

By the time a Christian decides to embrace Torah-keeping, they have typically given it a lot of thought. Sometimes through self-directed studies—but more often through Torahist teachers—they have come to believe that the teachings of Torahism ring more true than what they understand the doctrines of mainstream Christianity to be. Their new position is based on passages in the same Bible, which they now see in a new light, thanks to the "clarity" Torahism has given them. Now they see the "true" story of Scripture, as set in its proper Jewish context.

This means that, as Christians, we need to know our stuff. Any serious discussion with our Torah-keeping friends will occur at the level of theological and historical facts and concepts. The arguments of Torahism are often complex and nuanced. At any given time, we might find ourselves quoting and interpreting Scripture, debating doctrine, contesting church councils, and tackling many "ologies," from soteriology to eschatology to replacement theology. It is my hope and prayer that this book will serve as a useful tool in helping you navigate those discussions.

4

A Biblical Framework

We don't see things the way they are.
We see them the way we are.

TALMUD

HERE IS AN INTERESTING CONUNDRUM. Scripture is full of passages that teach us to love the Law of God, that God's law is eternal, that we are to meditate on it day and night, that it revives our soul, and so on.[1] At the same time, other passages teach things like,

> now we are released from the law, having died to that which held us captive, so that we serve in the new way of the Spirit and not in the old way of the written code. (Romans 7:6).

And we read that Jesus "abolished the law of commandments expressed in ordinances" (Eph 2:15), and Christians "are not under law but under grace" (Rom 6:14).

As Bible-believing Christians who accept all of Scripture as true, how can we reconcile these two seemingly contradictory teachings about God's law? This tension is at the very heart of the debate between Torah-observant and mainstream Christianity. Allow me to introduce a biblical framework that can help us make sense of the seemingly competing passages we find about the law.

---

[1] Deuteronomy 6:6-9; Psalm 1:1-2, 19:7-8, 110:111-113, etc.

Principle & Expression

One way to view the storyline of Scripture is through a framework called *Principle & Expression* (P&E). This interpretive lens offers a significant degree of explanatory power[2] and can be a helpful key for unlocking difficult passages about the law. It is a framework that we will refer to throughout this book. And the concept behind it is nothing new. The P&E framework is based on the distinction between a *general principle* and the *various expressions* of that principle.

By way of example, consider the moral principle "murder is wrong." All cultures at all times have regarded murder—the unlawful killing of one human being by another—to be immoral. However, different cultures express this principle differently. For example, did you know that prior to 2005, a husband in Haiti who killed his wife immediately after discovering her in the act of adultery was to be pardoned? In 2005, the Haitian government abolished the right of a husband to kill his wife due to infidelity. So, while the moral principle "murder is wrong" never changed, there is a difference in how the Haitian government expressed it before and after 2005. What was allowed under one expression became prohibited under the next. Yet, the principle that "murder is wrong" remained unchanged.

Notice that while the Haitian government modified the law that explicitly addressed killing an unfaithful wife, the rest of their murder laws were untouched. So the newer expression did not completely wipe out the previous. The two expressions are vastly more alike than different because each is grounded in the same unchanging principle.

When it comes to Scripture, the premise of the Principle & Expression framework is this: There exists a set of perfect principles grounded in God that never change, and He has expressed these principles differently at different times in history. Every commandment given by God in every expression across time is grounded in one or more of His unchanging principles. And although Scripture reveals that God's expressions have changed over time—and we will look at many examples of this in Part Two—the various expressions all reflect the immutable heart of God and are therefore more alike than different.

One might ask, "If there is a universal law grounded in God that never changes, why would He vary the way He expresses it to mankind?" It is not because God has changed, but because His people have, in two

---

[2] In philosophy, the phrase *explanatory power* refers to the ability of a hypothesis or theory to effectively explain the subject matter to which it pertains.

important ways. First, like a maturing child, God's People have grown in their knowledge of Him throughout history. He first spoke directly to men like Adam, Noah, Abraham, and Moses. Later, Yahweh communicated His law in writing. First on stone tablets (Ex 31:18), then through the writings and prophets of the Tanakh. And centuries after the Old Testament writings, Yahweh gave His people a new revelation through Jesus and the New Testament authors. Mankind's knowledge of Yahweh has continually grown as He revealed more about Himself.

The second reason for the difference in expressions is that Yahweh has stepped into human history to affect change in the world. As a result, the circumstances of God's people have changed dramatically over time. Many of these acts of God brought with them a new expression of His unchanging principles. Initially, it was just God and the first two humans living in the Garden of Eden together. Later, there came a period of four centuries in which God's People were living in slavery in Egypt. They grew from a small tribe into a massive people group, and Yahweh ultimately stepped in and rescued them. Shortly afterward, He gave His people the Law of Moses to mature them from a ragtag mass of recently freed slaves into an orderly nation that would serve Him and show the world His greatness. And later still, God sent His only Son, Yeshua, to inaugurate a new covenant. Scripture reveals a Living God Who moves in and through the timeline of history.

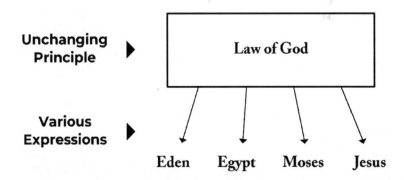

God does not tell us everything He plans to do all at once. Rather He reveals His will to us on a need-to-know-basis in what theologians refer to as *progressive revelation*. So while God is outside of time—He is, in fact, the Creator of time—He chose to condescend to humanity by stepping into our timeline of history and working out his plan of redemption there.

For reasons we can't know, God did not choose to send Jesus to save His people at Mount Sinai. Instead, He made a covenant with Israel there and issued a set of laws to serve as the terms of that contract. Yahweh told the Israelites that He would bless them if they obeyed His commands and if they disobeyed, they would be cursed.[3] The Bible refers to these regulations as the *Law of Moses*[4] because God chose Moses as His mediator. And the moral aspect of this law was nothing new. Yahweh had embedded moral direction into the heart of mankind from the very beginning.[5] So God did not appear to Israel at Sinai to present a moral code but to deliver laws that would create a unique nation.

Establishing Our Terminology

Consistent terminology is crucial to the arguments we're exploring. For the purposes of the Principle & Expression framework, we will use the phrase *Law of God* to refer to the unchanging, universal principles that God established for mankind from the very beginning. It is important to note that our definition of the *Law of God* may not always correspond to the definition intended by the biblical authors. Each use of "Law of God" in Scripture must be interpreted in its own context.

The Law of God (as we're defining it) has been in effect and unchanging since creation. However, Yahweh has expressed it in various ways throughout history. The biggest and most formal expression occurred at Mount Sinai, where God gave Israel His law through Moses. We will use the phrase *Law of Moses* (or *Mosaic Law*) to refer to that body of commandments. Scripture later reveals the reason God gave the Mosaic Expression to Israel. It served as a tutor or guardian to help guide His People until Christ came. Galatians 3 says,

> So then, the law was our guardian until Christ came, in order that we might be justified by faith. But now that faith has come, we are no longer under a guardian. (Galatians 3:24-25)

This passage offers an excellent opportunity to test an application of the Principle & Expression framework. Seen through the P&E lens, we might interpret this text as saying something like,

---

[3] The list of blessings and curses is found in Deuteronomy 28.
[4] Joshua 8:31-32, 23:6; Judges 4:11; 1 Kings 2:3; 2 Kings 23:35; 2 Chronicles 23:18, 30:16; Ezra 3:2, 7:6; Nehemiah 8:1; Daniel 9:13; Luke 2:22, 24:44; John 7:23; Acts 13:39, 15:5, 28:23; 1 Corinthians 9:9; Heb 10:28.
[5] Genesis 1:26-27; Romans 1:18-20.

The Mosaic expression of the Law of God was our guardian until Christ came. And now that Christ has come, we no longer live by that expression, but rather by a New Expression of the same Law of God. (Galatians 3:24-25, *P&E interpretation*)

In other words, God's people have always been, and always will be, under the Law of God. God's Law did not change with the advent of the New Covenant. But because of the work of Christ, it is now expressed differently. Thus, we will refer to the Law of God as articulated under the New Covenant as the *New Expression*. And it is vital to remember that the Mosaic and New Expressions are overwhelmingly more similar than different.

The P&E framework reveals that the running disagreement between Torahism and mainstream Christianity happens at the level of *expression*, not *principle*. And it allows us to affirm two seemingly paradoxical truths at the same time.

1. The Law of God is unchanging
2. Christians are not obligated to keep the Law of Moses.

In Part Two, we will use the P&E framework to examine the claims of Torahism in several contexts. But for now, let's close Part One with a look at one compelling thread of Scriptural evidence for the P&E framework.

Atonement as an Example

Scripture reveals the principle in the Law of God that *atonement for sin comes through the shedding of blood* (See Lev 17:11). This is first hinted at in the Garden when, as a result of their disobedience, Adam and Eve suddenly became aware of their nakedness. What did God do in response to this first sin? He instituted the first shedding of blood in history.

And the Lord God made for Adam and for his wife garments of skins and clothed them. (Gen 3:21)

The phrase "garments of skins" suggests the institution of blood sacrifice. Ross explains it this way,

An animal was sacrificed to provide garments of skin, and later all Israel's animal sacrifices would be part of God's provision to remedy the curse—a life for a life. The sinner shall die! (Ezek.

18:20; Rom. 6:23) Yet he will live if he places his faith in the LORD, who has provided a Substitute. The skin with which God clothed Adam and Eve perpetually reminded them of God's provision. Similarly in the fullness of time, God accepted the sacrifice of Christ, and on the basis of that atonement. He clothes believers in righteousness (Rom. 3:21–26).[6]

Centuries after getting kicked out of Eden—just prior to the giving of the Mosaic Law—God's unchanging principle of blood atonement became even more apparent. While His People were in slavery in Egypt, God gave them the commands to sacrifice the Passover lamb. It is here that we first explicitly see the shedding of blood secure the salvation of God's people.

> The whole assembly of the congregation of Israel shall kill their lambs at twilight. Then they shall take some of the blood and put it on the two doorposts and the lintel of the houses in which they eat it . . . The blood shall be a sign for you, on the houses where you are. And when I see the blood, I will pass over you, and no plague will befall you to destroy you, when I strike the land of Egypt. (Exodus 12:6b–7, 13)

This first Passover was a foreshadowing of the blood of Christ, writ large. And not long after, God's People arrived at Mount Sinai where they received the Mosaic Expression of the Law of God. It was here that Yahweh revealed more about the nature of His principle of blood atonement.

> For the life of the flesh is in the blood; and I have given it to you for making atonement for your lives on the altar; for, as life, it is the blood that makes atonement. (Lev 17:11).

At the end of Israel's slavery in Egypt, the Passover marked the beginning of ritual sacrifice. Then, under the Mosaic Law, the expression of God's unchanging principle of blood atonement took the form of animal sacrifices at the tabernacle. God annually required the blood of bulls and goats to atone for sin (Lev 16). His universal principle was now expressed as a regular ceremony in the temple services. And centuries

---

[6] Ross, A. P. (1985). Genesis. In J. F. Walvoord & R. B. Zuck (Eds.), *The Bible Knowledge Commentary: An Exposition of the Scriptures* (Vol. 1, p. 33). Victor Books.

later, under the New Covenant, things changed dramatically. In the New Testament, the author of Hebrews teaches,

> For if the blood of goats and bulls, and the sprinkling of defiled persons with the ashes of a heifer, sanctify for the purification of the flesh, how much more, then, will the blood of Christ, who through the eternal Spirit offered himself unblemished to God, cleanse our consciences from acts that lead to death, so that we may serve the living God! (Hebrews 9:13-14)

Under the New Expression, God's law of blood atonement remains. It wasn't abolished, and it didn't come to an end. But the expression of this principle changed considerably. Atonement was now satisfied by the blood of Christ.

Thus, using the issue of blood atonement, we can trace the evolution of the various expressions of the Law of God. His unchanging principle was first expressed in the Garden through animal skins, which served as a "shadow" of Christ's sacrifice. Later, the "shadow" took on more detail, as expressed in the Passover sacrifice. Then came the ritual sacrifice of bulls and goats under the Mosaic Expression. And finally, under the New Expression, the "shadow" (Heb 10:1) gave way to the real thing. Yahweh's blood atonement principle was ultimately expressed in Christ, "whom God put forward as a sacrifice of atonement by his blood, effective through faith" (Rom 3:25).

Do Christians today still have a sacrifice? Yes, we do! Christ is our sacrifice. Under the New Covenant, "we have been sanctified through the offering of the body of Jesus Christ once for all" (Heb 10:10). Christ has eternally fulfilled the blood sacrifice required by God's Law. And thus, in contrast to the commands of the Mosaic Expression, under the New Expression, "there is no longer any offering for sin" (Heb 10:18b).

5

A Biblical Response

In essentials, unity; in non-essentials,
liberty; in all things, charity.

AUGUSTINE[1]

SHOULD TORAH-KEEPERS BE OPPOSED as false teachers preaching a false Gospel? Or should they be pulled aside like brothers wandering off the path? Because Torahism spans a range of beliefs, the answer is often a little of both. This is not a simple, black-and-white issue. There is a spectrum of thought on the role the Law plays in the life of a Christian, and I'm convinced there is room for honest disagreement.

The Gospel is about repenting of our sin and acknowledging faith in Christ as the only way to salvation. Torahists who affirm this biblical understanding of the Gospel can be categorized as brothers and sisters in Christ. Those who teach anything else are preaching a false Gospel. Paul warned the church in Galatia, "If anyone is preaching to you a gospel contrary to the one you received, let him be accursed" (Gal 1:9).

> We know that a person is not justified by works of the law but through faith in Jesus Christ, so we also have believed in Christ Jesus, in order to be justified by faith in Christ and not by works of the law, because by works of the law no one will be justified. (Galatians 2:16)

---

[1] This quote has been variously attributed to Augustine of Hippo (354–430), John Wesley (1703–1791), and a number of theologians in between.

When Torahism focuses on how our faith should be lived out, rather than how we are justified (saved), we have a family disagreement—a matter between brothers and sisters of the faith—on par with disputes about spiritual gifts, election versus free will, and end times. These are not unimportant issues. But they are secondary in the sense that there is room for honest disagreement among believers.

But when Torah-keepers begin emphasizing Moses over Christ or insinuating that keeping the Law makes one a little more righteous, they swim in treacherous waters. The border between a family dispute and the riptide of heresy is often hard to make out. And many well-meaning Torah-keepers with genuine faith in Christ have inadvertently crossed that boundary without realizing it. At the end of the day, any teaching that all Christians are required to keep the Law of Moses is unbiblical.

What Can I Do About It?

The most popular question I hear is, "What can I do about my family member or friend who has fallen into Torahism?" Many people are looking for advice on how to respond to the things their loved one is telling them. They want to know the best way to reason with them and get them to leave these false teachings behind. Unfortunately, there is no one-size-fits-all solution.

For the last few years, I have been searching for a "silver bullet" that would take down Torahism once and for all. I hoped to find a biblical passage clear enough that it would take the legs out from under the theology in one fell swoop. And guess what? I found many such passages! (See Part Two.) Unfortunately, I underestimated the complexity of the issue of Torah-observant Christianity. It's not merely an intellectual enterprise in which a well-meaning Christian miscalculated his sums and ended up at the wrong conclusion. It goes much deeper than that. There are emotional and spiritual factors at play that often carry greater weight than the intellectual aspect. And these factors cause Torah-keepers to automatically reject any biblical interpretation that does not align with their presuppositions.

Torahism has singled out a handful of Bible passages that could be interpreted as supporting the idea of Torah observance for Christ-followers and built a theology around them. Passages that teach the opposite are re-interpreted or sometimes even rejected. The old political adage "you can make the data say whatever you want" applies to Torahism. Not necessarily in the nefarious sense of trying to swindle people out of their money or loyalty, but on the personal level of confirmation bias. The theology of Torah-keeping "feels right" to its followers for many reasons. For some, it confirms suspicions about historical conspiracies concerning corruption, power grabs, and racism. For others, it seems to provide a sense of spiritual or intellectual superiority. (*Those silly, misled Christians. If only they could see what we see.*) For others, it is borne out of a sincere disappointment with the direction of modern Christianity.

And if we're honest, the criticism leveled at the modern Church is not entirely off-base. Some factions of Christianity *are* drifting away from our faith's genuine Jewish roots. Some are distancing themselves from deep Scriptural study, choosing instead to preach spiritually shallow self-help sermons. Others are engaged in a dangerous syncretism in which the moral values of secular culture are imported—and sometimes even replace—biblical values. The whole of Christendom has not veered off course. But we would be naive to deny the existence of such strains of thought. That said, choosing to respond to these issues by teaching a return to Torah-keeping for all Christians is a bit like removing graffiti from a wall using dynamite. It gets rid of the vandalism, but at what cost?

As I see it, we are dealing with two distinct questions.

1. Does your friend or loved one believe wrong things?
2. If so, how should you deal with it?

We will tackle these questions in reverse order. Part Two addresses the first question. There we will examine the theological claims of Torahism and gain a deeper understanding of where they are right and wrong, why, and to what degree. The remainder of this chapter will address the second question. Here are five areas to consider when dealing with Torahism in your life.

Maintain Perspective
It is essential to keep Torahism in perspective. Yes, it can be dangerous, but it is not as scary as other heresies out there. Most Torah-observant followers of Jesus confess that salvation comes only through faith in Christ. And if your loved one confesses faith in Yeshua, you have a lot to celebrate! Keeping Saturday Sabbath or skipping Christmas may disrupt family traditions or schedules, but it does not endanger their salvation. We have a great deal of freedom in Christ. Even though Christians are not required to keep the Law of Moses, we are also not

prohibited from doing so. For Christ-followers, keeping those Mosaic traditions is technically permitted but not required.

Value the Relationship

For the reasons above, I believe we should not make the Hebrew Roots beliefs of our loved ones a test of fellowship. In other words, their adoption of Torahism, as wrong as the theology might be, should not necessarily cause us to cut ties with them. "If possible, so far as it depends on you, live peaceably with all" (Rom 12:18). Sometimes it is not up to us, of course. But as far as they are willing to continue doing life with us, let's welcome it, remembering the words of our Lord. "By this, all people will know that you are my disciples if you have love for one another" (John 13:35). Treating others with love and grace is not just wise; it is biblical. It is never wrong. And when it comes to Torahism, maintaining relationships is so important. At some point, our loved ones will begin to realize how off-base their theology is. And if we're still in a relationship with them, showing love and grace, we will be in a position to lovingly guide them back when God says it is time.

The flip side is that we do not want to condone false theology. Often an "agree to disagree" truce is the best solution. *I don't agree with you on everything you're saying about the Bible, but I love you, and I want us to still be in each other's lives.* Act in love and extend grace wherever you can. As the famous quote says, "In essentials, unity, in non-essentials, liberty, in all things, charity."

Know Your Stuff

When dealing with Torahism in a loved one, our job is to understand the difference between essentials and non-essentials. We need to be reading our Bibles and working to understand the fundamentals of the Christian faith. Knowing exactly where we can extend grace on theological matters can get tricky.

For example, what does the Bible teach about Christmas that can help us when Torah-keeping threatens to damage our long-held family traditions? How should we respond to a Hebrew Roots family member who refuses to participate in Christmas anymore? (Christmas is dealt with in-depth in Chapter 17.) The bottom line is that the Bible teaches celebrating Christmas is permitted but not required. Our loved ones are free to skip Christmas if they choose. And in that case, it is probably best, as painful as it might be, to respect their wishes and tell them you'll miss them. Better to miss them at Christmas than risk them cutting ties altogether. At the same time, we need to acknowledge that they have no biblical basis on which to criticize us for choosing to celebrate the birth of Christ. Nor do they have a biblical reason to demand we stop doing so.

When to Engage

Whether or not you should engage with someone on their Torahism is a question only you can answer. If they're not open or able to have civil, productive conversations, then an "agree to disagree" truce may be in order. If you choose to engage, acknowledging areas where you agree is a great place to start. And it is beneficial for both sides. Highlighting common ground can help avoid the other person feeling attacked or criticized. And the good news is that mainstream Christianity has far more in common with Torahism than not; same Scripture, same God, same story of redemption, same Savior, and so on.

I often battle with teachers and keepers of Torahism in the arena of ideas by establishing theological cases and arguing biblical concepts. And that approach has its place. But when we deal with people we love and want to be in a relationship with, a different approach is often required. Rather than proving them wrong, try getting them to think about what they believe by asking honest questions. It can be as simple as *How did you come to that conclusion?* or *Have you ever considered...?* This approach aims not to win arguments or prove them wrong but simply to "put a pebble in their shoe," as apologist Greg Koukl says. Ask questions that help them recognize the flaws in their current beliefs and become less comfortable with them. Koukl also offers this wise advice:

> Always make it a goal to keep your conversations cordial. Sometimes that will not be possible. If a principled, charitable expression of your ideas makes someone mad, there's little you can do about it. Jesus' teaching made some people furious. Just make sure it's your ideas that offend and not you, that your beliefs cause the disruption and not your behavior.[2]

To date, I've not heard of anyone being argued out of the Hebrew Roots movement. At least not in one fell swoop. Like any of us,

---

[2] Koukl, Gregory. *Tactics, 10th Anniversary Edition* (p. 39). Zondervan. Kindle Edition. I highly recommend this book. It was written for conversations between Christians and non-Christians but applies equally well to conversations between Christians and Torahists.

Torahists typically need to find their own way out. And it sure helps when a loving friend or family member is there to lovingly guide them along the way.

It is Not Up to Us

Lastly, and most importantly, this is not our fight to win. The outcome is up to God. Without the working of the Holy Spirit, no argument we mount, no point we raise will make a difference. God invites us to join in His work. And He does so knowing that we, too, are flawed in our own ways. None of us have a perfect or complete understanding of God or Scripture. We all have some level of surprise in store for us when we get to Heaven. And because we don't have all the answers, we must approach our Torah-keeping friends and family members in prayer and humility. And, in the end, trust God to bring about the best outcome.

PART TWO

*Claims About
the Torah*

6

The Torah Is Eternal

Forever, O Lord, your word is firmly fixed in the heavens.

PSALM 119:89

NOW THAT WE'VE ESTABLISHED A FOUNDATION for our discussion, let's examine some of Torahism's specific claims and see how they stack up against Scripture. We'll start with the belief on which all its teachings are predicated. Namely, that the Law of Moses is eternal. This belief is why Torah-keepers claim we are still under that Law today.

Could the claim be true? Was the Mosaic Law intended to remain binding and unchanged forever? According to Torahism, the answer is a resounding yes! But what does the Bible teach? Let's first look at the verses in the Torah that our Hebrew Roots friends point to when they claim the Law of Moses is eternal and everlasting. Then we'll examine what the New Testament has to say on the subject.

Eternality in the Torah

The dictionary definition of *eternal* is "without beginning or end; lasting forever; always existing (opposed to temporal)." Yahweh is our point of reference for eternality. Christianity and Torahism agree that He is eternal,[1] without beginning or end.

---

[1] Genesis 1:1; Psalm 90:2; John 1:1; Romans 1:20; 1 Timothy 1:17.

Before the mountains were born or you brought forth the whole
world, from everlasting to everlasting, you are God. (Psalm
90:2)[2]

On the other hand, the Law of Moses—although it was given by an
eternal God—is not itself eternal. Why? Because it had a beginning.
According to Rabbi Even-Israel, the Mosaic Law was given to mankind
at Mount Sinai.[3] The apostle Paul agrees, teaching that "sin indeed was
in the world before the law was given" (Rom 5:13). Galatians says the
Law came 430 years after God's promise to Abraham (Gal 3:17). Jesus
also taught that the Law of Moses is not past-eternal. In response to the
Pharisees testing Him on the issue of divorce, He said, "Because of your
hardness of heart Moses allowed you to divorce your wives, but from the
beginning it was not so" (Matt 19:8). These words not only verify that
the Mosaic Law had a beginning, but they also reveal that it was not the
ultimate expression of the Law of God. Instead, the Law of Moses
contains concessions that Yahweh, in His great mercy, allowed for the
sake of His beloved Israel.

Indeed, God created the universe and humanity, including a host of
Old Testament saints—Adam, Noah, Abraham, Isaac, Jacob, Joseph,
etc.—who all lived and died before the Law was given. The world saw
the Fall and the Flood and the Tower of Babel before it saw the Law.
The Jews spent 430 years in slavery in Egypt before the Law of Moses
existed. So the Mosaic Law is not eternal. It was given at a specific time
in history (~1400 B.C.) at a particular place (Mount Sinai) through a
specific man (Moses).

How About Everlasting?

The Law of Moses is not technically *eternal* because it had a
beginning. But once given, was it intended to remain binding and
unchanged forever, as our Torahist friends affirm? There are a number
of passages that seem to support their position.

- Your word, Lord, is eternal; it stands firm in the heavens. (Psalm
  119:89)
- Yet you are near, Lord, and all your commands are true. Long ago I
  learned from your statutes that you established them to last forever.
  (Psalm 119:151-2)

---

[2] Also see Deuteronomy 33:27; Isaiah 26:4; Jeremiah 10:10.
[3] Even-Israel, "Torah Eternal," *Chabad.org*.

- All your words are true; all your righteous laws are eternal. (Psalm 119:160 NIV)
- Know therefore that the Lord your God is God; he is the faithful God, keeping his covenant of love to a thousand generations of those who love him and keep his commandments. (Deuteronomy 7:9)

Two points can be made by way of response. First, many of the verses cited by our Torah-keeping friends do not teach that the Law of Moses, in particular, will last forever. This is where Torahist teachers often misunderstand (or perhaps take advantage of) the grey area between terms such as *Torah*, *Law*, God's *Word*, and God's *commandments*. This is why the *Principle & Expression* framework we discussed in chapter four is so helpful. By revealing that the Mosaic Law does not contain the entirety of God's laws and commands, it allows us to affirm that the Law of God is eternal and unchanging while recognizing that the Law of Moses is not.

It should be noted that Torahism tends to adopt a Jewish understanding of these terms and concepts. Which is not an unreasonable approach. After all, these are words initially written in Hebrew and found in the Hebrew Scriptures. Who would better understand the Jewish Bible than Jewish sages and rabbis? Yet, our Torah-keeping friends can miss an important detail in their zeal for Hebrew culture. Jewish sages and rabbis—as erudite and wise as they indeed are—interpret these terms within a theology that rejects Jesus as Messiah and rejects the New Testament writings. Their commitment to Judaism colors their interpretation. Christians, on the other hand, do not believe God's story ended with the Old Testament. So we find the best and most accurate interpretation of these Hebrew terms on the pages of the New Testament. The NT authors offer an inspired, Christ-centered, Jewish interpretation of the Hebrew Scriptures.

The second response to the claim that the Law of Moses is everlasting is to examine what the Bible means by "everlasting." And here we will need to wade into slightly more technical waters. Nearly all of the Old Testament was written in biblical Hebrew.[4] When translating any text, there is not an exact one-to-one correlation between languages. This is especially true when translating biblical Hebrew—which has less than 9,000 words—into modern English, which has well over 200,000 words! In most cases, the English translations give us what we need. But

---

[4] According to the International Bible Society, a few chapters of Ezra and Daniel and one verse in Jeremiah were written in biblical Aramaic rather than Hebrew.

when it comes to examining the claims of Torahism, with its error by degrees, it is sometimes necessary for us to parse the English translations a bit more carefully.

For example, in Leviticus 16, God lays out His instructions to Israel regarding Yom Kippur (the Day of Atonement). We find detailed commands regarding the sacrifice of bulls and goats and what the priest is to do with the blood. Leviticus 16 ends with the following decree:

> And this shall be *a statute forever* for you, that atonement may be made for the people of Israel once in the year because of all their sins. (Leviticus 16:34, *emphasis added*)

In this verse, the Hebrew word עוֹלָם (*olam*) is translated into English as *forever* (ERV, ESV, NCV), *permanent* (CSB, NASB, NLT), or *lasting/everlasting* (KJV, NIV, NRSV). These English words all refer to something that never ends. Yet the New Testament teaches that the sin sacrifices *have* ended. They were replaced by the "once for all" sacrifice of Christ (Heb 10:10), thus "there is no longer any offering for sin" (Heb 10:18). How do we account for this discrepancy? Did the Torah err in saying Yahweh would require those sacrifices forever? Of course not. The problem is not with the Torah but with the English translation.

In ancient Hebrew, the word *olam* is not as cut-and-dry as the English word *forever*. It has a much broader definition that does not always carry the concept of eternity contained in the English word. In fact, according to the NAS Old Testament Hebrew Lexicon, *olam* can be used to mean:

> long duration, antiquity, futurity, forever, ever, everlasting, evermore, perpetual, old, ancient, world;
>
> *(of past) ancient time, long time;
>
> *(of future) forever, always, continuous existence, perpetual, everlasting, indefinite or unending future, eternity

This wide range of definitions explains why, in the New American Standard Bible translation, the single Hebrew word *olam* is translated into 25 different English words or phrases:

ages (1)	ever (10)	long time (3)
all successive (1)	everlasting (112)	never (17)

always (1)	forever (206)	old (11)
ancient (13)	forever and ever (1)	permanent (10)
ancient times (3)	forevermore (1)	permanently (1)
continual (1)	lasting (1)	perpetual (29)
days of old (1)	long (2)	perpetually (1)
eternal (2)	long ago (3)	
eternity (3)	long past (1)	

So, when we come across the Hebrew word *olam*, we need to determine the author's intended meaning based on the context in which it is used. Fruchtenbaum points out that *olam*,

> is used of someone's lifetime (Ex. 14:13), of a slave's life (Ex. 21:6; Lev. 25:46; Deut. 15:17), of Samuel's life (I Sam. 1:22; 2:35), of the lifetimes of David and Jonathan (I Sam. 20:23), and of David's lifetime (I Sam. 27:12; 28:2; I Chr. 28:4). While the English reads *forever*, obviously from the context it does not mean "forever" in the sense of eternity, but only up to the end of the person's life.[5]

This range of meaning raises an important question. In Leviticus 16:34, how do we determine if *olam* meant the sacrifices would continue "for all time" or "for a long, indefinite duration," or something else?

> And this shall be *a statute forever* for you, that atonement may be made for the people of Israel once in the year because of all their sins. (Leviticus 16:34, emphasis added)

In Judaism, the context for determining the meaning of this verse is limited to the Tanakh. Christians and Torahists, on the other hand, accept the New Testament as the Word of God. Therefore they interpret this verse within the larger context of the Old *and* New Testaments. This makes a big difference. God has sovereignly chosen to reveal His will to mankind over time rather than all at once. So when new information is introduced along the biblical timeline, we have to interpret the former Scriptures in light of the latter. They are both the inspired Word of God, of course. But often, the newer information helps to explain and illuminate the older.

It is like the movie *The Sixth Sense*. Near the end of the film, we get the shocking revelation that the psychiatrist Malcolm (played by Bruce

---

[5] Ariel Ministries Manuscript 176, Dr. Arnold G. Fruchtenbaum.

Willis) has been dead the whole time. This revelation does not change the content of the earlier scenes or make them untrue. In fact, there is a sense in which it makes them even *more* true. Re-watching the movie reveals clues that had been sitting in plain sight the whole time. For example, Malcolm's wife wasn't ignoring him or being cold. She acted like he didn't exist because he was dead, and she couldn't see him. And Malcolm never touches or moves objects in front of anyone other than his young patient, Cole, who can see dead people. Also, Malcolm never directly interacts with the Cole's mother. These clues were there for us all along, but it is not until we receive the revelation later in the film that we fully understand what they mean.

The same is true of the Bible. Once our eyes are opened to Yahweh's new revelation through Yeshua and the New Testament authors, the Old Testament comes into sharper focus. We begin noticing clues left by the Author that were sitting in plain sight the whole time. The Old Testament was not wrong and it is not to be thrown away. Because of God's later revelations, it means something *more* than we thought. And our new understanding makes it even more real and amazing. Augustine put it this way, "The Old Testament is in the New revealed; the New Testament is in the Old concealed."[6] Kennedy writes:

> Jesus Himself is the key that unlocks the meaning of every biblical text. Understanding who Jesus is—both who He claims to be and how He Himself reads the Scriptures—is the first and most critical hermeneutical task . . . His life, death, resurrection, and ascension fulfill the old covenant law and restore a desolate humanity to communion with God (Eph. 2:11–16). Without His divinely ordained and obedient sacrifice for sinners, the whole Bible, but especially the Old Testament, is rendered incoherent.[7]

Returning to Leviticus 16:34, it is easy to understand why, prior to Jesus and the New Covenant, the Jewish sages and rabbis interpreted the phrase "a statute forever" to mean that the sin sacrifices commanded on the Day of Atonement would last literally until the end of time. Israel had no idea there would be a New Covenant at that time. That wouldn't be revealed until the prophet Jeremiah. And we wouldn't even begin to understand it until Christ.

---

[6] Augustine, *Seven Questions Concerning the Heptateuch*, dated 419-420 CE.
[7] Anne Carlson Kennedy, "The Theological Legacy of Rachel Held Evans," *Equip*.

In hindsight, we now know Yahweh promised a New Covenant (Jer 31:31-34), which was inaugurated in the first century through Yeshua's death on the cross.[8] And we know the Old Covenant was made obsolete and outdated because of Christ's sacrifice (Heb 8:13), which, among other changes, replaced the Mosaic sin sacrifices "once for all" (Heb 10). In light of this newer information, we can conclude that *olam* must have been used in Leviticus 16:34 to refer to "a long duration" rather than "forever."

The same reasoning holds true for Exodus 40:15, which tells of the appointing of the Levitical priesthood.

> And their anointing shall admit them to a *perpetual priesthood* throughout their generations. (Exodus 40:15, *emphasis added*)

If the word *olam* in this passage meant "forever," then the priesthood prescribed in the Mosaic Law—which was strictly limited to descendants of the tribe of Levi[9]—would have been the only priesthood until the end of time. However, the New Testament says that Jesus—who descended from the tribe of Judah, not Levi—is now our High Priest (Heb 7:14-18). And further, *all* Christians, whether Jew or Gentile, are now a royal priesthood through the indwelling of the Holy Spirit (1 Pet 2:4-10). And when God allowed the Romans to destroy the temple in Jerusalem in 70 CE, the Levitical priesthood ended and has never returned. Therefore, when the Torah describes the Levitical priesthood as *olam*, it cannot mean it will literally last until the end of time. Instead, it is best interpreted to indicate that the priesthood was to last for "a long duration."[10]

There are numerous examples throughout Scripture where English words and phrases like *forever, eternally, throughout your generations, unto a thousand generations,* and *as long as you're living on the earth* could not literally mean "until the end of time."[11] However—and here is where it gets tricky—there are also many passages where that is *precisely* what those words mean. For example, Yahweh and His attributes are literally

---

[8] Matthew 26:28; Luke 22:20; 1 Corinthians 11:25.
[9] See Exodus 40:15 and Deuteronomy 18:5. The end of the Levitical priesthood is one of many clues that tell us the Law of Moses is no longer in effect. This issue is discussed in greater detail in chapter fourteen, *The Temple, Priests, Sacrifices & Worship.*
[10] This is evident in how the word *olam* is rendered in other Bible translations. For example, in the NIV, the English word "everlasting" is not used in this verse at all. Instead, it refers to "a priesthood that will continue throughout their generations."
[11] Exodus 21:6; 1 Kings 8:13; Jonah 2.

eternal,[12] His Word will actually endure forever,[13] and His love is truly unending.[14]

This is why context is so critical. In pursuing an understanding of the true Hebrew roots of the Christian faith, we need to be careful not to abandon or undermine the later revelations found in the New Testament. When we see older verses that seem to indicate a thing will last forever and find newer verses which indicate that thing has ended, it should give us pause. As we work to reconcile potential contradictions, we must view them in light of the entire Bible.

The Law in the New Testament

Another way to examine the eternality of the Law of Moses is to survey what the New Testament says about it. There are various passages that reveal that at least parts of the Mosaic Law have been fulfilled and come to an end. For example, the Jerusalem Council, as recorded in Acts 15, gathered to discuss whether Gentile Christians were required to be circumcised and keep the Law of Moses. Their final answer? Nope. And consider Galatians 3.

So then, the law was our guardian until Christ came, in order that we might be justified by faith. But now that faith has come, we are no longer under a guardian. (Galatians 3:24-25)

Here the apostle Paul uses the analogy of a guardian[15] to describe the Law of Moses. He begins by stating that (a.) the law was our guardian (b.) until Christ came so that (c.) we might be justified (declared righteous) through faith. The Faithlife Study Bible commentary on this passage notes, "The law had a temporary and protective role. It kept people mindful of their condition and guided them toward maturity in God's ways."[16] Paul completes his analogy by teaching that now that faith in Christ has come, we are no longer under the Mosaic Law.

Let's close this chapter by looking at two other New Testament passages that teach that the Law of Moses has ended and, therefore, cannot be eternal.

---

[12] Genesis 21:33; Deuteronomy 32:40; Isaiah 40:28; Psalm 100:5, 117:2.
[13] Isaiah 40:8; Psalm 33:11, 119:89.
[14] Isaiah 54:8-10; Jeremiah 31:3; Psalm 109:2.
[15] In the Greek παιδαγωγός (paidagógos). Some translations render this word into English as custodian (NASB), or tutor (NKJV).
[16] Barry, J. D., Mangum, D., Brown, D. R., Heiser, M. S., Custis, M., Ritzema, E., ... Bomar, D., Faithlife Study Bible (Ga 3:24) (Lexham Press, 2012, 2016).

2 Corinthians 3

Wiersbe describes the context of Paul's second letter to the church in Corinth as follows.

> No sooner did the Gospel of God's grace begin to spread among the Gentiles than a counterfeit "gospel" appeared, a mixture of Law and grace. It was carried by a zealous group of people that we have come to call "the Judaizers." Paul wrote his letter to the Galatians to refute their doctrines, and you will find him referring to them several times in 2 Corinthians.[17]

In chapter 3, Paul discusses how Christians are ministers of the New Covenant. There we find a short passage that presents a tremendous challenge to the theology of Torahism.

> Now if the ministry of death, carved in letters on stone, came with such glory that the Israelites could not gaze at Moses' face because of its glory, which was being brought to an end, will not the ministry of the Spirit have even more glory? For if there was glory in the ministry of condemnation, the ministry of righteousness must far exceed it in glory. Indeed, in this case, what once had glory has come to have no glory at all, because of the glory that surpasses it. For if what was being brought to an end came with glory, much more will what is permanent have glory. (2 Corinthians 3:7-11)

The phrase "carved in letters on stone" in v. 7 is an obvious reference to the Mosaic Law (Ex 31:18). And it is labeled a "ministry of death." Those are strong words. Of course, Paul does not mean that the Mosaic Law literally kills us. Rather he presents a contrast and underscores the fact that the Law cannot save us; it can only identify our sin and condemn us.[18] Paul continues,

> Now if the ministry of death, carved in letters on stone, [*the Law of Moses*] came with such glory that the Israelites could not gaze at Moses' face because of its glory, which was being brought to an end, will not the ministry of the Spirit have even more glory? (2 Corinthians 3:7-8, *comments added*)

---

[17] Warren W. Wiersbe, *The Bible Exposition Commentary*, vol. 1 (Victor Books, 1996), p. 637.
[18] This is the same thing taught in Romans 3:20, 7:7-25, 8:2.

Paul is contrasting the glory of the Mosaic law, which was written on stone by the finger of God, with something he calls "the ministry of the Spirit." There are a couple of things to point out here. First, although the Mosaic law is called a *ministry of death* and a *ministry of condemnation*, it was attended by the glory of God. So the Law of Moses is not some ancient, pointless code that we can toss out. No, it is "holy, righteous and good" (Rom 7:12). It just wasn't intended to remain unchanged forever.

Second, Paul is referring to Exodus 34:29–35 where, after being in God's presence to receive the Law, Moses' face shone so brightly that the Israelites were afraid to get close to him. He had to put on a veil. And if the Mosaic Law came with such amazing glory, Paul asks, how much more glory will the *ministry of the Spirit* have?

What is the ministry of the Spirit? Because the indwelling of the Holy Spirit is a sign of saving faith in Christ, Paul often used the concept of the "Spirit" when contrasting the Law and Sinai Covenant with Jesus and the New Covenant.[19] So, 2 Corinthians 3:7-8 is essentially saying, "If the Law of Moses came with such glory that the Israelites couldn't look at Moses' face because of it, how much more glory does the ministry of Christ have?"

Additionally, the glory on Moses' face is described as "being brought to an end." Scripture doesn't say how long Moses had to wear the veil. After the giving of the Law, it is never mentioned again. But here in Second Corinthians, Paul teaches that, at some point, the reflection of God's radiant glory on Moses' face ended. That idea is linked to the temporary nature of the Mosaic Law, and contrasted with the eternal ministry of the Spirit. In other words, when God gave the Law to Moses, it was accompanied by His glory. And just like the radiant glow on Moses' face eventually ended, so would the Law that came with it.

The next verse extends the contrast. "For if there was glory in the ministry of condemnation, the ministry of righteousness must far exceed it in glory" (2 Cor 3:9). Paul contrasts the glory of the *ministry of condemnation* with that of the *ministry of righteousness*. He is carrying forward the comparison introduced in verses 7-8. There was glory in the Mosaic Law, but the ministry of Jesus is far more glorious. Jesus and the new covenant are superior to Moses and the Old Covenant. Paul doubles down on this idea in the last two verses of the passage.

Indeed, in this case, what once had glory has come to have no glory at all, because of the glory that surpasses it. For if what was

---

[19] Romans 2:29, 7:6, 8:2; 2 Corinthians 3:3; Galatians 5:18.

being brought to an end came with glory, much more will what is permanent have glory. (2 Corinthians 3:10-11)

The glory of Jesus and the New Covenant is so overwhelming that, by contrast, the Mosaic Law and the Sinai Covenant have "come to have no glory at all." This idea is echoed in Hebrews.

But in fact, the ministry Jesus has received is as superior to theirs [the Levitical priests] as the covenant of which he is mediator is superior to the old one, since the new covenant is established on better promises. (Hebrews 8:6, bracketed comment added)

And the author of Hebrews ends this chapter with the following statement:

In speaking of a new covenant, he makes the first one obsolete. And what is becoming obsolete and growing old is ready to vanish away. (Hebrews 8:13)

Don't miss the import and the timing of this statement. The Sinai Covenant—for which the Mosaic Law served as the terms—is called *obsolete*. The Greek word is παλαιόω (*palaioō*), which means to be *become old, wear out*. And just a few years after these words were written, the temple in Jerusalem was destroyed. The old covenant and its law became obsolete and vanished away.[20]

Torahism teaches that Christians today are required to keep the Law of Moses. But look at the ways the text of our passage describes that law:

- ministry of death
- ministry of condemnation
- came with great glory
- being brought to an end
- once had glory
- came to have no glory at all

Second Corinthians reveals that the Mosaic Law has been outshined and come to an end because of the exceedingly glorious and superior ministry of Christ. Thus, we might paraphrase our passage as follows:

---

[20] This unique historical period is discussed in greater detail in chapter nine, *Yeshua Kept Torah*.

If the Law of Moses came with such glory that the Israelites could not gaze at Moses' face because of it, how much more glory does the ministry of Christ have? There was glory in the Law, but the righteousness of Jesus far exceeds it. In fact, the Law, which enjoyed a temporary glory that has ended, has been surpassed by the glory of Christ which will never end. (2 Corinthians 3:7-11, *author's paraphrase*)

Torahism's assertion that the Mosaic Law is eternal (or everlasting) does not align with what Scripture teaches. And here we bump into the thorny issue of terminology once again. Is God's *Word* eternal? Yes. Is His *Torah* eternal? Of course! Are His *promises* eternal? Absolutely. But the *Law of Moses* was never intended to last forever.

Ephesians 2

In Ephesians 2, we find a beautiful description of the unity that Yeshua's sacrifice made possible between Jews and Gentiles.

But now in Christ Jesus you who once were far off [*Gentiles*] have been brought near by the blood of Christ. For he himself is our peace, who has made us both [*Jew and Gentile*] one and has broken down in his flesh the dividing wall of hostility by abolishing the law of commandments expressed in ordinances, that he might create in himself one new man in place of the two, so making peace, and might reconcile us both, to God in one body through the cross, thereby killing the hostility. (Eph 2:13-16, *comments added*)

The text goes on to teach that, because of Christ, Gentiles "are no longer strangers and aliens" but "fellow citizens with the saints and members of the household of God" (v. 19). This encouraging message of unity begs the question, why were Jews and Gentiles at odds in the first place? The *Bible Exposition Commentary* offers some helpful insight.

The cause of that enmity was the Law, because the Law made a definite distinction between Jews and Gentiles. The dietary laws reminded the Jews that God had put a difference between the clean and unclean (Lev. 11:44–47). But the Gentiles did not obey these laws; therefore they were unclean. Ezekiel the prophet reminded the priests that their task was to teach the Jews "the difference between the holy and the profane" (Ezek.

44:23). The divine ordinances given by God to Israel stood as a wall between the Jews and the other nations. In fact, there was a wall in the Jewish temple, separating the court of the Gentiles from the rest of the temple areas. [21]

The Law of Moses was the source of the "dividing wall of hostility" (Eph 2:14) between Jews and Gentiles. And Yeshua broke that wall down "in His flesh" (v. 14), meaning through His sacrificial death. And what effect did Christ's death have? It "abolish[ed] the law of commandments expressed in ordinances" (v. 15), which was the source of the division in the first place. And what do you suppose the phrase "the law of commandments expressed in ordinances" would have meant to Paul's first-century Jewish audience? It is an unambiguous reference to the Mosaic Law, under which the Jewish people had been living for 1,500 years. And what does the text say Jesus did to that law? He *abolished* it. The Greek word is καταργέω (*katargeō*), meaning "to render inoperative, annul, make of no effect." How could Paul have written such a thing if the Law of Moses was, as Torahism claims, eternal?

Our point about the temporary nature of the Law of Moses has been made. But because this is a foundational issue on which Torah-keeping hangs, and because there is even more Scriptural evidence available to us, let's consider one final argument.

New Commandments

Some of the commandments given to us by Yeshua are not found in the Torah,[22] and this is a game-changer. It means the Torah-keeper cannot follow the Law as Yahweh gave it to Moses *and* follow Yeshua at the same time. This idea is met with strong resistance by Torahists. When I asked about the new commandments given by Yeshua in an online discussion, one Torahist replied:

> You are a lawless Christian if you want to make Yeshua break Torah by adding new commands to it. You're making Yeshua sin by breaking the command in Deuteronomy that says you shall not add to this book of the Torah. Therefore, you just made Yeshua out to be a sinner who could not have been the messiah.

---

[21] Warren W. Wiersbe, *The Bible Exposition Commentary*, vol. 2 (Victor Books, 1996), p. 23.
[22] Matthew 4:19, 5:23-24, 5:34, 5:44; Mark 16:15; John 13:34.

Beware lawless Christians who are always trying to make you follow a false messiah! (Tim C.)

I asked the group why Yeshua called it a "new" command when He said, "A new command I give you: Love one another. As I have loved you, so you must love one another" (John 13:34). I was curious to see how our Torahist friends would interpret this verse. Following are a few of the responses I received.

Yeshua was getting to the new command. They hadn't probably gone over it yet, just like if you were to give someone who was just learning to play guitar a lesson, you wouldn't tell them how to shred on a solo without first teaching the basics first. Then would come a day that you would tell your student (disciple), "A new lesson I give you, shred until people's faces fall off." So did you just come up with the concept of shredding or has shredding always been around? Or is it just a *new lesson* to your student that you haven't gone over yet? Please...try a little harder to make Yeshua break the commands by adding something to the Torah, because if he added one thing, he isn't the messiah. (Rocky S.)

Just know this, Yeshua could not have added anything to the Torah or he wouldn't be the messiah, he was sinless. Unlike us, we love to add to the Torah or take away from the Torah and say it has been abolished. (Ben F.)

You actually think Yeshua was coming up with the brand-new concept of love?? He is teaching from the Torah, the Torah tells us: Do not take revenge on others or continue to hate them but love your neighbors as you love yourself. I am the Lord. (Leviticus 19:18) The command of *love one another* isn't a new command he just came up with on the spot! The disciples are just that: *His* disciplines. He's supposed to teach them the way of Torah. (Jodie S.)

Based on their passionate responses, our Torah-keeping friends seem aware that Torahism falls apart if we can show that Yeshua added any new commandments.[23] In defense of their position, they point to the words of Moses in Deuteronomy:

> Do not add to what I command you and do not subtract from it but keep the commands of the Lord your God that I give you. (Deuteronomy 4:2)
>
> See that you do all I command you; do not add to it or take away from it. (Deuteronomy 12:32)

Based on passages like this, our Torahist friends conclude that when Yeshua said He was giving us a "new" command, it must mean one of two things. Either it was not actually new, in which case we're left wondering why He called it new (καινός kainos). Or Jesus was adding to the Law of Moses, which means He is not the Messiah.

However, there is a third and much more biblical option they are not considering: Yeshua's new commandments were not added under the Sinai Covenant because that was coming to an end. Instead, they were given under the New Covenant, which was being inaugurated. This third option makes the most sense of the text of Scripture. Let's look at a few of the new commands Yeshua gave us.

Love One Another

> A new commandment I give to you, that you love one another: just as I have loved you, you also are to love one another. (John 13:34)

Why did Yeshua call this command "new"? We can certainly agree with our Torah-keeping friends that the commandment to love was not new. Jewish tradition highly values love. Rabbi Hillel, a contemporary of Yeshua and one of the most influential figures in Jewish history, preached love and taught things such as, "Be of the disciples of Aaron, loving peace and pursuing peace, loving mankind and bringing them nigh to the law."[24] And the Torah commands both love for God and love

---

[23] It is interesting to note that the admonition not to add or remove any Torah commands was given to Israel. So Jesus as a man was subject to that restriction, but as God incarnate, He was not. Make of that what you will.

[24] Ethics of the Fathers 1:12.

for one's neighbor.[25] In fact, Jesus taught, "All the Law and the Prophets hang on these two commandments" (Matt 22:40).[26]

If the commandment to love already existed in the Torah, why did Yeshua refer to His commandment as new? I believe the answer is found in the qualifying phrase "as I have loved you." Barry notes,

> Jesus inserts this phrase into the commandment from Lev 19:18. The new part of the commandment is that Jesus' disciples are instructed to love other people the way Jesus loved them— serving them like a slave would, as He does in this scene, even to the point of laying down their lives for others.[27]

What makes His commandment new is the standard He set for our love. We are to love *as Christ loved us*. And what kind of love did Yeshua model for us? A love not limited to His family, friends, and disciples. Jesus taught us to love our enemies and pray for those who persecute us. And He demonstrated this kind of love by laying down His life not only for His friends but also for His enemies. "God shows his love for us in that while we were still sinners, Christ died for us" (Rom 5:8). This kind of unmerited, selfless love is not commanded in the Torah.

Elwell and Beitzel elaborate on this newness.

> The character of the new commandment comes from the "new covenant" which Jesus inaugurated at the Last Supper. Under the new covenant, God "writes" his law on the hearts of believers (Heb 10:16). That is, he actively works in them in the person of the Holy Spirit and gives them a new willingness to obey him (Rom 8:4; Gal 5:16). The new commandment of love is the all-embracing, single requirement of the new covenant (Rom 13:8, 10; Gal 5:14) . . . Anticipating his ascension into heaven, Jesus left one inclusive commandment to preserve his disciples in the new age until its consummation at the judgment day (Jn 5:28, 29; 1 Jn 4:17). Obedience to the new commandment was supposed to identify them as Jesus' disciples during his absence

---

[25] Leviticus 19:18; Deuteronomy 6:5.
[26] The phrase "the Law and the Prophets" is a Hebraic idiom that refers to the entirety of the Jewish Scriptures (Tanakh).
[27] John D. Barry et al., *Faithlife Study Bible* (Lexham Press, 2012, 2016), Jn 13:34.

(Jn 13:35; 17:21–23). The love command was thus new in the sense that it had a special function in the new age.[28]

I Am the True Vine

In addition to John 13:34, Jesus gave other commandments not found in the Mosaic Expression. His teaching in John 15:1-17 is one example. Here Yeshua reorients His followers to a new way of living in God. Under the Mosaic Expression, God told His people that He would bless them if they kept His laws and precepts (Deut 28:1-14). And as we will examine in chapter fourteen, there was a sense of serving God at a distance in the Mosaic temple system. The people brought their sacrifices to the priests, who would then offer them to God. The priests could enter holy places where the average person was not allowed.

But in John 15, Jesus reveals that relationship has changed. He teaches us to abide in *Him*, not the temple, or the Law, or even the Father. Christ is the true vine (v. 1). And we aren't just commanded to get close to Him; we are to be *in* Him. In the same way a vine supplies life-giving nutrients to its branches, we draw our life-giving identity and righteousness from being directly connected to Christ. Our blessings are no longer linked to legal obedience. They come in a whole new way.

Abide in me, and I in you. As the branch cannot bear fruit by itself, unless it abides in the vine, neither can you, unless you abide in me . . . If you keep my commandments, you will abide in my love, just as I have kept my Father's commandments and abide in his love . . . This is my commandment, that you love one another as I have loved you . . . These things I command you, so that you will love one another. (John 15:4, 10, 12, 17)

The imagery alludes to the Tanakh's depictions of Israel as Yahweh's vineyard (Isa 5:1–7). Jesus is the embodiment of Israel, the central focus of God's plan of salvation. He fulfills the role of Israel as the true vine.

Sermon on the Mount

In many cases in the New Testament, we find an elevation of a Mosaic command. Under the New Expression, it is given a higher meaning. Or perhaps it is more accurate to say the command is elevated

---

[28] Walter A. Elwell and Barry J. Beitzel, "Commandment, The New," *Baker Encyclopedia of the Bible* (Baker Book House, 1988), pp. 501–502.

to more closely conform to the ultimate principles of the Law of God. We see this in the Sermon on the Mount.

> You have heard that it was said, "Love your neighbor and hate your enemy." But I tell you, love your enemies and pray for those who persecute you. (Matthew 5:43-44)

Here Yeshua is both elevating and transforming the Torah's teaching to include the radical new concepts of loving your enemies (as opposed to just your neighbors) and praying for those who persecute you. In the Torah, enemies are fought against, resisted, shattered, and scattered.[29] There are no Torah commands about praying for our enemies or loving them. This is a profound new commandment given by Jesus. It is underscored in His teaching about an eye for an eye.

> You have heard that it was said, "An eye for an eye and a tooth for a tooth." But I say to you, Do not resist the one who is evil. But if anyone slaps you on the right cheek, turn to him the other also. And if anyone would sue you and take your tunic, let him have your cloak as well. And if anyone forces you to go one mile, go with him two miles. Give to the one who begs from you, and do not refuse the one who would borrow from you. (Matthew 5:38-42)

This profound posture of humility and sacrificial love for one's enemies is not found in the Torah.

The Great Commission

The passage known as the Great Commission also reveals a distinction between the Mosaic and New Expressions of God's Law. And it should be noted that Jesus gave this command after His resurrection and, thus, it was clearly issued under the New Covenant.

> Go therefore and make disciples of all nations, baptizing them in the name of the Father and of the Son and of the Holy Spirit, teaching them to observe all that I have commanded you" (Matt 28:19-20).

---

[29] See Genesis 22:17, 24:60; Exodus 15:6, 23:27; Leviticus 26:7-8; Numbers 10:35, 24:8; Deuteronomy 32:41-43.

This passage introduces four teachings not found in the Torah. First is the idea of making disciples "of all nations," which is echoed in Mark 16:15 where Jesus says, "Go into all the world and proclaim the gospel to the whole creation." In this evangelical command, there is a fulfilling of God's promise to Abraham that "in you all the families of the earth shall be blessed" (Gen 12:3). But the Torah nowhere commands Israel to make disciples of other nations. In fact, the Jewish people have never evangelized other nations. Yet, that's what Jesus commands here.

In Judaism, the fundamental laws of morality apply to everyone, but the Mosaic Laws of the Torah are only for the Jewish people. This was as true before Christ as it is today. Although Judaism allows converts, the Jewish people have never believed it necessary for everyone to adhere to Judaism. Further, the kind of "disciple" Jesus is talking about in the Great Commission has come to saving faith in *Him* and wants to follow *Him* as their Savior and Lord. They are called to follow in the ways of Christ, not Moses. Yeshua's consistent teaching in the Gospels is "follow Me."

The second new teaching in the Great Commission is Jesus' command to baptize. The word *baptize* is not found in the Jewish Bible, much less the Torah. Nor is the Christian concept of baptism. The Law of Moses commands ritual cleansing by bathing in water,[30] especially as a purification rite for those who have committed certain unclean offenses. And later, in second temple Judaism, water immersion was used as part of the conversion ceremony for Gentiles who wanted to join the Jewish community.

> The purpose of this entry requirement, known as proselyte baptism, was to remove any hint of ceremonial uncleanness from the Gentile (b. Yebam 46a–48b; b. Gerim 60a–61b). Gentiles were considered spiritually and ritually unclean and needed purification in order to enter Israel and the temple (Josephus, *Jewish War* 2:150; Philo, *On the Embassy to Gaius* 212; Acts 10:28). Ritual cleansing for Jews was symbolic of inward cleansing, as "one who has become a proselyte is like a child newly born" (b. Yebam 48b).[31]

---

[30] Leviticus 14:8-9, 15:5-13, 16-27, 16:4, 24-28, 17:15, 22:6; Numbers 19:7-8, 19; Deuteronomy 23:11.
[31] Benjamin Espinoza, "Baptism," ed. John D. Barry et al., The Lexham Bible Dictionary (Lexham Press, 2016).

Although the concept is not taught in the Tanakh, beginning around the second century BCE, the Jewish people began to view water immersion as an act of repentance. This set the groundwork for the Christian concept of baptism. It was this "baptism of repentance" that John the Baptist engaged in. He recognized the symbolism and what was to come, saying, "I baptize you with water, but he who is mightier than I is coming, the strap of whose sandals I am not worthy to untie. He will baptize you with the Holy Spirit and fire" (Luke 3:16). Jesus later reminded the apostles of this when He appeared to them after His resurrection. "For John baptized with water, but in a few days you will be baptized with the Holy Spirit" (Acts 1:5).

Christian baptism was given as a foreshadowing of the baptizing of the Holy Spirit and a powerful symbol of passing from death into life through Christ's resurrection.

> Or don't you know that all of us who were baptized into Christ Jesus were baptized into his death? We were therefore buried with him through baptism into death in order that, just as Christ was raised from the dead through the glory of the Father, we too may live a new life. For if we have been united with him in a death like his, we will certainly also be united with him in a resurrection like his. (Romans 6:3-5)

The imagery is incredible and altogether new. Our descent beneath the surface of the sacramental water symbolizes Christ's death. Our raising again represents participation in His resurrection into new life. Christian baptism is not a purification rite like the Torah commands concerning bathing in water. It is a symbolic ritual unlike anything previously commanded by Yahweh.

The third new teaching in the Great Commission is Yeshua's command that disciples be baptized "in the name of the Father and of the Son and of the Holy Spirit." In the Tanakh, we frequently see people calling on, blessing, proclaiming, and doing things "in the name of" the Lord. In Hebrew categories, a name is a big deal. It is not merely a term of identification but a symbol of someone's essence and presence. Hence the Mosaic commandment not to carry the Lord's name in vain.[32]

The newness Jesus adds to the ancient Hebrew understanding of "in the name of" is the presence and authority of the Trinity. The Tanakh does not speak directly to the triune nature of God, which is why Judaism

---

[32] Exodus 20:7; Leviticus 19:12.

rejects the Christian doctrine of the Trinity. It is seen as a violation of the *oneness* of God. "Hear, O Israel: the Lord our God, the Lord is one" (Deut 6:4). God did not fully reveal His tri-unity until Christ and the New Covenant. Moreover, Yeshua identified Himself as a member of the Trinity and, thus, taught that He is co-equal with Yahweh. The idea that the Messiah would be divine—much less Yahweh incarnate—was a shocking revelation to the Jewish people (Mark 14:60-65). And His command to baptize "in the name of the Father and of the Son and of the Holy Spirit" (Matt 28:19) would have been inconceivable under the Mosaic expression. This was a new command.

The final aspect of newness found in the Great Commission is that Jesus' new disciples should be taught to observe "all that I (Jesus) have commanded you" (Matt 28:20). This is significant. Yeshua did not instruct His disciples to keep everything Moses commanded or everything required in the Law and the Prophets. Of course, Jesus endorsed and taught many of the Torah commands. But not all of them. He never directed anyone to eat kosher, be circumcised, keep Shabbat and the feasts, or make sin offerings. So when Jesus said, "all that I have commanded you," He was not necessarily teaching the Law of Moses.

Summary

Torahism hinges on the belief that the Law of Moses was given without end. However, this belief stems from a biased interpretation of Scripture. When viewed against the overarching storyline of the Bible, the Mosaic Law cannot have been intended to last literally forever. This is evidenced in three significant ways. First, several of the institutions the Torah describes as lasting "forever"—such as animal sacrifices, the Levitical priesthood, and the Sinai Covenant—have come to an end. Second, the impermanent nature of the Law of Moses is explicitly taught in the New Testament.[33] And lastly, Yeshua issued many new commands not given in the Torah.

---

[33] For example, 2 Corinthians 3:7-11; Galatians 3:24-29; Ephesians 2:13-16.

7

The Torah Is for All Nations

*Fish die when they are out of water,
and people die without law and order.*

TALMUD

I N THE LAST CHAPTER WE ESTABLISHED that the Law of Moses was not eternal or everlasting but instead was given for a specific time. Now we turn our focus to the *who* of the Mosaic Law. Was it given solely to Israel, as mainstream Christianity and Judaism affirm? Or was it given, as many Torah-keepers argue, to Gentiles as well? We begin with the words of the Torah itself.

> The Lord called to [Moses] out of the mountain, saying, "Thus you shall say to the house of Jacob, and tell the people of Israel: 'You yourselves have seen what I did to the Egyptians, and how I bore you on eagles' wings and brought you to myself. Now therefore, if you will indeed obey my voice and keep my covenant, you shall be my treasured possession among all peoples, for all the earth is mine; and you shall be to me a kingdom of priests and a holy nation.' These are the words that you shall speak to the people of Israel." (Exodus 19:3-6)

The first thing to note is to whom Yahweh made this promise. Whom does God say will be His treasured possession and a kingdom of priests and a holy nation? His words were addressed to "the house of Jacob" and "the people of Israel." In biblical Hebrew, "house of" refers to a person's physical descendants or family. Thus, the phrase לְבֵית יַעֲקֹב (*l'bayit ya'akov*, house of Jacob) is an explicit reference to the descendants of Abraham through Jacob.

Recall that, after Jacob wrestled with Yahweh, the Lord told him, "Your name shall no longer be called Jacob, but Israel, for you have striven with God and with men, and have prevailed" (Gen 32:28). Thus, the phrase "people of Israel" in Exodus 19:3 is a synonym for "house of Jacob."[1] At Sinai God entered into a covenant with the descendants of Jacob, not the Egyptians who enslaved them. Yahweh told Israel, "You yourselves have seen what I did to the Egyptians" (19:3); He sent them ten plagues and drowned their army as they pursued the Israelites. And at Mount Sinai, Yahweh entered into a covenant with His people who had been enslaved in Egypt for 400 years. This is the ethnic group referred to in the Torah as "the Israelites"—or sometimes just "Israel"— and known today as the Jewish people.

In the opening verses of Exodus 19, Yahweh promised Israel that if they kept His covenant, out of all nations, they alone would be His treasured possession. Although the whole earth belongs to the Lord, Israel would be His holy nation. The word *holy* (קָדוֹשׁ *qadosh*) means "set apart, removed from common use." So the idea of a holy or "set apart" nation further underscores the exclusivity of God's covenant with Israel alone.

Yahweh did not command the Amalekites to circumcise their men or the Hittites to keep the Sabbath. And He certainly didn't require the Amorites to make sacrifices in His temple. What Yahweh commanded in the Mosaic Law He required of Israel alone to set them apart from all the other nations and peoples. This is further demonstrated when Moses gave the Law for a second time. He told the Israelites,

> When your son asks you in time to come, "What is the meaning of the testimonies and the statutes and the rules that the Lord our God has commanded you?" then you shall say to your son, "We were Pharaoh's slaves in Egypt. And the Lord brought us out of Egypt with a mighty hand." (Deuteronomy 6:20-21)

The Law was given specifically to the people who were slaves in Egypt and later rescued by Yahweh. Leviticus makes this set-apartness

---

[1] This is a common Hebrew literary technique known as *parallelism*, which involves restating the same idea in different ways.

abundantly clear and reveals the connection between unclean foods and unclean people.

> You shall therefore separate the clean beast from the unclean, and the unclean bird from the clean. You shall not make yourselves detestable by beast or by bird or by anything with which the ground crawls, which I have set apart for you to hold unclean. You shall be holy to me, for I the Lord am holy and have separated you from the peoples, that you should be mine. (Leviticus 20:25-26)

The reason for the kosher food laws was to identify and set aside Israel as God's people. And this sense of holy separateness extends well beyond the Torah into the rest of the Tanakh. In a prayer of gratitude, King David taught the national uniqueness of Israel.

> And who is like your people Israel, the one nation on earth whom God went to redeem to be his people, making himself a name and doing for them great and awesome things by driving out before your people, whom you redeemed for yourself from Egypt, a nation and its gods? And you established for yourself your people Israel to be your people forever. And you, O Lord, became their God. (2 Samuel 7:23-24)

The psalmist describes Israel in ethnic terms, "O offspring of Abraham, his servant, children of Jacob, his chosen ones!" (Ps 105:5-6). In Nehemiah, we read how "the Israelites separated themselves from all foreigners"—all non-Israelites—to confess their sins, read from the books of Moses, and worship Yahweh (Neh 9:1-3). And did you know that the expression "My people" is never used by Yahweh to refer to other nations, only Israel?

This is not to say that Yahweh did not allow Gentiles into His ways or worship. He certainly did, up to a point. He did not afford them the full rights and privileges of the Israelites. Bird notes,

> Though not given full citizenship in Israel, they were protected and—if they maintained ritual purity—even allowed to participate in the Passover (Ex 12:47–48) and other sacrifices (Num 15:14).[2]

---

[2] Chard Bird, *Unveiling Mercy*, (New Reformation Publications, 2020), p. 123.

God supernaturally created the nation of Israel in the womb of 90-year-old Sarah (Gen 21:1-7). And generations later, He set the nation of Israel apart from all other nations, the Israelites from the non-Israelites. This dividing wall is affirmed in the New Testament teachings that Yahweh's distinction between Jews and Gentiles had come to an end. Echoing the words God spoke to Israel at the giving of the Sinai Covenant (Ex 19:3-6), Peter proclaims to Gentile believers under the New Covenant,

> But you are a chosen race, a royal priesthood, a holy nation, a people for his own possession, that you may proclaim the excellencies of him who called you out of darkness into his marvelous light. *Once you were not a people, but now you are God's people*; once you had not received mercy, but now you have received mercy. (1 Peter 2:9-10, *emphasis added*)

Imes notes,

> "Race" or "people" and "nation" are ironic ways to refer to Peter's audience, made up of a variety of ethnic groups and scattered throughout an entire region. The gospel has made possible something impossible in the physical realm. It's also audacious in another sense. Before Peter's letter, the word "people" (*am* in Hebrew or *laos* in Greek) was used only to designate Jews.[3]

The Mixed Multitude

A common argument of Torahism is that when God rescued Israel out of Egypt, a mixed multitude of Gentiles left with them, as indicated in Exodus 12:38, "A mixed multitude also went up with them, and very much livestock, both flocks and herds." And this mixture of Jews and Gentiles was later present at Mount Sinai when the Law was given. On that basis, our Torah-keeping friends declare that the Law was given to Jews *and* Gentiles.

Although the Torah does not explicitly mention Gentiles at Sinai, it is not unreasonable to believe that some of the mixed multitude were still with Israel when Moses delivered the Law.[4] If that were the case, does it mean that the Law was given to both Jews and Gentiles? Not at all. Regardless of the ethnic make-up of the Sinai attendees, as we saw above,

---

[3] Carmen Joy Imes, *Bearing God's Name: Why Sinai Still Matters* (IVP Academic, 2019), p. 169.
[4] In fact, Jewish tradition holds it was this mixed multitude who stirred up trouble at Sinai by introducing the idea of a golden calf and declaring "These are *your* gods, O Israel" (Exodus 32).

Yahweh made His Covenant exclusively with the descendants of Abraham through Jacob.

Imagine a public business rally at a hotel conference room where the CEO of the company promises a $10,000 bonus check to each of his employees. Although everyone in attendance hears the promise—TV reporters, security guards, waitstaff—only those who meet the criteria, only his employees, are eligible for the bonus. It's the same thing with the Torah. Despite who else may have been at Sinai, God's words in Exodus 19 make it clear that the criteria of eligibility in His promise— the people with whom He was making this Covenant—were the descendants of Jacob.[5]

Same Law for Foreigners

Another common argument from our Torahist friends is that when a foreigner lived among the Israelites, they were required to live under the Law of Moses. Therefore, the Law applies to Gentiles as well. They will typically point to Exodus 12:49 as evidence that the Law was given to both Jews and Gentiles: "The same law shall apply to the native as to the stranger who sojourns among you." However, when that verse is read in context, it tells a different story.

Exodus 12:43-51 records the institution of Passover. The text begins by stating, "And the Lord said to Moses and Aaron, 'This is the statute of the Passover: no foreigner shall eat of it'" (v. 43). Yet, in this passage, Yahweh *does* allow a provision for non-Jews who want to keep the Passover. They must first show their allegiance to Yahweh by being circumcised (v. 48). So when verse 49 then says that the "same law" applies to the native and the stranger, it is not a reference to the entirety of the Law of Moses. It's talking about God's specific command that everyone who participates in the Passover feast must be circumcised. That is the law that applies both to the Israelites and foreigners among them.

The same is true of a similar passage in Leviticus, "There shall be one standard for you; it shall be for the stranger as well as the native, for I am the Lord your God" (Lev 24:22). In context, the "standard" Yahweh is speaking of here is not the entirety of the Mosaic Law but rather the standard of punishment for murder. "Whoever takes a human life shall surely be put to death" (Lev 24:17).

---

[5] See Exodus 19:1-6, 25:22, 30:31, 31:13-17, 35:1-4; Leviticus 4:2, 7:23, 7:29, 7:38, 9:3, 16:34, 22:18; Numbers 2:2, 5:6, 5:12, 6:2, 9:2, 15:38; Deuteronomy 1:3, 4:1, 4:44-45, 32:52, etc.

And again in Numbers: "One law and one rule shall be for you and for the stranger who sojourns with you. (Num 15:16). This verse comes from a passage discussing laws about sacrifices. The specific process for offering sacrifices is spelled out in verses 4-12, and then the LORD says,

Every native Israelite shall do these things in this way, in offering a food offering, with a pleasing aroma to the LORD. And if a stranger is sojourning with you, or anyone is living permanently among you, and he wishes to offer a food offering, with a pleasing aroma to the LORD, he shall do as you do. One law and one rule shall be for you and for the stranger who sojourns with you." (Numbers 15:13-16)

The "one law and one rule" (v. 15) is not a reference to the entirety of the Law of Moses but the common rules for offering sacrifices in Israel. And yet, even when bound by the same rules about sacrifice, the Torah maintains a distinction between the "native Israelite" (v.13) and the "stranger" (v. 14). Indeed, the fact that the Torah refers to non-Israelites as "sojourners," "foreigners," and "strangers" confirms they were considered other than Israel.

Assyrians, Babylonians, Egyptians, and all other Gentiles were not expected to eat kosher, keep Shabbat, circumcise their men, or keep the annual feasts. And even the sojourner in Israel was not subject to the Mosaic Law in the same way the native Israelites were. For example, there was a different dietary standard. Yahweh commanded Israel,

You shall not eat anything that has died naturally. You may give it to the sojourner who is within your towns, that he may eat it, or you may sell it to a foreigner. For you are a people holy to the Lord your God. (Deuteronomy 14:21)

This is the Torah telling us in no uncertain terms that non-Jews are allowed to eat things that Jews are not. Notice the Israelites' holiness— their set-apartness—from the foreigners and the sojourners among them. This is also evident in God's commands about loaning money. Every seventh year the Israelites were commanded to release what they had lent to their Jewish neighbor.

And this is the manner of the release: every creditor shall release what he has lent to his neighbor. He shall not exact it of his neighbor, his brother, because the Lord's release has been proclaimed. Of a foreigner you may exact it, but whatever of yours is with your brother your hand shall release. (Deuteronomy 15:2-3)

You may charge a foreigner interest, but you may not charge your brother interest, that the Lord your God may bless you in all that you undertake in the land that you are entering to take possession of it. (Deuteronomy 23:20)

The Torah teaches a clear difference in the treatment of Jews and Gentiles under the Law of Moses. Israelites can require repayment and charge interest on loans made to Gentiles, but not so with their fellow Israelites. Which makes sense if the Mosaic Law was for national Israel. Would we say that the laws of Ireland were given to everyone in the world because when a foreigner stays in Ireland, they are required to live under Irish law? Of course, not. Passages like those above underscore the fact that the Torah was the national law of Israel rather than a universal law given to all people.

Lastly, consider the perspective of Messianic Judaism on the application of the Law. As ethnic Jews who have come to faith in Jesus, they are keenly aware of how Yahweh explicitly gave the Mosaic Law to the ancient people of Israel for their specific needs at their particular time in history.

Let's jump a few thousand years back to the time of the ancient Near East, a culture and mindset completely foreign to ours today, whose social structures are badly damaged by the Fall. Within this context, God raises up a new nation with new laws to live by, in order to create a new culture for them. In doing so, He adapts His expectations to a people whose attitudes and actions are subject to influence by the pagan nations around them. These laws aren't the permanent, divine ideal for all peoples everywhere at all times. They are specific to that people with their specific needs in that ancient era . . . Take for example God's ideal for marriage—a monogamous union joining husband and wife as one flesh (Gen. 2:24). When God is dealing with Israel, a nation of fallen humans affected by their surroundings in the ancient Near East, God's ideals are distorted and forgotten. Therefore, God is on the move to restore His ideals through this small new nation. The laws of Moses are a first step in that process.[6]

Gentiles & The Law

What is the relationship of the Gentile Christian to the Law of Moses? That question was asked and answered at the Jerusalem Council (Acts 15:1-29). The apostles and elders in Jerusalem determined that what "seemed good to the Holy Spirit and to us" (Acts 15:28) was that Gentile believers were not required to be circumcised or keep the Law of Moses. The Council did not require them to keep Shabbat, the feasts, the kosher food laws, the purity laws, or any other civil or ceremonial observances. Instead, they were given just four restrictions to foster unity with their Jewish brothers and sisters in Christ. (We will look at the Jerusalem Council in more detail below.) In short, the Bible teaches that Christians are not subject to the Law of Moses under the New Covenant.

Commands vs. Traditions

Once given, the Law of Moses became the heartbeat of Jewish culture. This lasted for 1,500 years until Jesus established the New Covenant. And under the New Covenant, many things changed. The definition of the "People of God" was expanded to include both Jews and Gentiles (Gal 3:28-29, Eph 2:11-16). The Sinai Covenant became obsolete (Heb 8:13). And the Law of Moses ceased to be binding on God's people, Jew or Gentile. We see these changes taught in several places in the New Testament. For example,

> The law was our guardian until Christ came, in order that we might be justified by faith. But now that faith has come, we are no longer under a guardian, for in Christ Jesus you are all sons of God, through faith. (Galatians 3:24-25)

Now that Christ has come, we are no longer under the Law. This teaching would have been primarily aimed at Jewish believers because, as we've seen, Gentiles weren't under the Law of Moses. The Law wasn't given as a guardian for the Gentiles but for the Jews. And now that Jesus has come, we are no longer under that guardian. Paul further teaches that the "People of God" are no longer determined by their Jewish ethnicity.

---

[6] Seth D. Postell, Eitan Bar and Erez Soref, *Reading Moses, Seeing Jesus: How the Torah Fulfills its Goal in Yeshua*, (One For Israel Ministry, 2017), Kindle location 1814-1816.

Rather we "are all sons of God, through faith" (v. 25). He then expounds on this idea,

> For as many of you as were baptized into Christ have put on Christ. There is neither Jew nor Greek, there is neither slave nor free, there is no male and female, for you are all one in Christ Jesus. And if you are Christ's, then you are Abraham's offspring, heirs according to promise. (Galatians 3:27-29)

This would have been a shocking revelation to Paul's first-century Jewish audience, who were literally Abraham's offspring and heirs of the promise God gave him. It's important to note that Paul is not arguing here for a complete lack of distinction between Jews and Gentiles any more than he is teaching a complete lack of difference between males and females. He is teaching unity, not uniformity. Under the New Covenant, the identity of "Abraham's offspring" was expanded to include anyone who has placed their faith in Jesus; Jew or Gentile, man or woman, slave or free. However, as we will see, Jewish followers of Jesus still have a calling to maintain the boundary markers of their Jewish identity.

The Commandments Today

The Law of Moses given to Israel under the Sinai Covenant is no longer in effect, but that does not mean Christians today are lawless. Under the New Covenant, God's Law is written on our hearts.[7] Moreover, the moral and spiritual commandments given under the Law of Moses are repeated, re-taught, and endorsed under the New Covenant.

As we saw in chapter four, although the New Expression of the unchanging Law of God differs from the previous Mosaic Expression, it does not amount to anything like a wholesale change. Because the two expressions flow from the same unchanging set of Divine principles, they are far more similar than different. Nothing has changed concerning right and wrong or loving God or loving people. But there have been changes, especially in the Mosaic commands given to distinguish Israel from the Gentile nations. For example,

> Therefore let no one pass judgment on you in questions of food and drink, or with regard to a festival or a new moon or a

---

[7] Jeremiah 31:31-34; Ezekiel 37:26; 2 Corinthians 3:2-3; Hebrews 8:10, 10:16

Sabbath. These are a shadow of the things to come, but the substance belongs to Christ. (Colossians 2:16-17)

For Jewish believers in Jesus, many of these observances understandably continue as important, even sacred, traditions. And it makes sense they would want to maintain them. These rituals were part of their cultural identity as Jewish people. And they were not forbidden; they only ceased to be obligatory. Thus, what was initially given as law continued under the New Covenant as customs or tradition. And we are free in Christ to observe such traditions. Provided, of course, they are undertaken as a matter of personal preference or conscience rather than a requirement of salvation or a condition of obedience.

When it comes to Gentiles who want to be "Torah observant," things start to get a little strange, in my opinion. I understand the motivation behind wanting to adopt the Mosaic traditions. These are the same rituals Jesus kept! However, an important distinction is often overlooked by our Torah-keeping friends: *Jesus was Jewish.* Therefore, unlike Gentiles, He was born under the Law of Moses (Gal 4:4-5).

Biblically speaking, Gentiles are free in Christ to observe whatever Jewish traditions they want. I've attended a Passover Seder and a couple of Sabbath services at a local Messianic synagogue, and I loved it. I learned a lot and was blessed by the experiences. But adopting the Jewish traditions and food laws as a regular part of a Gentile's practice of their Christian faith is not necessary. The danger in Torah-observant Christianity is the belief that these traditions are *required* of all Christians. Torahism often looks down on Christians who choose not to keep those traditions, labeling them "lawless" and "walking in sin." But the bottom line is this: if you're not Jewish, the Law of Moses has never applied to you.

The Jerusalem Council
In Acts 15, the apostles and elders directly addressed the question at the heart of this book. *Are Christians required to keep the Law of Moses?* Roughly twenty years after Yeshua's resurrection (~50 CE), a council was convened in Jerusalem. And in my opinion, the outcome of this discussion is enough to disprove Torahism once and for all.

As the gospel spread in the early years of the church, certain Jewish believers in Christ (sometimes referred to as *Judaizers*) began to teach other believers they needed to be circumcised and follow the Mosaic Law to be saved. As a result, they found themselves in a sharp dispute with

Paul and Barnabas. So they all decided to head to Jerusalem to discuss the issue with the apostles and elders (Acts 15:1-2). The assembly of church leaders who convened in Jerusalem to address this dispute is known as the *Jerusalem Council*, and you can read all about it in Acts 15:1-29. This was the first official council convened by the Christian church.

The fact that this council was necessary provides an important clue to understanding the unique relationship between Jewish followers of Jesus and the Torah. If the earliest Jewish believers viewed Torah-keeping as merely optional for the Jewish people, they surely wouldn't have needed to discuss whether Gentiles were obligated to keep it. Yet this issue was significant enough that it prompted a "sharp dispute and debate" (Acts 15:2) in the early church. Which reveals a distinction in Scripture between how Jewish and Gentile believers approached keeping Torah. More on that in a bit.

In attendance at this council were Paul, Barnabas, Peter, James, and the elders of the church in Jerusalem. Some who belonged to the religious party of the Pharisees stood up and began the discussion by saying, "The Gentiles must be circumcised and required to keep the Law of Moses" (Acts 15:5). This is the exact position held by Torahism today. How amazing that Scripture provides us with an account of how the apostles handled this issue. God foresaw Torahism.

The council considered the Pharisee's statement carefully. Peter began by putting to rest the notion that either circumcision or keeping the Law were required for salvation.

> Why do you try to test God by putting on the necks of Gentiles a yoke that neither we nor our ancestors have been able to bear? No! We believe it is through the grace of our Lord Jesus that we are saved, just as they are. (Acts 15:10–11)

This reference to law as a yoke (ζυγος *zygos*) was not original to Peter. Yeshua used the same term (Matt 11:29–30, 23:4), as did Paul (Gal 5:1). And it does not require us to view the Mosaic Law as a restrictive, binding mechanism.[8] However, Peter's statement in Acts 15 *does* indicate that the Law of Moses was something Israel could never live up to. Indeed, the entire storyline of the Tanakh was driven by

---

[8] A Jewish rabbi's set of rules and teachings about how to live the Torah was called his "yoke." When they invited people to learn to keep the Torah, it was often referred to as "the yoke of Torah" or "the yoke of the kingdom of heaven."

Israel's inability to maintain loyalty to Yahweh by keeping that Law. It is the very reason God promised a New Covenant (Jer 31:31-34).

Next at the Council, James, the brother of Jesus, addressed whether circumcision and keeping the Mosaic Law should be required as a matter of obedience. He declared, "we should not trouble those of the Gentiles who turn to God" but instead give them just a few restrictions (v. 19-21). Rather than the Law of Moses, he offered four things from which they were to abstain. The rest of the elders and apostles agreed, and together they drafted a letter informing Gentile believers of this decision. This letter is recorded in its entirety in Acts 15:23-29 and it ends as follows:

> It seemed good to the Holy Spirit and to us not to burden you with anything beyond the following requirements: You are to abstain from food sacrificed to idols, from blood, from the meat of strangled animals and from sexual immorality. You will do well to avoid these things. Farewell. (Acts 15:28-29)

This was a groundbreaking decision. If there was ever a time during the forming of the nascent Christian church to require the keeping of the Law of Moses, this was it. But the Council determined it was neither a requirement of salvation *nor* obedience. Instead, the Gentiles were simply told, "You will do well to avoid these things" (Acts 15:29). And the decision not to require the Mosaic Law enjoyed a divine endorsement. It carried the full weight of the Apostles, the elders, *and* the Holy Spirit. "For it has seemed good *to the Holy Spirit and to us* to lay on you no greater burden than these requirements" (Acts 15:28).

This decision is a point on which Torahism as a belief system crumbles. How can Torah-keepers teach that the Law of Moses is binding on all believers when Scripture says it isn't? There is just no way to reconcile the decision of the Jerusalem Council with the theology of Torahism.

The Four Restrictions

When faced with the Jerusalem Council's decision, our Torah-keeping friends will try to defend their beliefs by focusing on the four restrictions given. They categorize them as a "starter pack" of commandments that would stop the Gentiles from doing a whole lot of sinful things right off the bat. Then, over time, the new Gentile believers would learn the rest of the Law of Moses as they heard the Torah read in the synagogues every Sabbath. Here are just a few of the many comments I've received promoting that theory.

Isn't it interesting that the council in Acts 15 chose four random instructions (laws) for the Gentiles to follow? Is this the exhaustive list? Or perhaps these are where the Gentiles are to *start*, and they will learn the rest when they come and hear the scriptures preached every Sabbath day. (William T.)

Gentiles were coming to Faith in a Jewish Messiah—they were given very basic things to follow at first. They were being discipled in Jewish houses of worship by Jewish believers. Who would expect them to adopt everything all at once? (Josh A.)

It is not a requirement; it is a starting point. They are coming to learn truth. (Angela L.)

These four starter commands would cut off believers from the Pagan temples. Now that these people were cut off from their former religious lives, where will they be worshipping? We know the expectation is that new believers will gradually learn the Torah because they would be entering the religious life of the nation *in the synagogue*. (Jodie S.)

These theories, while perhaps interesting, all suffer from an absence of biblical support. The New Testament nowhere teaches, or even hints at, a gradual approach to the Law of Moses for Gentile believers in Yeshua. Indeed, we never see them taught or expected to learn the Torah, gradually or otherwise. And the idea that uncircumcised Gentile believers in Jesus would have been welcomed into non-believing Jewish synagogues where the Torah was taught is a bit problematic.

Moreover, if the Council intended to start the new Gentile believers off with a few basic things until they learned the rest of the Law, how do we explain the absence of the two most distinguishing characteristics of Yahweh's covenant people? Namely, the Sabbath and the kosher food laws. Dunn notes,

[Jewish] dietary rules constituted one of the clearest boundary markers which distinguished Jews from Gentiles. The observance of the Sabbath was another. Thus, eating unclean food and violating the Sabbath ranked together as the two chief hallmarks of covenant disloyalty, while strictness in both was of fundamental importance in maintaining covenant faithfulness.[9]

Neither of these observances would have been difficult for a new Gentile believer to understand or immediately put into practice. Yet the Jewish-run Council decided they should not be required. Don't miss the significance of that decision.

James explains that the four specific restrictions should be given because "from ancient generations Moses has had in every city those who proclaim him, for he is read every Sabbath in the synagogues" (Acts 15:21). His point is not precisely explained. But notice this is a statement of historical fact rather than a future proclamation. James is not linking the four restrictions to the Torah but to the widespread presence of Judaism at the time. The council recognized that the stage was set for a clash of cultures within the body of Christ and that is something they wanted to avoid. Consider the unique theological and cultural landscape in which they were operating at the time.

- Jews were discussing how to let Gentiles into what they saw as the natural evolution of the Jewish faith. At that time, Christianity was called *The Way*,[10] because it taught the way of *Yeshua HaMashiach*, the Jewish Messiah.

- The Jewish believers had "from ancient generations" heard the Law of Moses read every Sabbath in the synagogue. It was their heritage, the ancient constitution of their holy nation. As God's covenant people, the Mosaic ways were baked into their cultural DNA.

- The Council recognized that Gentile believers, having been newly welcomed into God's family, would live and serve alongside Jewish believers. A blending of backgrounds and traditions was inevitable as Jews and Christians gathered to pray, break bread, and worship the same God.

- The four restrictions given by the Council were activities that would have been inherently offensive to Jewish believers. Yet the average Gentile from a pagan background may not have realized this. Gentiles understood moral issues such as murder, theft, and adultery. But the Council's four instructions would not have been so obvious.

---

[9] James D.G. Dunn, *Romans in The Word Biblical Commentary* (1988)
[10] See Acts 9:2, 19:9, 19:23, 24:14, 24:22.

In light of that cultural and theological backdrop, allow me to suggest a different reason those restrictions were given which *does* enjoy biblical support. A universal theme in the ministry of Jesus—indeed throughout the whole of the New Testament—is unity among believers.

By this all people will know that you are my disciples, if you have love for one another. (John 13:35).

Let us therefore make every effort to do what leads to peace and to mutual edification. Do not destroy the work of God for the sake of food. All food is clean, but it is wrong for a person to eat anything that causes someone else to stumble. It is better not to eat meat or drink wine or to do anything else that will cause your brother or sister to fall. (Romans 14:19-21)

Therefore, if what I eat causes my brother or sister to fall into sin, I will never eat meat again, so that I will not cause them to fall. (1 Corinthians 8:13)[11]

The Jerusalem Council's four restrictions were part of this biblical theme of unity between Gentile and Jewish believers. Verses 19-21 could be paraphrased as follows:

Let us not make it difficult for the Gentiles turning to the God of Israel. Instead, let us offer a few instructions to help them keep the peace with their new Jewish brothers and sisters, who have been steeped in the Law of Moses for generations. Here are four guidelines that should be sufficient to keep relations agreeable between them. (Acts 15:19-21, author's paraphrase)

Additional support for this interpretation is found in how these restrictions are introduced. "Therefore my judgment is that we *should not trouble* those of the Gentiles who turn to God" (Acts 15:19, *emphasis added*). The Greek word used for "trouble" is παρενοχλεῖν (*parenochlein*), which means to "cause difficulties" (CSB, EHV, HCSB, NIV), "put obstacles in the way of" (AMP, CJB), "create problems" (CEB), or "bother" (EXB, ICB, NCV). This would be a bizarre phrase to use if the council's intention was to point the Gentiles to the Law of the Torah.

---

[11] See also Romans 12:3-8, 14:1-23; 1 Corinthians 8:7-13, 10:25-30, Galatians 3:23-29, 5:1-15; Ephesians 4:1-16; Philippians 2:1-11; 1 Peter 3:8-22.

No, their goal was to avoid bothering (or causing trouble or difficulty for) those coming to faith. In the words of Peter, they wanted to avoid "putting on the necks of Gentiles a yoke that neither we nor our ancestors have been able to bear" (Acts 15:10). Categorizing the four restrictions as a "starter pack" of laws does not align with Acts 15, and it presents an idea foreign to the New Testament. Those instructions were, instead, a directive for maintaining harmony and unity in the new and growing Christian church.

It is Only About Salvation

A second common Torahist argument about the Jerusalem Council is that the discussion was only about salvation. Therefore, the Council's decision only proves that we are not required to follow the Law of Moses *to be saved*. However, says the Torah-keeper, we still need to follow the Mosaic Law as a matter of obedience. Acts 15 indeed opens with a statement about salvation.

> Certain people came down from Judea to Antioch and were teaching the believers: "Unless you are circumcised according to the custom taught by Moses, you cannot be saved." (Acts 15:1)

To which Peter ultimately argued, "it is through the grace of our Lord Jesus that we are saved" (Acts 15:11). It's true that the keeping of the Law was not considered a matter of salvation by the Council. However, as we have seen, they *also* decided not to require the Gentiles to keep the Law of Moses as a matter of obedience. In other words, the Council agreed two things were true at the same time.

1. Salvation comes through the grace of Jesus, not the Law (Acts 15:11).
2. Gentiles are not required to obey the Law of Moses. The Council gave the Gentiles "no greater burden" than the four restrictions listed in the letter (Acts 15:28).

The Four Today

A Torahist friend once asked, "How do you think the church, in general, is doing with regard to observing the four prohibitions given by the Jerusalem Council?" It's an interesting question. The unspoken assumption is that the four restrictions were biblical commands given to all Gentile Christians for all times. But I'm not convinced that is what this passage teaches. For one thing, the three food restrictions are not repeated anywhere elsewhere in the New Testament. In fact, as we will see in chapter thirteen, the opposite is taught regarding food. The fourth restriction regarding sexual immorality is repeated elsewhere and obviously applies to all Christians. And I have to be honest. I do not think the modern church is doing very well on that issue.

Jewish Believers and the Torah

A few years back, when I first dug into the Jerusalem Council in earnest, a question formed in my mind that I have not able to resolve until recently. As we've just seen, Acts 15:1-29 unambiguously teaches that Gentile followers of Jesus are not required to be circumcised or keep Torah. But what about *Jewish* believers in Jesus? Because my primary area of study and work has been the 100% Gentile movement of Torahism, I have not had occasion to pursue the answer to my unresolved question with much rigor. But thanks to some deep Messianic Jewish thinkers including Dr. David Rudolph, Rabbi Eduardo Arroyo, Dr. Michael Brown and others, a few dots have started to connect for me.

My understanding has evolved since I wrote the first edition of Torahism. In all honesty, I am still working through it. But I want to share one important insight I am confident about. I have come to believe that Jewish followers of Jesus have a different relationship to the Torah then do Gentile followers of Jesus. Neither are required to keep Torah as a matter of salvation or righteousness, of course. There is nothing any of us can do to add to what Jesus has already done on our behalf. But I have come to see how Jewish believers in Yeshua may have a sort of calling to maintain the boundary markers of their Jewish identity by keeping Torah, at least in a fashion that is appropriate under the New Covenant. But that is for another book. And in either case, the Bible is crystal clear. Gentiles are not—and have never been—obligated to keep Torah.

Summary

Torahism teaches that the Law of Moses was given to all nations. Yet, the Torah itself makes it clear it was given solely to Israel in order to set her apart from all other nations. The Torah's requirement that foreigners who lived among the Israelites keep the Mosaic Law is no different than any nation requiring foreigners within its borders to keep its laws. And the decision of the Jerusalem Council in Acts 15 made it abundantly clear that the Mosaic Law is not binding on Gentile Christians today as a matter of salvation *or* obedience.

8

The Law Was
Not Abolished

But now that faith has come, we are no longer under a guardian.

GALATIANS 3:25

I
N THE PREVIOUS CHAPTER WE SAW that the Law of Moses was
not given to Gentiles and they have never been subject to it. Despite
this fact, our Torah-keeping friends point to Matthew 5:17-20 as
Exhibit A in their argument that the Mosaic Law is binding on all
Christ-followers today. It is the lynchpin passage on which the full
weight of Torahism hangs. And for Exhibit B, Romans 3:31 is a trendy
choice. Let's dig into these two passages and see what they teach about
the Law.

Matthew 5:17-20
Our Hebrew Roots friends will often quote one or two verses from this
passage (usually verse 18) to make their case. But verses 17-20 go
together as one thought. This passage appears early in Yeshua's famous
Sermon on the Mount, which spans Matthew chapters 5-7. The text of
5:17-20 presents a self-contained idea in which Jesus teaches,

> Do not think that I have come to abolish the Law or the
> Prophets; I have not come to abolish them but to fulfill them.
> For truly, I say to you, until heaven and earth pass away, not an
> iota, not a dot, will pass from the Law until all is accomplished.
> Therefore, whoever relaxes one of the least of these
> commandments and teaches others to do the same will be called

least in the kingdom of heaven, but whoever does them and
teaches them will be called great in the kingdom of heaven. For
I tell you, unless your righteousness exceeds that of the scribes
and Pharisees, you will never enter the kingdom of heaven.
(Matthew 5:17-20)

Before breaking down the full passage, let's briefly address a specific
Torahist teaching on verse 17.

Bauer & the Word Fulfill

Hebrew Roots teacher Zachary Bauer holds up Matthew 5:17 as
proof that the Mosaic Law remains in effect on all Christ-followers. He
begins his argument by claiming that the word *fulfill* in this verse cannot
mean "to abolish or do away with," and of course, he's right.[1]

Do not think that I have come to abolish the Law or the
Prophets; I have not come to abolish them but to fulfill them.
(Matthew 5:17)

Bauer goes on to claim that the word fulfill here means "to do." In
other words, "I have not come to destroy, but to *do*." He labors the point
that the English words fulfill and do are synonyms, and the Merriam-
Webster Thesaurus agrees. The original Greek word in this passage
(from the root πληρόω, *pleroo*) also supports Bauer's argument that
Yeshua came to do what the Mosaic Law required. Bauer stresses that
Yeshua fulfilled the Law in the sense that He was fully obedient to it—
not in the sense of bringing it to completion. He knows that if we
interpret this verse to mean Jesus brought the Law to completion in some
way, Torahism would crumble. And ironically, in taking pains to make
his point, Bauer shows how Torahism is false.

If Yeshua came to obey the Law and do what it requires, it raises an
important question. What did the Law require? Scripture says it required
the shedding of the blood of an unblemished offering sufficient to satisfy
God's justice.[2] And the blood of animals could never atone for sin (Heb
10:4). Those sacrifices were only a reminder of sin, a display of faith to
which Israel was called. The fact that animal sacrifices were continually
repeated shows that the ultimate sacrifice had yet to be offered (Heb

---

[1] New2Torah video "Moral Laws & The Covenant."
[2] Hebrews 10; 1 Peter 1:18-20.

10:2). It is not the blood of animals but the blood of Jesus that atones (Heb 10). And that's exactly what He provided.

Yeshua fulfilled the Law by laying down His life as a ransom for many,[3] which ushered in the New Covenant promised by God[4] and rendered the Old (Sinai) Covenant obsolete (Heb 8:13). And as we will see in the coming chapters, when the Old Covenant ended, the Law of Moses, which served as the terms of that Covenant, ended as well. Thus, according to Bauer's definition of *fulfill*, Jesus *did* what the Law required, thus fulfilling its requirements and bringing it to completion.

Fulfilling the Hebrew Scriptures

Let's expand our study to the entirety of Matthew 5:17-20. And it is essential to remember that, although our Torah-keeping friends base their entire theology on this one passage, and although we are about to do a focused study of it, this text does not exist on an island.[5] It contains just four of the 31,000+ verses in the Bible. So anything we conclude about this passage must align with the rest of what Jesus taught and with the entirety of Scripture.

Let me begin by calling your attention to a particular phrase Jesus uses in the opening verse of this passage.

Do not think that I have come to abolish *the Law or the Prophets*;
I have not come to abolish them but to fulfill them. (Matthew
5:17, *emphasis added*)

The phrase "the law and the prophets" refers to the Tanakh—the Hebrew Scriptures—and it is used many times in the New Testament. For example, Jesus says, "whatever you wish that others would do to you, do also to them, for this is the Law and the Prophets (Matt 7:12). And after teaching the Greatest Commandments are to love God and love people, He adds, "On these two commandments depend all the Law and the Prophets" (Matt 22:40). And speaking of John the Baptist, Yeshua said, "For all the Prophets and the Law prophesied until John…" (Matt 11:13). The book of Acts talks about Paul preaching in synagogues where they read from the Law and the Prophets (Acts 13:14-15).

---

[3] Matthew 20:28; Mark 10:45.
[4] Jeremiah 31:31-34; Matthew 26:28; Luke 22:20; 1 Corinthians 11:25.
[5] Some have suggested that Jesus' audience for this passage was exclusively Jews, who had a different relationship to the Law than Gentiles. However, assigning any single portion of the Sermon the Mount exclusively to Jewish believers is problematic.

So verse 17 is speaking of the entirety of the Hebrew Scriptures, rather than just the Law of Moses, as our Torah-keeping friends often assume. The Hebrew scriptures *include* the law of Moses, of course. But Yeshua's message is bigger than that. He is saying, *"Do not think that I have come to abolish the [Hebrew Scriptures]. I have not come to abolish them but to fulfill them."* And that brings us back to the question: What does it mean for Jesus to fulfill the Hebrew Scriptures?

The Bible unambiguously teaches that Jesus is the Messiah promised in the Tanakh. In fact, the word "Christ" (Χριστός *Christos*) appears more than 500 times in the New Testament, and it is not Yeshua's last name. Christos is a title that means "anointed one." It is the Greek version of the Hebrew word מָשִׁיחַ (mashiach). And as the Messiah, what does it mean for Jesus to fulfill the Hebrew Scriptures? It means satisfying everything that spoke of Him or pointed to Him, including the messianic prophecies. The theme of fulfillment is all over the New Testament. In Matthew alone, we read:

- Then was fulfilled what was spoken by the prophet Jeremiah (2:17)
- So that what was spoken by the prophets might be fulfilled... (2:23)
- So that what was spoken by the prophet Isaiah might be fulfilled (4:14)
- The prophecy of Isaiah is fulfilled... (13:14)
- But all this has taken place that the Scriptures of the prophets might be fulfilled... (26:56)
- Then was fulfilled what had been spoken by the prophet Jeremiah... (27:9)

Thus, in verse 17, Jesus is saying, *"Do not think that I have come to abolish the [Hebrew Scriptures]. I have not come to abolish them but to fulfill [what they told of Me]."* And He develops this idea further in verse 18, which is the part of this passage that generates the most emotion among Torah-keepers.

For truly, I say to you, until heaven and earth pass away, not an iota, not a dot, will pass from the law until all is accomplished. (Matthew 5:18)

If there is one verse on which all of Torah-observant Christianity hangs its hat, this is it. They view verse 18 as a clear and unambiguous teaching that not an iota or dot of the Mosaic Law will change until heaven and earth pass away. And there are a couple of things we can all agree on regarding this verse.

First, Jesus is teaching that there won't be even the slightest change in the Law of Moses until some condition is met. Either until *heaven and earth pass away,* or until *all is accomplished,* or both. (Depending on how you want to interpret these two clauses.) Second, we all agree that heaven and earth have not passed away. I think we would have noticed if that had happened! So we agree on these two things.

And there is a third point on which we can all agree, although it causes our Torah-observant friends to squirm a bit. The uncomfortable third point is this: *some things have already passed from the law.* Scripture teaches that, because of the work of Yeshua, some of the commands in the Law of Moses have passed away. That's a big deal. Because if the Law has changed—even one iota—it leaves us with only one valid interpretation of 5:18. Namely, that the condition Jesus was talking about was "until all is accomplished," not "until heaven and earth pass away." Why? Because we all agree that heaven and earth have not passed away, yet things have passed from the Law.

What Has Passed from the Law?

It's important to note that Yeshua wasn't referring to general changes or shifts in the Law of Moses. He said not even the *tiniest* bit will change: "not an iota or a dot will pass from the law." Therefore, if even the slightest change to the Law of Moses is indicated in Scripture, it would confirm that Jesus was not teaching that the Law will remain unchanged "until heaven and earth pass away."

When Yeshua says nothing will "pass from the law," what does He mean? The Greek word used is παρέρχομαι (*parerchomai*), which literally means "to pass by." It is used twice in this verse.

> For truly, I say to you, until heaven and earth *pass away* (*parerchomai*), not an iota, not a dot, *will pass* (*parerchomai*) from the law until all is accomplished. (Matthew 5:18)

In both cases, *parerchomai* communicates the idea of passing out of sight, passing away, ending. Jesus is saying that nothing commanded in the Law of Moses will cease to be required until all is accomplished. And yet things *have* passed from that Law. Let's look at four examples. First, the Torah says,

Aaron shall present the bull as a sin offering for himself, and
shall make atonement for himself and for his house . . . Then he
shall kill the goat of the sin offering that is for the people . . .
because of their transgressions, all their sins. (Lev 16:11, 15-16)

These are laws about the high priest and the sin offerings required
annually on Yom Kippur, the Day of Atonement. Yahweh required the
sacrifice of animals under the Mosaic law to atone for sin. But the New
Testament teaches that Jesus was our sin offering "once for all"[6] and,
therefore, "there is no longer any offering for sin" (Heb 10:18). The
animal sacrifices commanded in the Torah are no longer required. Even
if the temple is rebuilt one day, even if the Levitical priesthood is re-
established, even if many of the sacrifices prescribed in the Torah
resume, God will never again require sin sacrifices. Why? Because
"When Christ had offered *for all time a single sacrifice for sins*, he sat down
at the right hand of God" (Heb 10:12, *emphasis added*).

To suggest that sin offerings will one day resume—as many of our
Torah-observant friends do—is to propose the insufficiency of Christ's
sacrifice on the cross. The animal sacrifices required in the Torah were
just a reminder of sin (Heb 8:3-4).

For since the law has but a shadow of the good things to come
instead of the true form of these realities, it can never, by the
same sacrifices that are continually offered every year, make
perfect those who draw near. (Hebrews 10:1)

The animal sacrifices for sin were not the "true form of these
realities." They *pointed* to the true form, Christ. Indeed, "we have been
sanctified through the offering of the body of Jesus Christ *once for all*"
(Heb 10:10). Do Christians today still have a sacrifice for sin?
Absolutely. It is the eternal sacrifice that Jesus made on the cross. This
is why there is no longer any offering for sin. As Yeshua declared on the
cross, "It is finished" (John 19:30).

The Torah expressly commanded a regular sin offering. The New
Testament says sin offerings are no longer required. That is a change of
more than an iota or dot.[7] The commands given in Leviticus 16
regarding sin sacrifices have passed from the law. Not because they were
abolished, but because they were fulfilled (Matt 5:17).

---

[6] Hebrews 7:27, 9:12, 9:26, 10:10.
[7] If you want to study this for yourself, read Leviticus 16 and then read Hebrews 10. You will see a
number of changes.

The second example of a change in the Law of Moses is found in the commands regarding circumcision. This ritual goes all the way back to Abraham. It served as a unique identifier of God's covenant people and was a sign of the Abrahamic covenant. In fact, throughout the Bible, the words "circumcised" and "uncircumcised" are often used to refer to "Jews" and "non-Jews" (Gentiles), respectively.

At Sinai, Yahweh gave the command that every Israelite male child was to be circumcised on the eighth day after birth (Lev 12:3). But under Yeshua and the New Covenant, circumcision ceased to be required of God's people. The New Testament says that if anyone was uncircumcised when God called him to salvation, "let him not seek circumcision" (1 Cor 7:18). And the Jerusalem Council in Acts 15 determined that circumcision was not required of Gentile believers.

> For it has seemed good to the Holy Spirit and to us to lay on you *no greater burden than these requirements*: that you abstain from what has been sacrificed to idols, and from blood, and from what has been strangled, and from sexual immorality. (Acts 15:28-29, *emphasis added*)

The apostle Peter was criticized by some fellow Jews in Jerusalem who said, "You went to uncircumcised men and ate with them" (Acts 11:3). Peter ultimately replied,

> If then God gave the same gift to them [the uncircumcised] as he gave to us [the circumcised] when we believed in the Lord Jesus Christ, who was I that I could stand in God's way? (Acts 11:17, bracketed comments added)

Moreover, Paul "had been entrusted with the gospel to the uncircumcised" (Gal 2:7), and we never see him instruct anyone to be circumcised. In Galatians 2 he wrote, "But even Titus, who was with me, was not forced to be circumcised, though he was a Greek" (Gal 2:3). And even though "false brothers" tried to impose the laws of circumcision— or as Paul described it, "bring us into slavery" (v. 4)—"to them we did not yield in submission even for a moment, so that the truth of the gospel might be preserved for you" (v. 5).

Even in the case of Timothy, Paul did not require him to be circumcised as a matter of righteousness or obedience. Rather, Paul "took him and circumcised him because of the Jews who were in those places, for they all knew that his father was a Greek" (Acts 16:3). Wiersbe notes,

Timothy would be working with both Jews and Gentiles in the churches, and it was essential that he not offend them. That was why Paul had Timothy circumcised (see 1 Cor. 9:19–23). Again, it was not a matter of Timothy's salvation or personal character, but rather of avoiding serious problems that would surely become stumbling blocks as the men sought to serve the Lord (Rom 14:13–15).[8]

This is how Paul can teach that "in Christ Jesus neither circumcision nor uncircumcision counts for anything, but only faith working through love" (Gal 5:6). Indeed, just a few verses earlier, Paul said, "Look: I, Paul, say to you that if you accept circumcision, Christ will be of no advantage to you" (Gal 5:2). Some interpret these various teachings as forbidding Gentile Christians from being circumcised.

The bottom line is this: the Torah explicitly commands circumcision (Lev 12:3), including for Gentiles who want to participate with Israel in the Passover (Ex 12:48). Yet, as we saw above, the New Testament teaches that circumcision is no longer required. This is another change to the Law of Moses. The commands regarding circumcision have passed from the law.

We find a third change in the laws concerning the priesthood. The Mosaic Law required all priests to come from the tribe of Levi.[9] That's why it was called the *Levitical* priesthood. And further, priests must be descendants of Aaron, the first high priest. Only Levitical priests were allowed to enter the tabernacle's Holy Places.

You shall make for [the priests] linen undergarments to cover their naked flesh. They shall reach from the hips to the thighs; and they shall be on Aaron and on his sons when they go into the tent of meeting [tabernacle] or when they come near the altar to minister in the Holy Place, lest they bear guilt and die. This shall be a statute forever for him and for his offspring after him. (Ex 28:42-43, bracketed comments added)

Under the New Covenant, all that changed. Jesus was appointed our High Priest,[10] despite being from the tribe of Judah (Heb 7:14).

---

[8] Warren W. Wiersbe, *The Bible Exposition Commentary, vol. 1* (Victor Books, 1996), pp 466–467.

[9] Exodus 40:12-15; Deuteronomy 18:1-5

[10] Hebrews 2:17, 3:1, 4:14-15, 5:5-10, 7:26, 8:1, 9:11.

> Now if perfection had been attainable through the
> Levitical priesthood (for under it the people received the law),
> what further need would there have been for another priest to
> arise after the order of Melchizedek, rather than one named after
> the order of Aaron? (Hebrews 7:11)

The author of Hebrews teaches that the priesthood of Yeshua was
"after the order of Melchizedek," an ancient priest who ministered to
Abraham long before the Mosaic Law was given (Gen 14:17-20). And
on that basis, he shows how the Levitical priesthood (which he refers to
as "the order of Aaron") was not the intended final state of Yahweh's
priesthood. A high priest from the tribe of Judah is unquestionably a
change in the Law of Moses. But there is more.

Paul describes himself as "a minister of Christ Jesus to the Gentiles
in the *priestly service* of the gospel of God" (Rom 15:16, *emphasis added*).
Yet Paul was from the tribe of Benjamin, not Levi (Phil 3:5), so he did
not meet the Torah's qualifications to be a priest. Before we think Paul
might have been using the term "priestly" in a loose sense, consider that
he was "educated at the feet of Gamaliel according to the strict manner
of the law of our fathers" (Acts 22:3). The Mishnah reveres Gamaliel as
one of the greatest Jewish teachers of the law of all time, saying, "Since
Rabban Gamaliel the Elder died, there has been no more reverence for
the law, and purity and piety died out at the same time."[11] And his pupil,
the apostle Paul, called himself "a Pharisee, a son of Pharisees" (Acts
23:6). The Pharisees were the Jewish sect known for their strict
observance of the traditional and written law. Paul knew the Law of
Moses inside and out. He had the modern equivalent of a Ph.D. in
Mosaic Law. And yet he felt perfectly free to offer "priestly service" for
the sake of the Gospel.

And the apostle Peter, also born and raised a Jew, taught that Christ-
followers—without distinction to race, much less tribe—are "a holy
priesthood" (1 Pet 2:5) and a "royal priesthood" (1 Pet 2:9). And
Revelation tells us that Yeshua has made His followers—again, without
distinction to race or tribe— "*priests* to serve his God and Father" (Rev
1:6, NIV). The Jewish New Testament authors did not just casually
throw around the term "priest." These were theological statements.
Statements that the authors would not have made if they thought the
priestly laws of Moses were still in effect.

---

[11] Sotah 9:15

Moreover, under the Mosaic Law, only Levitical priests were allowed to enter the holy places, and they did so by the blood of animals and the veil (Lev 16:15). Under Yeshua, the priestly rights and privileges were conferred on everyone who has placed their faith in Him.

> Therefore, brothers, since we have confidence to enter the holy places by the blood of Jesus, by the new and living way that he opened for us through the curtain, that is, through his flesh, and since we have a great priest over the house of God, let us draw near with a true heart in full assurance of faith, with our hearts sprinkled clean from an evil conscience and our bodies washed with pure water. (Hebrews 10:19-22)

Notice that even the purity requirements of the priesthood (sprinkling and washing) are satisfied differently. This is another discernible change in the Law of Moses.

In the Torah, Yahweh unambiguously commands not only that all His priests come from the tribe of Levi, but they also must be descended from Aaron, the first high priest (Deut 18:5). Under the New Covenant, Christ is our High Priest, and every follower of Jesus is a priest even if they are not from the tribe of Levi. Indeed, even if they are not Jewish. Every believer is a holy priest able to "offer spiritual sacrifices acceptable to God through Jesus Christ" (1 Pet 2:5). The commands regarding the priesthood have passed. Not because they were abolished, but because Jesus fulfilled them (Matt 5:17). And this brings us to the last change I want to highlight.

The Mosaic Law required a big, beautiful curtain in the temple to separate the Most Holy Place from the Holy Place (Ex 26:31-35). The Torah describes it as "a veil of blue and purple and scarlet yarns and fine twined linen. It shall be made with cherubim skillfully worked into it" (Ex 26:31). At the very moment Jesus died on the cross— inaugurating the New Covenant in His blood (Luke 22:20)—God Himself ripped that temple veil in two from top to bottom.

> And Jesus cried out again with a loud voice and yielded up his spirit. And behold, the curtain of the temple was torn in two, from top to bottom. And the earth shook, and the rocks were split. (Matthew 27:50-51)

Our Torah-keeping friends will sometimes challenge which "curtain of the temple" this verse refers to. Was it really the veil between the Holy

Place and the Most Holy Place? Indeed, Matthew does not specify which curtain was torn. The Torah commanded two curtains; an outer curtain separating the Holy Place from the court (Ex 26:36-37), and an inner curtain dividing the Most Holy Place from the Holy Place (Ex 26:31-35). It is the inner veil that seems presupposed by the author of Hebrews:

> Therefore, brothers, since we have confidence to enter the holy places by the blood of Jesus, by the new and living way that he opened for us through the curtain, that is, through his flesh... (Hebrews 10:19-20)[12]

Whichever curtain it was, it signified a change in Yahweh's temple laws. The curtain that God required under Moses, He tore down under Christ.

Torah-keepers eager to avoid acknowledging this change may attempt two objections. They might suggest Matthew was referring to some other temple curtain not required in the Torah. But the fact that Matthew used the definite article "*the* curtain of the temple" leaves little doubt it was the veil separating the Holy Place from the Most Holy Place. First, because when Matthew's first-century audience read the phrase "the curtain of the temple," they would have naturally thought of that specific curtain, which the Torah repeatedly refers to as simply "the veil."[13] Second, why would Matthew interrupt His dramatic narrative of the death of Christ to share an insignificant detail about a random curtain?

The other potential objection is that God did not tear down the curtain; it was the earthquake Matthew mentioned. Yet, Matthew directly links the tearing of the temple veil with the death of Christ, the opening of tombs, and the resurrection of the dead (Matt 27:51-53). This was no random geological event. Even if the earthquake physically caused the tearing of the curtain, God was ultimately behind it. In light of Jesus' prophecies of the destruction of the temple,[14] and the subsequent teaching about the veil in Hebrews 10, it seems evident the tearing of the curtain symbolized the opening of access to God at Christ's death. It was Yahweh Himself bringing the old system of worship to an end. Surely no one would suggest we sew back together the curtain that God tore asunder.

---

[12] See also Hebrews 4:16; 6:19–20; 9:11–28.

[13] Exodus 40:21-26; Leviticus 4:6, 4:17, 16:12-15, 21-23; Numbers 4:5, 18:7, etc.

[14] Matthew 24:1-2; Mark 13:1-2; Luke 21:5-6.

Before we move on, allow me to offer one additional area of change to consider. It is perhaps not as concrete an example as the four listed above, but it certainly points to a change—if not in law, then in relationship. Consider what the Torah teaches about righteousness.

> And the Lord commanded us to do all these statutes, to fear the Lord our God, for our good always, that he might preserve us alive, as we are this day. And it will be righteousness for us, if we are careful to do all this commandment before the Lord our God, as he has commanded us. (Deuteronomy 6:24-25)

Contrast this with what Paul wrote about his fellow Jews who refused to accept Christ as their Messiah.

> Brothers, my heart's desire and prayer to God for them is that they may be saved. For I bear them witness that they have a zeal for God, but not according to knowledge. For, being ignorant of the righteousness of God, and seeking to establish their own, they did not submit to God's righteousness. For Christ is the end of the law for righteousness to everyone who believes. (Romans 10:1-4)

There are more biblical examples of changes to the Mosaic Law, but in the interest of space, and because the point has been made, we'll stop here. It is simply untenable to suggest that not an iota or a dot of the Law of Moses has changed. Because heaven and earth have not passed away—and at the same time, there have been significant changes to the Law of Moses—I believe the most reasonable interpretation of our Lord's words in Matthew 5:18 is that nothing will pass from the Law *until all is accomplished.*

Until Heaven & Earth Pass Away

What, then, are we to make of the clause "until heaven and earth pass away" in 5:18? There are two general schools of thought on how best to understand this statement, and, in the end, they each seem to end with the same general conclusion.

On the one hand, this phrase could be validly interpreted as a Hebraic idiom, a standard teaching method for Jesus. For example, just a few verses earlier, He calls His followers salt (5:13) and light (5:14). And a few verses after this passage, He tells His listeners that if their right eye or right hand causes them to sin, they are to remove those body parts and throw them away (5:29-30). These passages were undoubtedly meant figuratively. Those who follow Christ are not literally salt or light, nor are we expected to maim our bodies to avoid sin. (Even a man with no right eye can still lust after a woman with his left eye!)

If Jesus' statement in 5:18 is likewise interpreted metaphorically, it communicates the importance of His mission. *Sooner Heaven and Earth would pass away than I will fail to fulfill what the Scriptures foretold.* He is repeating for emphasis the same idea stated in 5:17: "Do not think that I have come to abolish the Law or the Prophets." Yeshua is vehemently underscoring the importance of the Hebrew Scriptures.

A second valid approach is to view this passage more literally. In this case, the question becomes, how are we to understand the two "until" clauses?

> For truly, I say to you, *until heaven and earth pass away*, not an iota, not a dot, will pass from the Law *until all is accomplished.* (Matthew 5:18, *emphasis added*)

As we established above, Jesus could not have meant there would be no change in the Law until heaven and earth pass away. The best interpretation, then, is that the first "until" clause sets the scope for the second. Jesus meant something like: *the following statement shall remain true until heaven and earth pass away: nothing will pass from the law until all is accomplished.* Thus, we could paraphrase 5:17-18 as follows:

> Do not even think that I have come to abolish the Hebrew Scriptures. I have not come to abolish them but to fulfill them. For truly, I say to you, until heaven and earth pass away, not an iota, not a dot, will pass from them until all these things have taken place as prophesied. (Matthew 5:17-18, author's paraphrase)

A few chapters later, Jesus repeats this same idea when He teaches, "For all the Prophets and the Law prophesied until John" (Matt 11:13). Barbieri provides a helpful summary of this understanding of the passage.

> This section presents the heart of Jesus' message, for it demonstrates His relationship to the Law of God. Jesus was not presenting a rival system to the Law of Moses and the words of the Prophets, but a true fulfillment of the Law and the Prophets—in contrast with the Pharisees' traditions . . . Jesus'

fulfillment would extend to the smallest Hebrew letter . . . These things are important because letters make up words and even a slight change in a letter might change the meaning of a word. Jesus said He would fulfill the Law by obeying it perfectly and would fulfill the prophets' predictions of the Messiah and His kingdom. But the responsibility of the people was made clear. The righteousness they were currently seeking—that of the Pharisees and the teachers of the Law—was insufficient for entrance into the kingdom Jesus was offering. The righteousness He demanded was not merely external; it was a true inner righteousness based on faith in God's Word (Rom. 3:21–22). This is clear from what follows.[15]

Viewed through the Principle & Expression framework, we can understand why Jesus said that He did not come to abolish the Law and the Prophets. He did not come to tear down the Law of God (the universal principles grounded in the nature of the Father). Rather He came to fulfill them, to live them out perfectly. And in doing so, He ushered in the New Covenant and, with it, a new and superior expression of those same unchanging Laws of God.

The Fulfillment Described

Jesus' post-resurrection appearance to the disciples is often left out of the discussion about Matthew 5:17-20. Here Yeshua stands before His disciples, having just eaten some fish to prove that He was genuinely resurrected in the flesh, and reminds them of the words He spoke at the Sermon on the Mount.

Then he said to them, "These are my words that I spoke to you while I was still with you, that everything written about me in the Law of Moses and the Prophets and the Psalms[16] must be fulfilled." Then he opened their minds to understand the Scriptures, and said to them, "Thus it is written, that the Christ should suffer and on the third day rise from the dead, and that repentance for the forgiveness of sins should be proclaimed in

---

[15] L. A. Barbieri, Jr., *The Bible Knowledge Commentary: An Exposition of the Scriptures* (Vol. 2, p. 30).

[16] Interestingly, this is the only place in the New Testament where Jesus refers to the Hebrew Scriptures using all three categories: the law, prophets, and Psalms. He is stressing that He has fulfilled the *entirety* of Jewish Scripture.

his name to all nations, beginning from Jerusalem. You are witnesses of these things." (Luke 24:44-48)

We need to break down what is happening here because it's amazing. Jesus starts by reminding His disciples of what He said while He was still with them—namely, that everything written about Him must be fulfilled (v. 44). And when did He say that? In Matthew 5:17-20. There Jesus proclaimed that He came to fulfill the Law and the Prophets and that not an iota or a dot would pass away until that was accomplished. And now, after His resurrection, Jesus explains to his disciples what He meant. To do so, He had to open their minds to understand the Scriptures (v. 45). "Thus it is written," He begins (v. 46) as He reveals what the Hebrew scriptures said about him: that He was going to suffer and rise from the dead on the third day (v. 46), and repentance for the forgiveness of sins will be proclaimed in His name to all nations, beginning at Jerusalem (v. 47).

And then Yeshua tells his disciples, "You are witnesses of these things" (v. 48). In other words, *the Hebrew scriptures were fulfilled before their very eyes*. Before He died, the qualifier Jesus put on these changes was "until all is accomplished" (Matt 5:18). And the resurrected Jesus now tells His disciples that *all has been accomplished*. Osborne notes,

> All of history has prepared for this moment, and the entire future of the human race rests on these three days from the cross to the empty tomb. Note that the divine "must" (dei) covers "everything ...written about me." He is saying that every single iota of Scripture pointed to him, and the true purpose of the old covenant was to prepare Israel for the coming of Christ.

> As the Father opened their eyes, Jesus now "opened their minds" to the Scripture truths (v. 45). In spite of all the times this had been addressed, none of his followers had been able to grasp the reality of what was coming. It was too far out of their religious experience and expectations, and so they misunderstood the God-intended meaning of the prophecies. Jesus now clears away the debris of false understandings and enables them to grasp the truth. The doubts that dominated their thinking are now over once and for all. Not only the reality of the cross and empty tomb

but also the scriptural prophecies that foretold these events are now clearly perceived.[17]

Relaxing One of These Commands

We've spent a lot of time on verses 17-18 because that is where the primary skirmish between Torahism and mainstream Christianity occurs. But the remaining two verses of this passage have some important ideas to add to the conversation. Verse 19 says,

> Therefore whoever relaxes one of the least of these commandments and teaches others to do the same will be called least in the kingdom of heaven, but whoever does them and teaches them will be called great in the kingdom of heaven. (Matthew 5:19)

Some Christians suggest the phrase "these commandments" refers to the commands Jesus is about to give his audience beginning in Matthew 5:21. But I don't believe that is the best interpretation. First, because in Matthew, the Greek word οὗτος (houtos, meaning "this" or "these") never points forward. But more importantly, verse 19 begins with the word "therefore." It is a conclusion based on the previous two verses. Jesus is saying, "Because nothing shall pass from the Law until all is accomplished...whoever relaxes one of the least of these commandments..." etc. So "these commands" most likely refers to the Torah commands, none of which shall pass until all is accomplished.

This interpretation aligns with what Yeshua taught in verses 17-18. He is not here to abolish the Law and the Prophets—the Hebrew Scriptures—but to fulfill them. And even the least of their commands will remain in effect until He does so. France notes,

> Like the previous two verses, this one warns the disciples against altering or setting aside any part of the law, however small. (*Relaxes* is from the same root as *abolish* in v. 17, and means to 'set aside' or 'teach against' a commandment, rather than to disobey it . . .) That this is Jesus' teaching for his own disciples,

---

[17] Grant R. Osborne, *Osborne New Testament Commentaries (Luke: Verse by Verse)*, ed. Jeffrey Reimer, Elliot Ritzema, and Danielle Thevenaz, Awa Sarah, (Lexham Press, 2018), p. 575-576.

not a traditional Jewish saying, is indicated by *the kingdom of heaven.*[18]

Yeshua is, for the third verse in a row, affirming the law as it stood. His admonition in verse 19 is an unmistakable echo of His many clashes with the Pharisees,[19] who added their rules and traditions to the Law while claiming to uphold it unchanged. Jesus not only rebuked hypocritical religious leaders for elevating their traditions above God's Law, but He also focused on their responsibility to rightly teach others. This is exactly what He teaches in verse 19, and that idea is carried forward into verse 20:

> For I tell you, unless your righteousness exceeds that of the scribes and Pharisees, you will never enter the kingdom of heaven. (Matthew 5:20)

The final two verses in the passage teach against behaving as the scribes and Pharisees did toward the Law. Indeed, throughout this entire passage, Yeshua labors the point that the Law must not be messed with. He "did not come to abolish" it (v. 17), not an "iota or dot" will pass from it (v. 18), do not relax "the least of these commands" (v. 19). Our Torah-keeping friends' intuition about this passage is not wrong. Yeshua is stressing the importance of the Hebrew Scriptures, including the Law of Moses, in no uncertain terms.

However, the way Torahism applies this passage is problematic. Torah-observant Christians (directly or indirectly) seem to interpret Yeshua's words to mean that we need to keep the Law *even better than the Pharisees.* They use their interpretation of Matthew 5:17-20 as a sort of Rosetta Stone by which we must understand every other passage in the New Testament. Their error in teaching that Gentiles are subject to the Law of Moses is compounded by the faulty conclusion that Jesus "plainly teaches" that Law will not change in the slightest until heaven and earth pass away. From there, all other NT passages, no matter how clear or unambiguous, are re-interpreted to align with Torahism's erroneous presuppositions.

I often get the sense that Torahism stems from a subconscious attempt to outdo the Pharisees in their study of, and dedication to, the Mosaic Law. Although few Torah-keepers would openly admit it, their

---

[18] R. T. France, "Matthew: An Introduction and Commentary," *Tyndale New Testament Commentaries* vol. 1 (InterVarsity Press, 1985), p. 121.

[19] Matthew 14:1-9, 23:1-36; Mark 7:1-19; Luke 12:1-3, 13:10-17, etc.

theology is based on an underlying, perhaps even subliminal belief that at least some level of effort is required on our part to truly achieve righteousness before God. This is a mistake made by every Christian to some degree. It is just so utterly unfair that our righteousness should be wholly unearned and freely given to us solely based on our faith in Christ. Yet that is precisely what Scripture teaches. That's why it is called the Good News!

What, Then, Of the Law?

In the book *Reading Moses, Seeing Jesus,* a trio of Messianic Jewish scholars point out that Scripture describes several functions of the Mosaic Law under the New Covenant.

> The Law witnesses against us, points us to Yeshua, teaches us about God, offers us wisdom and insight, deepens our understanding of the person and work of Yeshua, and challenges us to love God and our neighbor."[20]

Just because we are no longer bound by the legal requirements of the Law of Moses, it does not follow that it serves no further purpose in our lives. The New Testament affirms—even after Christ's resurrection and ascension—that,

> All Scripture is breathed out by God and profitable for teaching, for reproof, for correction, and for training in righteousness, that the man of God may be complete, equipped for every good work. (2 Tim 3:16-17).

And that includes the Torah. At the same time, even the Hebrew Scriptures consider the Mosaic Law to be inferior to (and pointing toward) the better covenant to come.[21] Moses knew the Law would be broken even as he gave it.[22] But Yahweh did not bring the Mosaic Law to an end because it was defective. The Law was "holy and righteous and good" (Rom 7:12). It ended because it was only ever intended as a temporary guide to lead His people to Christ.

> So then, the law was our guardian until Christ came, in order that we might be justified by faith. But now that faith has come,

---

[20] Postell, Eitan, Soref, *Reading Moses, Seeing Jesus,* Kindle location 2221-2222.

[21] See Jeremiah 31 and Ezekiel 36. This idea is also found in Hebrews 8.

[22] Deuteronomy 30:1, 31:16-21, 32:13-21.

we are no longer under a guardian, for in Christ Jesus you are all sons of God, through faith. (Galatians 3:24-26)

Romans 3:31 We Uphold the Law

Another common "proof text" from Torah-keepers on the topic of the Law is Romans 3:31, which reads, "Do we then overthrow the law by this faith? By no means! On the contrary, we uphold the law." In this verse, the apostle Paul indicates that our faith in Jesus does not overthrow the law but upholds it. Torahism interprets these words as affirming that the Law of Moses is still valid and binding in every way. But is that what the text means?

The book of Romans is a letter written by Paul to the believers in Rome, which included both Jews and Gentiles at the time. It was written around 57 CE, while Paul was in Corinth, and this letter is a theological tour de force. The teachings here are dense and deep. To rightly understand what Romans 3:31 means, we will need to read through the larger passage in which it is found. The passage is teaching about the righteousness of God through faith, and the idea starts at verse 21. We will begin there and work our way up to the verse in question.

But now the righteousness of God has been manifested apart from the law, although the Law and the Prophets bear witness to it—the righteousness of God through faith in Jesus Christ for all who believe... (Romans 3:21-22)

"But now," the passage begins, signaling that a change has occurred. What has changed? "The righteousness of God has been manifested apart from the law" (v. 21). Under the Mosaic Law, righteousness came through obedience. "And it will be righteousness for us if we are careful to do all this commandment before the Lord our God, as he has commanded us" (Deut 6:25). Under Yeshua righteousness comes by believing. Picking up at verse 22,

For there is no distinction: for all have sinned and fall short of the glory of God, and are justified by his grace as a gift, through the redemption that is in Christ Jesus, whom God put forward as a propitiation [an atoning sacrifice] by his blood, to be received by faith... (Romans 3:22-25, bracketed comment added)

Paul reveals the universality of sin. All have sinned, both Jew and Gentile. "There is no distinction" (v. 22). Similarly, God's gift of justification is available to *all* who place their faith in Christ, whether Jew or Gentile. The salvation offered through Christ's atoning sacrifice is not received based on race, ancestry, or law but on faith. Continuing at verse 25,

> This was to show God's righteousness, because in his divine forbearance he had passed over former sins. It was to show his righteousness at the present time, so that he might be just and the justifier of the one who has faith in Jesus. (Romans 3:25-26)

God left the sins of previous generations unpunished under the Law of Moses. This statement is echoed in Hebrews chapters 9-10, where we learn that the blood sacrifice of bulls and goats—as required under the Mosaic Law—was only a *reminder* of sin. It could never actually take away sins. So it was Christ's sacrifice that redeemed even the sins committed under the first covenant (Heb 9:15). And here in Romans 3, Paul reveals that God did not leave those sins unpunished because he was indifferent toward them. Rather, it was to demonstrate His forbearance and kindness toward mankind. And if righteousness and justification are now available apart from the law through Christ—the apostle asks,

> Then what becomes of our boasting? It is excluded. By what kind of law? By a law of works? No, but by the law of faith. (Romans 3:27)

The law of faith eliminates our ability to boast about the works of the Law of Moses. We are saved by the "law of faith" (v. 27), which credits our salvation entirely to Christ. We did nothing to save ourselves, and therefore we have nothing to brag about, including any works of obedience to the Law. This does not mean that Law is abolished or useless. Boa & Kruidenier explain,

> It is the law which shows people that they have failed in all points to be righteous, forcing them to the conclusion that they must accept righteousness as a free gift of God. The law says, "You have nothing to boast in and I can prove it!"—and then proceeds to name all the places in which we have failed morally. Therefore, the free "gift of God" (Rom. 6:23) is the only way

that we can attain salvation, and it took the law to reveal it. Therefore, the law serves the gospel by removing all boasting about how one might be saved.[23]

Moving on to verse 28:

> For we hold that one is justified by faith apart from works of the law. Or is God the God of Jews only? Is he not the God of Gentiles also? Yes, of Gentiles also, since God is one—who will justify the circumcised by faith and the uncircumcised through faith. (Romans 3:28-30)

Paul explains that because justification is not based on keeping the Law, God can reconcile *all* people to Himself: both the circumcised (the Jews who were under the Law of Moses) and the uncircumcised (the Gentiles, who were never under the Law). Unlike the Law of Moses, the "law of faith" applies to both Jews and Gentiles. As Wright puts it,

> The message is simple: all who believe in Jesus belong to the same family and should be eating at the same table. This is what Paul's doctrine of justification is all about.[24]

With this broader context in mind, let's now turn to the verse so often cited by Torahism as affirming the ongoing obligation of the Mosaic Law. In Romans 3:31, Paul asks and answers a rhetorical question.

> Do we then overthrow the law by this faith? By no means! On the contrary, we uphold the law" (Romans 3:31).

What does Paul mean by "uphold"? Consider this. There is such a thing as sinful behavior. There is also such a thing as righteous behavior. How do we differentiate between the two? God's Law is the standard by which they are distinguished. Paul has elsewhere offered his own experience as a case study.

> If it had not been for the law, I would not have known sin. For I would not have known what it is to covet if the law had not

---

[23] Boa, K., & Kruidenier, W., *Romans* (Broadman & Holman Publishers, 2000), Vol. 6, p. 113.
[24] N. T. Wright, *New Tasks for a Renewed Church* (Hodder and Stoughton, 1992), p. 168.

said, "You shall not covet." But sin, seizing an opportunity through the commandment, produced in me all kinds of covetousness. For apart from the law, sin lies dead. (Romans 7:7b-8)

Once Paul understood what it meant to covet, his sin nature reared its ugly head and caused him to covet even more (Rom 7:7-8). He acknowledged, "I do not understand my own actions. For I do not do what I want, but I do the very thing I hate" (Rom 7:15).

Every human being struggles with this rebellious sin nature. The Law reveals our sin and underscores our need to be saved from it. And in Romans 3:31, when Paul says we "uphold the law," he means that when we come to faith in Jesus, we *validate the purpose of the Law of Moses*, which was to reveal our sin and point us to Christ. Stott notes that, in Paul's teaching of salvation,

> The function of the law is to expose and condemn sin, and so to keep sinners locked up in their guilt until Christ comes to liberate them through faith. (See Gal 3:21 ff.) In this way, the gospel and the law dovetail with each other, since the gospel justifies those whom the law condemns.[25]

The Righteous Requirement of the Law

Romans 3:31 can be equally understood from another perspective. It can interpreted as teaching that those justified by faith live according to the Spirit and "uphold" the Mosaic Law in the sense of fulfilling its righteous requirements. This is what Paul teaches a few chapters later.

> For God has done what the law, weakened by the flesh, could not do. By sending his own Son in the likeness of sinful flesh and for sin, he condemned sin in the flesh, in order that the righteous requirement of the law might be fulfilled in us, who walk not according to the flesh but according to the Spirit. (Romans 8:3-4)

In other words, the righteous requirement of the Law is fulfilled by believers who walk according to the Spirit. And again, in Romans 13:

> Owe no one anything, except to love each other, for the one who loves   another   has   fulfilled   the   law. For   the

---

[25] Stott, J. R. W., *The Message of Romans* (IVP Academic, 1994), p. 121.

commandments, "You shall not commit adultery, You shall not murder, You shall not steal, You shall not covet," and any other commandment, are summed up in this word: "You shall love your neighbor as yourself." Love does no wrong to a neighbor; therefore love is the fulfilling of the law. (Romans 13:8-10)

Romans 3:21-31 teaches that righteousness comes through faith, not obedience to the Law. And our faith in Jesus upholds the purpose of the Law of Moses, namely, to point us to Christ. Indeed, the righteous requirement of the Law is fulfilled by those who walk in love, according to the Spirit.

Summary

Torahism claims Yeshua did not come to abolish the Law of Moses, and therefore, it is binding on all Christ-followers. Jesus indeed came "not to abolish but fulfill" what the Law required. And what did the Law require? A perfect sacrifice for sin. Yeshua's sacrifice on the cross fulfilled what the Torah was pointing toward and, in doing so, fulfilled the Law and the Prophets. Thus, Christians today are not bound by the legal requirements of the Law of Moses. Jesus taught that not an "iota or a dot" shall pass from the Law until all is accomplished. And then He taught that all had been accomplished. The Mosaic Law was always intended to be temporary; its divine expiration date was the arrival of Jesus. However, just because we are no longer bound by the legal requirements of the Law of Moses does not mean it serves no further purpose in our lives. Among other things, the Law still reveals our sin and points us to Jesus, teaches us about our Heavenly Father, and challenges us to love God and neighbor. Under the New Covenant, our faith in Jesus fulfills what the Hebrew Scriptures foretold and the Law's righteous requirements.

9

Yeshua Kept Torah

But when the fullness of time had come, God sent forth his Son,
born of woman, born under the law.

GALATIANS 4:4

S URELY JESUS, AS THE SINLESS SON OF GOD born into a Jewish
family and culture, kept the Law of Moses, right? Absolutely!
We certainly cannot argue with our Torahist friends on this
point.

> But when the fullness of time had come, God sent forth his Son,
> born of woman, born under the law, to redeem those who were
> under the law, so that we might receive adoption as sons.
> (Galatians 4:4-5)

Jesus was not only born under the Mosaic Law, He is the only person
in history who ever kept it perfectly.[1] This qualified Him to serve as a
sinless representative of the nation of Israel (who had never been able to
keep the Law[2]) and pay the debt owed to God.

> And you, who were dead in your trespasses and the
> uncircumcision of your flesh, God made alive together with him,
> having forgiven us all our trespasses, by canceling the record of
> debt that stood against us with its legal demands. This he set
> aside, nailing it to the cross. (Colossians 2:13-14)

---

[1] 2 Corinthians 5:21; Hebrews 4:15; 1 Peter 1:18-19, 2:22; 1 John 3:5.
[2] Joshua 7:11; Judges 2:20; 1 Kings 11:11, 19:10-14; 2 Kings 17:15; Isaiah 24:5; Jeremiah 11:10,
31:31-34; Ezekiel 16:59; Hosea 8:1.

So, yes, Yeshua kept the Law of Moses. And it is here that our Torahist friends will advance the notion that, because Christ kept the Law, all Christians ought to keep it as well. This may appear to be sound, biblical reasoning at first glance. But there are several important factors to consider. The first of which is the distinction between *descriptive* and *prescriptive* passages in Scripture.

Descriptive passages simply describe what happened. For example, John 11:35 tells us, "Jesus wept." This short verse recounts a historical event; it does not teach that we should all be weeping. On the other hand, prescriptive passages instruct or prescribe what *ought* to happen; what we *should* do. For instance, "This is my commandment, that you love one another as I have loved you" (John 15:12). This verse is prescriptive. Why is this distinction important? Because the passages where we see Yeshua and the apostles keeping the Law of Moses are descriptive, not prescriptive. They tell us what happened rather than what we are supposed to do. For example:

Now Peter and John were going up to the temple at the hour of prayer, the ninth hour. (Acts 3:1)

Now at Iconium they entered together into the Jewish synagogue and spoke in such a way that a great number of both Jews and Greeks believed. (Acts 14:1)

Then Paul took the men, and the next day he purified himself along with them and went into the temple, giving notice when the days of purification would be fulfilled and the offering presented for each one of them. (Acts 21:26)

These passages do not teach that all Christians must visit the temple or the synagogue or engage in purification rituals. They are descriptions of historical events, a Scriptural record of the early church's activities. In the New Testament, we do not find any prescriptive passages that teach us to keep the ceremonial laws of Moses. This is true even of the texts where Jesus makes a Mosaic command of someone. For example, after healing the leper,

[Jesus] charged him to tell no one, but "go and show yourself to the priest, and make an offering for your cleansing, as Moses commanded, for a proof to them." (Luke 5:14)

This text, too, is descriptive. It tells us what Jesus instructed the Jewish leper to do after healing him. It does not prescribe what Christians are to do today.

Walk As Jesus Walked

Torah-keepers will invariably point to 1 John 2:6 as a biblical basis for their beliefs. "Whoever says he abides in [Jesus] ought to walk in the same way in which he walked" (1 John 2:6). Their argument is as follows: Jesus kept Torah and we are told to "walk as He walked," therefore, Christians are supposed to keep the Law of Moses, too.

Is that logic valid? Can we similarly conclude that because Jesus was a carpenter, His followers are all to be carpenters? Are we also to wander the countryside on foot telling people to "follow me"? These are obviously examples of following the logic of Torahism to its illogical conclusion, but they illustrate a valid point. Where do we draw appropriate boundaries around the notion of "walking as Jesus walked"?

The first thing to point out is that Jesus was Jewish, which is the only reason He was required to keep the Law of Moses. Non-Jewish followers of Jesus are not expected to keep Torah. And there are two other aspects to this line of thinking that need to be examined. First, what did John mean when he wrote, "Whoever says he abides in him ought to walk in the same way in which he walked" (1 John 2:6). Second, what is the historical context in which Jesus walked? Let's examine each in turn.

1 John 2:6

What do we know about how Jesus walked and lived out His mission? He lived in the first century as a poor Jewish man born under the Law (Gal 4:4-5). He was a tradesman who worked with his hands. He was also an itinerant teacher and preacher who walked from town to town, often sleeping outdoors, and didn't own any land. Jesus never earned a degree, held an office, wrote any books, visited a big city, or traveled more than 200 miles from His hometown. He taught others about God and ministered to them. He healed people, cast out demons, walked on water, stood up to the corrupt religious leadership (but never stood up to the government), sat with sinners (but never sinned with them), and spent a lot of time alone, praying to His Father. Yeshua lived in perfect love toward those around Him. And most importantly, He walked in sinless obedience to his Father, obedient even to death on the cross (Phil 2:6-8).

The question then is this. For Christians today who want to walk as Jesus walked, which of these attributes are we called to emulate? All of them? Some of them? To understand what John meant by "walk just as He walked," let's read those words in context. John's statement is part of a short passage in 1 John 2 that spans verses 3-6. Here, the apostle teaches how to determine if we truly know Christ. John begins in verse 3 with his main point: "This is how we know that we know him: if we keep his commands." He then develops this idea in the following two verses.

> The one who says, "I have come to know him" and yet doesn't keep his commands, is a liar, and the truth is not in him. But whoever keeps his word, truly in him the love of God is made complete. (1 John 2:4-5)

John then closes the short passage by restating his main point. "This is how we know we are in him: The one who says he remains in him should walk just as he walked" (1 John 2:5-6).

Although this passage was written in Greek, its author *Yohanan* (John) was Jewish. So it is not surprising to find him using the Hebrew literary device of *parallelism*—stating the same idea in different ways. Notice how John uses synonymous phrases to repeat the same concept for emphasis.

If we...	We will...
...know Him (v. 3, 4)	...keep his commandments (v. 3, 4)
...are in Him (v. 5)	...keep His word (v. 5)
...abide in Him (v. 6)	...walk as He walked (v. 6)

In other words, we know that we are right with Jesus when we obey what He taught us. John equates the concept of keeping Jesus' commands with walking the way he walked. We are to model the living out of our faith after the way Jesus lived out His faith, keeping His commandments and obeying all that He taught us. John is revisiting a concept he had introduced at the end of the previous chapter. In 1 John1, we read,

> This is the message we have heard from [Jesus] and declare to you: God is light, and there is absolutely no darkness in him. If

we say, "We have fellowship with him," and yet we walk in darkness, we are lying and are not practicing the truth. If we walk in the light as he himself is in the light, we have fellowship with one another, and the blood of Jesus his Son cleanses us from all sin. (1 John 1:5-7)

So a few verses later, in chapter two, when John says we are to "walk as Jesus walked," he is carrying this idea forward. We are to walk in the light as Jesus walked in the light.

Indeed, one of John's favorite metaphors is light. He mentions it over twenty times in his letters. To "walk in the light" means to live in the truth of God. And here in 1 John 2, the apostle teaches that walking in the light includes obeying God's Word. Psalm 119 says, "Your word is a lamp to my feet and a light to my path" (Ps 119:105). John says that to walk in the light is to "keep his commandments."

Torah-observant Christians want to interpret John's instruction to "walk as Jesus walked" as referring to keeping the Law of Moses since that is one of the ways Jesus lived out His faith. But that idea is not found in this passage. It is not even the general topic the apostle discusses in First John. Further, as we will unpack below, it is *because* Yeshua fulfilled the Mosaic Law by living it out perfectly that His followers do not need to. To "walk as Jesus walked" then is to live our lives in the truth of God, expressing our love for Him by obeying His commands. This is exactly what Jesus taught. "If you love me, you will keep my commandments" (John 14:15). Which raises the question, what did Jesus command of us?

Jesus' Commandments

It seems significant that neither 1 John 2:3-6 nor John 14:15 use the phrase "keep *the* commandments." The Greek does not use the definite article ἡ (hē), which would have indicated the Torah commands. Instead, in 1 John 2:3-4, the pronoun αὐτοῦ (*autou*) is twice used: "keep *His* commandments." And in John 14:15, we find the pronoun ἐμός (*emos*): "keep *My* commandments." What did Jesus command of us?

In the Gospels, Yeshua repeats and endorses many Torah commandments: do not murder, commit adultery, steal, bear false witness, etc. He instructs us to honor our mother and father, love our neighbors as ourselves, and love the Lord with all our heart, soul, and mind. Interestingly, we do not find Yeshua repeating or teaching what are commonly referred to as the "ceremonial" commandments. He does not teach we are to be circumcised, keep the Sabbath, keep the feasts, make our temple sacrifices, eat kosher, etc. At the same time, He never teaches against these things. They are simply left unaddressed.

It is curious that, although Jesus kept the whole of the Law of Moses Himself, He did not command His followers to do the same. How does that add up? It turns out there are two good reasons for this. First, Jesus was Jewish. Unlike every Gentile in history, Jesus was "born under the law" (Gal 4:4). And He knew His Gospel was also for the Gentiles. Second, at His resurrection, the entire world changed. That event split history in two and inaugurated the New Covenant.

The Bible teaches that the Law was given as a guardian until Jesus came, and now that He has come, we are no longer under that guardian (Gal 3:24-25). And Ephesians 2 says that Jesus "abolish[ed] the law of commandments expressed in ordinances" so that He might reconcile both Jews and Gentiles to God (Eph 2:14-16). At the Last Supper, Yeshua revealed that the New Covenant was in His blood (Luke 22:20, 1 Cor 11:25). So the Law of Moses was in effect for the Jewish people right up until His crucifixion. On that day, the New Covenant began. And upon His resurrection, Jesus became our new High Priest (Heb 4:14-5:10). And "when there is a change of the priesthood, there must be a change of law as well" (Heb 7:12). Jesus lived His life under the Law of Moses (Gal 4:4-5), and upon His death, He "redeemed us from the curse of the law" (Gal 3:13).

Walking as Jesus walked doesn't mean we have to hike from town to town on foot, teaching people about God. And it doesn't mean we have to take up carpentry. It also doesn't mean we have to keep the Law of Moses. (Especially if we're not Jewish!) To walk as Jesus walked is to walk in the light. It means living our lives in the truth of God, walking in love and obedience to Yeshua's commands.

Historical Context

There is also a historical aspect to Christ keeping the Law of Moses. By way of analogy, consider how a relay race works. Runners take turns racing around a track carrying a baton. When one runner completes her leg of the race, she hands the baton off to the next runner. By rule, this hand-off takes place within a short piece of track called the "changeover box," where the new runner gets up to speed as the old runner enters. The two athletes are running together on the track for a brief time. Then the hand-off happens, and the new runner takes off with the baton leaving the old runner behind.

Historically speaking, this is what happened when the Old Covenant handed the baton off to the New. The two systems ran together for roughly forty years. One covenant was winding down while the other was starting up. This historical "changeover box" began with the ministry of Christ (~30 CE) and ended with the destruction of the temple in Jerusalem (70 CE). And those who chose to follow Jesus (whether Jew or Gentile) went with the new runner.

Interestingly, there is a great deal of biblical precedent for Yahweh assigning the number forty to the length of *liminal periods*.[3] A liminal period is a time of transition, an in-between state during which a person has left their old status but not yet fully reached their new position. If you are in a liminal state, you're straddling what you are now and what you're about to be. Imes describes it this way,

> Every human ritual the world over includes an element of liminality, from coming-of-age rituals to funerals . . . For example, a wedding ceremony sets the bride and groom apart and lingers in liminal space. During the ceremony the couple is neither married nor unmarried. The congregation witnesses their change of status as a minister pronounces them "husband and wife." . . . [or] When a woman becomes pregnant, she enters liminality. She is officially on the threshold of motherhood, and yet has not experienced most of its aspects.[4]

God placed the entire world in a liminal state for forty days and nights during the flood (Gen 7). Moses entered liminality on the top of Mount Sinai when he spent forty days and forty nights receiving the Law from God (Ex 24:18, 34:28). After giving the Law, Israel sent out twelve spies who spent forty days scouting the promised Land (Num 13:25). And because of their unbelief, Yahweh sentenced Israel to the liminal space of the wilderness, where the Israelites wandered and ate manna for forty years (Ex 16:35; Num 14:33-34) before being allowed into the Promised Land. King David reigned over Israel for forty years (2 Sam 5:4; 1 Kings 2:11), as did his son Solomon (1 Kings 11:42). Jonah warned Nineveh, "Forty more days and Nineveh will be overthrown!" (Jonah 3:4). Yeshua spent forty days in the wilderness being tempted by Satan before beginning His ministry (Matt 4:2; Mark 1:13; Luke 4:2). And after His resurrection, He appeared for forty days, speaking about the

---

[3] The word liminal comes from the Latin word "limen," which means "threshold."
[4] Dr. Carmen Joy Imes, *Bearing God's Name: Why Sinai Still Matters* (IVP Academic, 2019), p. 17.

kingdom of God (Acts 1:3). These were all liminal periods of forty. So, it is not unreasonable to view the forty years between the ministry of Yeshua (the start of the New Covenant) and the destruction of the temple (the end of the Old Covenant) were equally indicative of a Divine period of transition.

This period would have been a confusing time for the Jewish people living in a culture that had been driven by the Mosaic Law for fifteen centuries. Many rejected Yeshua, considering Him a heretic or false prophet. But the Jews who understood He was their long-awaited Mashiach came to put their faith in Him. And for this first generation of new believers—the Jewish Christians—it would have been a challenging time.

Indeed, the uniqueness of this historical period provided a rich soil for change and revelation. Around the first century, a number of men claimed messiahship, garnered a following, and were ultimately executed.[5] However, as N. T. Wright notes,

> In not one single case do we hear the slightest mention of the disappointed followers claiming that their hero had been raised from the dead.[6]

Rather, they all faded into obscurity. Not so with Christ. Keller writes,

> The Christian view of resurrection, absolutely unprecedented in history, sprung up full-blown immediately after the death of Jesus . . . How could a group of first-century Jews have come to worship a human being as divine? . . . Jews believed in a single, transcendent, personal God. It was absolute blasphemy to propose that any human being should be worshiped. Yet hundreds of Jews began worshiping Jesus literally overnight.[7]

It is no wonder that the "changeover box" is the period of history the New Testament authors primarily wrote about.[8] Their texts begin with Yeshua's life, death, and resurrection, and trace the first few decades of the Christian church. So it is not surprising to find accounts of Jesus and His Jewish followers keeping the Mosaic customs. Those traditions were

---

[5] For example, Dositheos the Samaritan and Simon bar Kokhba.

[6] N. T. Wright, *Who Was Jesus?* (Eerdmans, 1993), p. 63.

[7] Timothy Keller, *The Reason for God* (Riverhead Books, 2008), pp. 218-220.

[8] Although a few of the New Testament documents are dated to after 70 CE, none of them record the destruction of the temple in Jerusalem.

deeply ingrained in the cultural DNA of the Jewish people. They drove the daily and annual rhythms of their lives. Indeed, it would have felt abnormal, even wrong, to a Jew *not* to keep them.

Moreover, for the Jews who had placed their faith in Yeshua as the promised Mashiach, following Him was the most Jewish thing they could do. And He nowhere taught against the Mosaic customs. Thus, there would have been no reason for the early Jewish believers *not* to keep Torah as they had always done. Especially prior to the destruction of the temple.

In fact, while the Law of Moses ceased to be binding as law, I believe Jesus and the Jewish New Testament writers fully expected that Jewish followers of Jesus would continue to keep Torah (in a manner appropriate under the New Covenant) as a matter of maintaining their Jewish identity. After all, the kingdom of God in the last days is not described as a homogenous, uniform group of people, but rather as "a great multitude that no one could number, from every nation, from all tribes and peoples and languages . . . crying out with a loud voice, 'Salvation belongs to our God who sits on the throne, and to the Lamb!'" (Rev 7:9-10). The Body of Christ is diversity in unity.

Scholarly Support

There is a great deal of scholarly support for the idea of a historical changeover box. Daniel Boyarin, professor of Jewish studies, views the two "new" religions of Christianity and Judaism as intensely and complexly intertwined during this period. He describes Christianity and Judaism as "part of one complex religious family, twins in a womb."[9] Professor of History and Judaic Studies Robert Goldenberg claims it is increasingly accepted among scholars that "at the end of the first century there were not yet two separate religions called 'Judaism' and 'Christianity.'"[10] Alan Segal, a Jewish scholar of ancient religions, says that "one can speak of a 'twin birth' of two new Judaisms, both markedly different from the religious systems that preceded them."[11]

Jewish historian Shaye J. D. Cohen describes the separation of Christianity from Judaism as "a process, not an event" in which the

---

[9] Daniel Boyarin, *Dying for God: Martyrdom and the Making of Christianity and Judaism* (Stanford University Press, 1999), p. 112.

[10] Robert Goldenberg, "Review of Dying for God: Martyrdom and the Making of Christianity and Judaism," *The Jewish Quarterly Review*, Vol. 92, No. 3/4 (Jan.–Apr. 2002), pp. 586–588.

[11] Alan F. Segal, *Rebecca's Children: Judaism and Christianity in the Roman World* (Harvard University Press, 1986), p. 77.

church became "more and more gentile and less and less Jewish."[12] According to Cohen, early Christianity ceased to be a Jewish sect when it ceased to observe Jewish practices, such as circumcision.[13] This process ended after the revolt in 70 CE when the temple was razed. At that time, Cohen says Pharisaic Judaism evolved into Rabbinic Judaism, various Jewish sects disappeared, and Christianity emerged as a distinct religion.[14] How this parting of the ways was handled (by both sides) is a matter of great debate. But the fact is that the Christian faith did not suddenly appear overnight fully formed. There was a long period of transition.

In addition to Scripture and scholarship, this changeover box is also confirmed in the Talmud. Although it is a collection of extra-biblical writings, not Scripture, the Talmud is a historical resource that can teach us a lot about the Second Temple period. And it contains a story that, perhaps without intending to, supports the New Testament teaching that the Mosaic Covenant had become obsolete.

> The Talmud says that at the end of the Day of Atonement (Yom Kippur) the high priest would wait for God's "miraculous stamp of approval," indicating the acceptance of Israel's atonement. How would God show His approval? According to the Talmud, inside the temple there was a red fabric (*lashon shel ze'hurit*). This piece of fabric would miraculously turn from red to white as a sign to the nation that God had indeed accepted their sacrifice, and that their sins would be covered for one more year. The sages write (see Tractate Yoma 39b) that forty years prior to the destruction of the temple in Jerusalem (around 30 CE, since the temple was destroyed in 70 CE), the red fabric stopped turning white on the Day of Atonement. The Talmud explains that this caused much panic and distress among the priests.

> From around the year 30 CE, according to the Talmud, God no longer honored the Sinai covenant as the way to cover Israel's sins. What happened to the Sinai covenant? The answer is that the Law is now fulfilled in a new way—not by something that

---

[12] Shaye J.D. Cohen, *From the Maccabees to the Mishnah* (Westminster Press, 1987), p. 228.
[13] Ibid., p. 168.
[14] Ibid., pp. 224-225.

will temporarily cover our sins for a year, but by Someone who atones for our sins once and for all.[15]

The End of An Era

Shabbat, the dietary restrictions, the feasts, temple offerings, circumcision, et al., began as commandments from Yahweh for Israel. They were required under the Mosaic Covenant and, thus, became the foundation of Jewish culture and tradition. And when Jesus came and, through His blood, initiated the New Covenant, those commandments ceased to be required, but they did not end. The Covenant Yahweh made with Israel at Mount Sinai—which had been in effect for 1,500 years—became obsolete after Yeshua's resurrection (Heb 8:13). Yet, these Mosaic traditions were deeply ingrained in the fabric of Jewish life. It would have felt strange and "wrong" for first-century Jewish Christians not to keep them.

Take, for example, the year my wife and I were on a Christmas tour in Norway.[16] We were in the U.S. for most of November as our nation began leaning into the upcoming Thanksgiving holiday. The weather turned cold, holiday specials and commercials saturated television, and grocery store coupons touted turkey and mashed potatoes. But on the day of the actual holiday, we found ourselves in a country that does not celebrate Thanksgiving. In Norway, it was just another Thursday. As Americans, it felt strange and "wrong" for us not to celebrate Thanksgiving, especially since our two daughters were there with us. So we decided to keep the tradition anyway and had a lovely ad hoc family Thanksgiving dinner overseas.

Thanksgiving to an American pales compared to the importance of the Law of Moses to a Jew. But you get the idea. The apostles and early Jewish Christians kept those traditions because they were part of their identity as a people. And they were never forbidden. Likewise, Messianic Jews today—those of Jewish ethnicity who fellow Yeshua as their Messiah—keep Shabbat, the kosher food laws, the feasts, circumcision, etc. As they should! Scripture maintains a clear distinction between Jews and Gentiles into the Last Days, calling them to dwell together in Messiah in unity and mutual upbuilding. The apostle Paul teaches that Jewish believers in Jesus should remain Jewish, and Gentiles should remain Gentiles (1 Cor 7:17-24). What was initially given as national law for Israel continued under the New Covenant as sacred tradition for

---

[15] Postell, Eitan, Soref, *Reading Moses, Seeing Jesus*, Kindle location 1882-1906.

[16] We are musicians who perform under the name *Dust & Daisies*.

the Jewish people. And we are free in Christ to observe such customs. Provided, of course, they are understood as a matter of personal preference/conscience rather than a requirement of salvation or a condition of obedience.

In the first century, the news of Yeshua and the New Covenant would have shocked all of Israel. The advent of Christ brought with it a paradigm shift in man's relationship with God. Changes of this magnitude can take generations to be fully understood and embraced. And in His mercy, Yahweh allowed a "grace period" where the initial impact could set in. But with the temple's destruction in 70 CE, the changeover was complete. The new runner had exited the changeover box with the baton. No longer could worship or sacrifices be offered at the temple, as required by the Law of Moses. Gone were the Levitical priesthood, the animal sacrifices, the temple ceremonies, and many civil laws. And the destruction of the temple was no accident. It was ordained by God and prophesied by Yeshua.

> Some of his disciples were remarking about how the temple was adorned with beautiful stones and with gifts dedicated to God. But Jesus said, "As for what you see here, the time will come when not one stone will be left on another; every one of them will be thrown down." (Luke 21:5-6)[17]

The temple's destruction in 70 CE was a pivotal plot shift in God's unfolding story of redemption. Looking back from two thousand years later, it is hard not to see this event as Yahweh telling mankind that the path for the old runner had ended. Christians no longer need a temple because *we* are the temple; God lives in us.[18] Atonement for sin no longer requires blood sacrifices because Yeshua is our sacrifice, once for all.[19] The baton has been handed off to the new runner. In the end, many first-century Jews missed the hand-off and continued to follow the old runner as he left the track. And this is precisely what Torahism is asking us to do today.

Imagine an ancient city where a rich man decided to build a giant temple. As workers constructed the tall outer walls they erected scaffolding around the building. Then they began working on the interior. The work dragged on for years, then decades, then centuries. Entire generations were born and died without the temple being

---

[17] Also see Matthew 24:1-3; Mark 13:1-4.
[18] 1 Corinthians 3:16-17; 2 Corinthians 6:16; Ephesians 2:19-22; 1 Peter 2:5.
[19] Hebrews 7:27, 10:10-18.

completed. Over time the people began to believe that the scaffolding *was* the finished temple. Then one day, centuries later, a man comes along and starts taking down the scaffolding. The people riot and want to kill him for tearing down their temple. But the man was only taking down the framing around the real temple because it had fulfilled its purpose. The scaffolding was just a shadow of the actual temple, which this man came to reveal. Torahism says, "No! We need to put the scaffolding back up. It is sacred!" This is where Torahism is at its most dangerous. By teaching we need to return to the scaffolding, Torah-keeping denies the adequacy and finality of the work of Christ.

Permitted but Not Required

This historical "changeover box" is also confusing for the theology of Torahism. Many of their beliefs are based on New Testament passages that indicate Jesus and the Apostles were keeping the Mosaic Law. Based on this, they argue:

> Our doctrine [*of keeping the Law of Moses*] makes so much better sense than what you preach: A lawless Messiah and hypocritical apostles who say the law is abolished and then keep eating kosher, going to the temple, circumcising traveling companions, celebrating feast days, making sacrifices and keeping the Sabbath 10, 20, and 30 years *after* the Messiah was resurrected! (Jodie S.)

> 1 John 2:6 says, "Whoever says he abides in Him ought to walk in the same way in which He walked." That means that if you abide in Yeshua, you need to walk in the same way as he walked. It doesn't say if you abide in him, you ought to tell people *not to do what I did.* You really need to get right with God and stop telling people to walk contrary to how Yeshua walked because he walked according to Torah. (Bob S.)

> Paul was confusing to me while in the Christian church. But once I unlearned the religion of Rome, I understood him better and the more Christianity confused me. Jesus was a Jew. He said to walk as He walked. He walked by the Torah. So that's what me and my family are doing. (Troy K.)

These statements raise the legitimate question we have been examining. Why do we see the apostles and disciples keeping the Mosaic traditions even *after* Jesus was resurrected and the New Covenant had begun? For example, in Acts 21, when Paul visited James, the people said,

> You see, brother, how many thousands there are among the Jews of those who have believed. They are all zealous for the law, and they have been told about you that you teach all the Jews who are among the Gentiles to forsake Moses, telling them not to circumcise their children or walk according to our customs. What then is to be done? They will certainly hear that you have come. Do therefore what we tell you. We have four men who are under a vow; take these men and purify yourself along with them and pay their expenses, so that they may shave their heads. Thus all will know that there is nothing in what they have been told about you, but that you yourself also live in observance of the law. (Acts 21:20-24)

And then Paul did it! What are we to make of this? Despite the case we are building that those observances are not required of Christians, Scripture nowhere teaches they have been forbidden, either. We are free in Christ to keep (or not keep) them as a matter of personal conscience. In other words, the New Testament teaches that the observance of Mosaic traditions *is permitted but not required*. We see this in Colossians.

> Therefore let no one pass judgment on you in questions of food and drink, or with regard to a festival or a new moon or a Sabbath. These are a shadow of the things to come, but the substance belongs to Christ. (Colossians 2:16-17)

And Paul modeled this freedom to keep or not keep the Mosaic customs in his own ministry.

> For though I am free from all, I have made myself a servant to all, that I might win more of them. To the Jews I became as a Jew, in order to win Jews. To those under the law I became as one under the law (though not being myself under the law) that I might win those under the law. To those outside the law I became as one outside the law (not being outside the law of God but under the law of Christ) that I might win those outside the law. To the weak I became weak, that I might win the weak. I have become all things to all people, that by all means I might

save some. I do it all for the sake of the gospel, that I may share
with them in its blessings. (1 Corinthians 9:19-23)

Paul seems far more concerned about spreading the Gospel than
whether (or to what degree) he kept the Mosaic commandments. This is
why in Acts 21, he did not hesitate when asked to purify himself at the
temple. It was a non-issue for him. The same idea is found in Romans
14:1-15:13. There Paul aligns himself with the "strong in faith" (Rom
15:1), who felt free to eat whatever meat they wanted. But he preached
freedom in Christ when it comes to deciding to what degree one wants
to keep the Mosaic customs regarding food.

> As for the one who is weak in faith, welcome him, but not to
> quarrel over opinions. One person believes he may eat anything,
> while the weak person eats only vegetables. Let not the one who
> eats despise the one who abstains, and let not the one who
> abstains pass judgment on the one who eats, for God has
> welcomed him . . . I know and am persuaded in the Lord Jesus
> that nothing is unclean in itself, but it is unclean for anyone who
> thinks it unclean . . . For the kingdom of God is not a matter of
> eating and drinking but of righteousness and peace and joy in
> the Holy Spirit. (Romans 14:1-3, 14, 17)

And again in 1 Corinthians. Notice the persistent theme of *permitted
but not required* in this passage.

> All things are lawful, but not all things are helpful. All things are
> lawful, but not all things build up. Let no one seek his own good,
> but the good of his neighbor. Eat whatever is sold in the meat
> market without raising any question on the ground of
> conscience. For "the earth is the Lord's, and the fullness thereof."

> If one of the unbelievers invites you to dinner and you are
> disposed to go, eat whatever is set before you without raising any
> question on the ground of conscience. But if someone says to
> you, "This has been offered in sacrifice," then do not eat it, for
> the sake of the one who informed you, and for the sake of
> conscience—I do not mean your conscience, but his. For why
> should my liberty be determined by someone else's conscience?
> If I partake with thankfulness, why am I denounced because of
> that for which I give thanks?

So, whether you eat or drink, or whatever you do, do all to the glory of God. Give no offense to Jews or to Greeks or to the church of God, just as I try to please everyone in everything I do, not seeking my own advantage, but that of many, that they may be saved. (1 Corinthians 10:23-33)

The freedom taught in the New Testament regarding the Mosaic traditions means that our Torahist friends are free in Christ to keep whatever Mosaic customs they want. Indeed, the problem with Torahism is not the keeping of the traditions, per se. It is the teaching that doing so is *required* of all Christians. That position denies the very freedoms the New Testament affirms for all believers and makes Torahism dangerous and unbiblical.

Post-Resurrection Appearances

There is one last aspect to the question of Jesus keeping Torah worth examining. After His resurrection, Jesus presented Himself to His apostles and gave many convincing proofs that he was alive (Acts 1:3). He later appeared to more than five hundred witnesses (1 Cor 15:6) and met with His disciples on a mountain in Galilee to deliver the Great Commission (Matt 28:19-20). All told, Yeshua walked the earth for forty days (Act 1:3) before finally ascending into heaven (Acts 1:9). The first few days after His resurrection would have included *Chag HaMatzot* (the Feast of Unleavened Bread), which concluded with a Shabbat. And He would have been around for at least four weekly Sabbaths during that time.

Interestingly, there is nothing written in Scripture about Jesus participating in the feast days or Sabbaths, teaching in the synagogues, or visiting the temple during these forty days. He did these things *before* His crucifixion. But following His resurrection, under the newly inaugurated New Covenant, we have no record of Yeshua engaging in any Torah-keeping activities. And the Great Commission— His final formal instruction for His new Church—contained no hint of the Torah (Matt 28:18-20). Nor did the last words He uttered before His ascension (Acts 1:8). Could this be because Yeshua had fulfilled the Mosaic Expression, and its commands were no longer a requirement?

Because Scripture does not mention something, it does not necessarily mean it did not happen. But if Yeshua *did* engage in any post-resurrection Torah keeping, God did not ordain that it should be recorded in His Word. And if keeping the Law of Moses was as important to Him as Torahism would have us believe—if that was truly the way Jesus intended all of His followers to rightly live out their faith in Him—one would think He would have mentioned it. Instead, prior to ascending to heaven to await His second coming, Yeshua's final victorious directive was a new command not found in the Torah.

Summary

We cannot separate the things Yeshua and the Apostles did during this period from what they taught. Torahism says that because Jesus and the Apostles kept Torah, all Christians are required to do the same today. But that is a myopic view that fails to consider that (a.) they were Jewish, and (b.) the Mosaic traditions were never forbidden. The New Testament teaches that Christ-followers are permitted but not required to observe them. So Torahism's teaching that all Christians are required to keep the Law of Moses as Yahweh gave it to Israel ultimately denies the sufficiency and authority of the work of Christ.

PART THREE

Claims About the Commandments

10

Moral & Ceremonial Law

"All things are lawful," but not all things are helpful.
"All things are lawful," but not all things build up.

1 CORINTHIANS 10:23

U NDER THE NEW COVENANT, we find ourselves with a set of commandments substantially different from the collection that made up the Law of Moses. This makes sense, even from a human perspective. For example, while there are many differences between the laws of India and the United States, there are also many similarities. The regulations that differ are typically social or cultural and concern issues such as property, traffic, taxes, national holidays, and so on. The laws that are similar are often moral in nature, governing issues like murder, rape, and theft. The same is true of the differences between the Mosaic Expression of the Law of God, which was given to Israel alone, and the New Expression, which is for Jew and Gentile alike.[1] Let's begin our examination of the issue of moral and ceremonial biblical commands by engaging again with the arguments of a popular Hebrew Roots teacher.

Those Phrases Don't Exist

A common target of Zachary Bauer's Torah-observant teachings is the idea that there are moral and ceremonial categories to the laws given in the Torah. He declares,

---

[1] The idea of the Mosaic and New Expressions of the Law of God is presented in chapter four, "A Biblical Framework."

If you're holding [to] the moral and ceremonial law—something that's not found in your entire Bible ever, not even once—I'm going to call you an idiot. Because that's what you are . . . The distinction between the two is never given in your Bible, never, not once. Those phrases do not exist![2]

Respectfully, if Bauer applied that same logic to his own statement, he would need to self-identify as an idiot since the word *bible* is not found in the Bible. He labors the point that the phrases *moral law* and *ceremonial law* are man-made terms not found in Scripture, and he's right. There are many man-made terms not found in the Bible: *heresy, omniscience, trinity, transfiguration.* But these extra-biblical terms refer to fundamental concepts that *are* found in Scripture.

For instance, the word *incarnation* is not in the Bible. It is a man-made term for a man-made doctrine. And why did man create that doctrine? To describe a crucial concept he found in the Bible. "And the Word became flesh and dwelt among us, and we have seen his glory, glory as of the only Son from the Father, full of grace and truth" (John 1:14). Although the word *incarnation* is not used in Scripture, the phenomenon it describes—that God assumed a human nature and became a man in the form of Jesus Christ—is a core tenet of the Christian faith with deep biblical roots.[3] Bauer's logic would require him to reject the doctrine of the incarnation because that word is not found in the Bible.

The issue isn't whether the Bible contains the phrases "moral law" and "ceremonial law." But instead, "Does Scripture contain the *concept* described by those phrases?" And the answer, of course, is yes. Let's take a look.

Cherry-picking

Bauer commonly argues that in the same book of the Torah where God forbids eating pork, He also prohibits homosexual activity. On that basis, Bauer accuses Christians of cherry-picking the verses they like. He suggests they hypocritically accept the laws against homosexual activity yet ignore the commands about kosher food:

---

[2] Zachary Bauer, New2Torah video, "The Moral and Ceremonial Doctrine of Men."
[3] Isaiah 7:14, 9:6; John 1:14, 3:16; Galatians 4:4-5; Philippians 2:6-8; 1 Timothy 1:15-17; Hebrews 1:1-2, etc.

In the book of Leviticus, it says a man should not lie with a man; that's an abomination. But just a few chapters before it says, "you should not eat these things because they are an abomination unto you." You're picking and choosing your abomination. There are some things you like and some things you don't, so the way you can navigate this gigantic minefield . . . is to take certain things and put them into categories that don't exist in your Bible. *They don't exist!* [Christians say] "We'll put that whole pork thing in the ceremonial law. And will put that whole 'man lying with a man' [issue] in the moral category. That's convenient for us. Because we love our piggie. We love our bacon."[4]

There's just one problem with Bauer's line of reasoning here. It is not true. The Christian position on these two laws—or any of the Laws of Moses—has nothing to do with personal preference. It is based on Scripture.

A Distinction in the Text

Bauer accuses Christians of cherry-picking because they keep the law about homosexual activity but do not keep the commandments about pork. In chapter thirteen, we will discover why Christians are not required to keep the kosher food laws. So why do we, at the same time, maintain the prohibition against homosexual activity found in the same book of the Bible?[5]

Again, it is not a matter of personal preference. It's about the authority of Scripture. Unlike the kosher food laws, the commands about sexual immorality—including homosexual behavior—are repeated and re-taught in the New Testament.[6] And therefore, unlike the kosher food laws, the moral laws about sexual immorality are still in effect. And that brings up a fascinating question.

Under the New Expression, why did God repeat and endorse the laws about sexual immorality but end the commands about food? Over the centuries, that question has made many Christians curious. They began studying the Bible and started to notice a pattern. Across the New Testament, many Mosaic laws are repeated, endorsed, or sometimes even

---

[4] Zachary Bauer from the video "The Moral and Ceremonial Doctrine of Men."

[5] A discussion of Christianity and homosexuality is beyond the scope of this book. But I feel it is important to affirm that, while homosexual behavior is clearly sinful, those in the LGBT+ community are loved by God and made in His image. They are beloved and valuable members of our families, friend groups, and communities. They should be treated with love, dignity, and respect as human beings, especially by Christians.

[6] Matthew 15:19; Romans 1:26-28; 1 Corinthians 6:9-11; 1 Timothy 1:8-11.

quoted directly.[7] These include the commandments against murder, adultery, stealing, greed, worshipping idols, bearing false witness, and so on.

At the same time, there are other Mosaic laws that the NT teaches are no longer in effect.[8] For example, under the New Expression, there is no more Levitical priesthood. Animal sacrifices are no longer required. Neither is the temple, or the feasts, or circumcision. What's going on here? Did God arbitrarily pick and choose which laws would continue and which would end?

As Christians continued to study Scripture, they started noticing a pattern.[9] The Mosaic laws that are repeated and endorsed under the Covenant primarily deal with issues of right and wrong. This makes sense if you think about it. Issues like murder, adultery, stealing, greed, and so on are objectively wrong; they are *always wrong for all people at all times*. These are moral values that transcend nations, cultures, and eras. The laws regarding these issues are grounded in God's unchanging moral perfection and therefore apply at all times to all people. As a shorthand, the biblical laws that deal with morality are sometimes referred to as the "moral laws." Not because the Bible uses the phrase *moral law*, but because we find the concept there. The Messianic Jewish organization IAMCS makes a great statement about morality and the Torah.

> The gift of the Torah to the Jewish people at Sinai was not revelatory in the sense of the moral aspect of it. Noah was an "ish tzadik" or "righteous man" (See Gen. 6:9); and Abraham obeyed God's statutes and commandments (Gen. 26:5), even long before the law at Sinai was even given. Torah is not a revelation of morality. Nor is the moral aspect of it unique in any way. A basic understanding of moral law is already embedded by God in the understanding of mankind. God did not appear to Israel at Sinai to present a moral code. God gave the law at Sinai, creating a unique nation.[10]

On the other hand, the commands that were fulfilled and, thus, came to an end as laws under the New Covenant are of a different type. Rather than morality, they dealt with issues that could be classified as ceremonial

---

[7] Matthew 15:19, 19:18; Mark 7:21, 10:19; Luke 18:20; Romans 13:9, etc.

[8] Mark 7:19; Acts 15:1-29; Romans 14-15; Colossians 2:16-17; Hebrews 7, 10, etc.

[9] And by the way, I'm summarizing centuries of theological discovery into just a few sentences here!

[10] "One Law, Two Sticks: A Critical Look at the Hebrew Roots Movement," International Alliance of Messianic Congregations and Synagogues.

or ritual in nature. For example, unlike murder or adultery, food in and of itself is morally neutral. It is not wrong for all people at all times to eat bacon. We know this because these dietary restrictions were not given to anyone before Sinai, nor to the Gentile nations. In fact, despite taking both clean and unclean animals onto the ark before the flood (Gen 7:2), God told Noah after the flood that they were *all* food for him (Gen 9:3).

And we never see God judging or denouncing Gentile nations for eating unkosher foods. Egypt, Assyria, Babylon and the rest of the Gentile nations could eat all the pork chops they wanted. Israel alone was given these unique food laws. And not as a matter of right and wrong, but as a matter of obedience and identity. The kosher food laws are part of a group of commands sometimes referred to as the *Holiness Laws*. These are regulations given by God to set Israel apart from all the other nations on earth.[11] Indeed, the word *holy* (קָדוֹשׁ, *qadosh*) means "set apart." It is about differentiation. Holy things are set apart from things that are common or profane. In antiquity, if you came across a tribe of people who did not eat pork or do any labor on the last day of the week, and all the males were circumcised, you knew they were Israelites, a people set apart for Yahweh, the one true God.

The Holiness Laws are part of a larger category of commandments that deal with food, sacred time (Sabbath, feasts, new moons, etc.), sacrifices, the temple, the Levitical priesthood, the feasts, and so on. These commands, which primarily concern matters of ritual and ceremony, are often collectively referred to as *ceremonial laws*. Not because the Bible uses the phrase "ceremonial law," but because the concept is found there.

Why Did the Ceremonial Laws End?

Under the Mosaic Expression, the *People of God* were defined by their ethnicity. The physical descendants of Abraham through Isaac—aka the Jews, the genealogical nation of Israel—were God's People. Everyone else was a Gentile, a non-Jew. That changed under the New Expression. Because of the redeeming work of Christ, the People of the God of Israel are now defined by faith in Yeshua rather than ethnicity.

> For as many of you as were baptized into Christ have put on Christ. There is neither Jew nor Greek, there is neither slave nor free, there is no male and female, for you are all one in Christ

---

[11] Exodus 19:4-6; Deuteronomy 7:6; 2 Samuel 7:23-24; Amos 3:2, etc.

Jesus. And if you are Christ's, then you are Abraham's offspring, heirs according to promise. (Galatians 3:27-29)

Under the Mosaic Covenant, the Jewish people alone were considered the offspring of Abraham and the inheritors of God's promises. But the passage above reveals that under the New Covenant, *anyone* who has placed their faith in Jesus is now considered Abraham's offspring and an heir of God's promise, whether they are Jewish or not. So, it makes sense that the specific laws given to set Israel apart from the Gentiles have ended as a legal obligation. Those laws were only given until Christ came. And now that He has come, we are no longer under the law. (Gal 3:24-25).

Consider how the change in relationship between Jews and Gentiles is described in Ephesians 2:

But now in Christ Jesus you who once were far off [Gentiles] have been brought near by the blood of Christ. For he himself is our peace, who has made us both one [Jew and Gentile] and has broken down in his flesh the dividing wall of hostility by abolishing the law of commandments expressed in ordinances, that he might create in himself one new man in place of the two, so making peace, and might reconcile us both, to God in one body through the cross, thereby killing the hostility. (Ephesians 2:13-16, bracketed comments added)

Because the "wall of hostility" (v. 14) between Jews and Gentiles had its foundation in the Mosaic Expression, the way Yeshua tore down that wall was "by abolishing the law of commandments expressed in ordinances" (v. 15).

Contrary to Bauer's strident protestations, Christians do not pick and choose which laws we want to keep based on our enjoyment of ham sandwiches. Scripture is our authority in these matters. That said, if Bauer wants to observe the kosher food restrictions, God bless him. He's entirely within his freedom in Christ to eat or not eat what he wants. The same goes for keeping the feasts and circumcision and so on. These Torah traditions have not been forbidden under the New Covenant. The New Testament teaches that they are *permitted but not required*. So Bauer—or any other Hebrew Roots or "Torah-observant" Christian—is free to observe whatever Mosaic traditions they want. Provided, of course, they acknowledge that doing so is a matter of personal preference, not a requirement of salvation or righteousness.

The problems begin when our Torahist friends start teaching—as Bauer often does—that all Christians are *required* to keep the Law of Moses. They argue that Christians who do not keep the Mosaic Law are rebelling against God and openly living in sin. And at that point, they've crossed the line into unbiblical territory. They are fomenting division in the body of Christ and undermining both the Gospel of Jesus and the sufficiency of His work in making us right with God. And it is these dangerous and errant teachings that motivate me to spend so much time and energy calling out these Hebrew Roots teachers on their false doctrine.

Summary

Torahism often claims that the phrases *moral law* and *ceremonial law* are nowhere to be found in the Bible and that Christians who make this distinction are cherry-picking the verses they like. However, because a particular word or phrase is not found in the Bible, it does not mean that the concept it describes is not there. (e.g., *incarnation, atheism, monotheism,* and *Bible.*) Moreover, there are clear distinctions in the text between laws related to right and wrong (morality), which are repeated and endorsed under Christ, and laws dealing with ceremonial or ritual matters that have been fulfilled and come to an end. God's People are defined differently and bound by a different collection of commandments under the New Covenant than under the Old Covenant.

11

Keep The Feasts

*The Sabbaths are for rest and the festivals for joy,
not for fasting and weeping and crying.*

MAIMONIDES

I N THE TORAH, YAHWEH GAVE ISRAEL a ceremonial calendar to
follow. Leviticus chapter 23 sums up God's appointed times. There
we find Yahweh giving Israel eight feasts—seven annual festivals
(four in the spring and three in the fall), plus the weekly Sabbath.

Feast	Hebrew Name	Hebrew Date
Passover	Pesach	Nisan 14-15
Unleavened Bread	Chag Hamotzi	Nisan 15-22
First Fruits	Yom HaBikkurim	Nisan 16-17
Pentecost, Feast of Weeks	Shavu'ot	Sivan 6-7
Feast of Trumpets; Jewish New Year	Yom Teru'ah (Rosh Hashanah)	Tishri 1
Day of Atonement	Yom Kippur	Tishri 10
Feast of Tabernacles	Sukkot	Tishri 15-22
The Sabbath Day	Shabbat	Weekly

Through these feasts, the Israelites were to celebrate their history and faith, worship Yahweh, and thank Him for His blessings. Torahism joins Judaism in keeping these feasts and teaches that all Christians are required to observe them as well. In fact, most Torah-keepers affirm that Christians who do not keep the feasts violate God's law and commit grievous sin.

> The reason you Christians don't keep the feasts is because you inherited the lies of the copycat religion that departed from keeping the feasts. Romanized Christianity departed from the faith practiced by Yeshua and the apostles. (Jim G.)

> Christmas, Easter and other celebrations sanctioned by the Catholic and Protestant churches are a departure from the biblical feasts given by Yahweh in Leviticus which the apostles taught the first-century believers to keep. (Brad B.)

> Christianity separated itself from the Lord's feasts and replaced them with pagan feasts because it didn't want anything to do with those detestable Jews. (Sue T.)

> Jesus was crucified on Passover, buried on the feast of Unleavened Bread, resurrected on the Feast of First Fruits, and sent us the Holy Spirit on Pentecost. It would seem that the feast days mandated by the Torah are pretty relevant. (Zachary Bauer, New2Torah)

There is nothing wrong with Christians observing these feasts. I have attended Shabbat services with a local Messianic Jewish congregation and celebrated the Passover seder. These were experiences I found enriching and a powerful connection to the ancient roots of my faith. So I agree with Torahism that the Torah feasts are important. Everything Yahweh gives is important! But, as we've seen, not everything He gives is required of all people. And the New Testament teaches the Torah feasts were foreshadows of Christ, and we are not to let others judge us on whether we keep them (Col 2:16-17).

It is also important to acknowledge that these feasts are distinctively Jewish, which is why most Jewish followers of Jesus still observe them today. Gentiles, however, have never been expected to keep the feasts.

They were given to Israel, not the nations,[1] which is why, even today, religious Jews find it offensive and a matter of cultural misappropriation when a Gentile Christian hosts a Torah feast, such as Passover. At the same time,

> Although it may be inappropriate for Gentiles to host a Passover Seder, it is an entirely different matter when a Jewish believer in Jesus hosts a Seder. Why? Because the Seder is part of their Jewish history. The Jewish person who interacts with Jewish tradition is doing so as an insider, not an outsider.[2]

The Torah feasts all share a major feature: sacrifice. And because Jesus was our sacrifice once for all,[3] believers in Him are not required to keep these feasts. He fulfilled them all. However, from our perspective as followers of Yeshua, understanding the feasts can enrich our faith and give us a unique insight into how they pointed to the coming Messiah. If you have a Torah-keeper in your life, this issue will come up sooner or later. So, let's take a brief look at the seven annual feasts and how they are related to Christ. We will save the weekly Sabbath for the next chapter.

The Seven Feasts

Pesach

Pesach (Passover)[4] commemorates Yahweh's final plague on Egypt when the angel of death "passed over" those Israelite families who applied the blood of the lamb to their doors (Ex 12). Thus, it is sometimes called the Feast of Salvation. When John the Baptist saw Yeshua and proclaimed, "Look, the Lamb of God, who takes away the sin of the world!" (John 1:29), and when Peter wrote that we are redeemed by "the precious blood of Christ, a lamb without blemish or defect" (1 Pet 1:19), and when John talked about triumph "by the blood of the Lamb" (Rev 12:11), their references to Pesach were not lost on their Jewish audiences.

---

[1] Gentiles, of course, were allowed to participate in certain feasts under certain conditions. For example, a non-Jewish male who wanted to "keep the Passover to the Lord" had to be circumcised (Ex 12:43-49), symbolizing his loyalty to Yahweh, the God of Israel.

[2] Gateway Center for Israel, "A Christian Guide to Passover," www.centerforisrael.com/papers/a-christian-guide-to-passover

[3] Hebrews 7:27, 9:12, 9:26, 10:10.

[4] In Torah-keeping communities, there is a great deal of controversy surrounding Passover and Easter. That issue is dealt with in chapter seventeen.

Yeshua is our Passover Lamb, an idea reflected in the taking of communion. The bread and wine represent the body and blood of Christ, which were foreshadowed by the bread and wine taken during Passover. Parsons notes,

> In both Testaments, the blood of the Lamb delivers from slavery—the Jew from Egypt, the Christian from sin. Think about the tenth plague in Exodus 12:5 when Egypt's firstborn sons died while the angel of death "passed over" the Jewish homes with the blood of the lamb on their doorposts. In the *B'rit Chadashah* (New Testament), Jesus serves as the sacrificial lamb. It is no coincidence that our Lord himself was sacrificed on the Passover. In Egypt, the Jew marked his house with the blood of the lamb. Today the Christian marks his house—his body, "the house of the spirit"—with the blood of Christ. Passover, then, represents our salvation.[5]

During the Last Supper, Yeshua equates the *matzah* (unleavened bread) of Passover with his body.

> The Lord Jesus on the night when he was betrayed took bread, and when he had given thanks, he broke it, and said, "This is my body, which is for you. Do this in remembrance of me." (1 Corinthians 11:23b-24)

Matzah is often used in Christian churches today to remember Yeshua's sacrifice during communion. It reminds us that His body was broken for our sins.

Chag HaMotzi & Bikkurim

The day after Pesach, *Chag HaMotzi* (the Feast of Unleavened Bread) begins. In Scripture, leaven (yeast) often symbolizes sin or evil. So the idea of avoiding yeast for seven days was symbolic of a sort of holy walk with the Lord. Then, "on the day after the Sabbath" following Unleavened Bread is *Yom HaBikkurim* (Day of First Fruits). At this feast, the Israelites brought the early crops of their spring planting, the "first fruits," which were specially dedicated to Yahweh by "wav[ing] the sheaf before the Lord" (Lev 23:11). The first fruits are not just the first to arrive chronologically. They also represent a hope of a greater harvest to

---

[5] John J. Parsons, "The Jewish Holidays," Hebrew4Christians.com.

follow. Scripture considers the "firstborn" (both human and animal) to be a type of first fruit and Yahweh's special possession (Ex 22:29, 34:19).

Bikkurim was celebrated on the third day of Passover, foreshadowing the "third day" on which Yeshua rose from the grave. When Paul declared, "Christ has indeed been raised from the dead, the firstfruits of those who have fallen asleep" (1 Cor 15:20), he knew what it would have meant to his Jewish audience. Yeshua represents the first fruits of the harvest of souls that will be given eternal life because of the new covenant in His blood.[6]

Shavu'ot

Fifty days after the Feast of Firstfruits comes a second harvest feast. Because it occurs seven weeks later—the fiftieth day is the day after the end of the seventh week—the festival was known as *Shavu'ot*, or Weeks. Robinson provides some helpful insight into the nature of this feast in the first century.

> The day God gave the Torah (Law of Moses) on Mount Sinai was [eventually] calculated as falling exactly on the day of Shavuot. By the time of Jesus, in addition to being the firstfruit holiday, it had also become the anniversary of the giving of the Law. It was on this very holiday, when tens of thousands of pilgrims were bringing their firstfruits, that the events of Acts 2 took place.[7]

Indeed, Pentecost (a word which means "fiftieth") occurred on Sahvu'ot.[8] Yahweh, in His divine timing, chose to give the Holy Spirit under the New Covenant on the same day He gave the Law under the Sinai Covenant. And if we step back and view the four spring feasts as a whole, we see that Yeshua was crucified on Pesach, buried on Chag Hamotzi, raised on Yom HaBikkurim, and He sent the *Ruach HaKodesh* (Holy Spirit) on Shavu'ot. This is no coincidence; it is Christ fulfilling the feasts. They were the shadows, He is the substance to which they pointed.

---

[6] Matthew 26:28; Luke 22:20; 1 Corinthians 11:25.

[7] Rich Robinson, "The Jewish Roots of the Feast of Pentecost," JewforJesus.org.

[8] There are some significant parallels between the account of the giving of the Law at Sinai (Exodus 19:16-20, 20:18-21) and the giving of the Holy Spirit on Pentecost (Acts 2:1-8). Robinson notes, "The loud sound and tongues of fire in Acts 2 would have brought Exodus 19-20 to mind for some in attendance—especially since this was the anniversary of the giving of the Law, and Mount Sinai would have been on the minds of many."

Sukkot

Sukkot (Feast of Tabernacles/Booths) is a fall festival during which many Jewish families construct a *sukkah* (hut) to commemorate the makeshift dwellings that Israel lived in during their forty years of wandering in the wilderness. After Israel entered the Promised Land, Sukkot became known as the "Feast of Ingathering" in association with the fall harvest. In this sense, it foreshadows the regathering of the Jewish people in the Last Days.[9] Zechariah's prophesy says, "everyone who survives of all the nations that have come against Jerusalem shall go up year after year to worship the King, the Lord of hosts, and to keep the Feast of Booths" (Zech 14:16). In this sense, Sukkot is a vision of the world to come.

Yeshua came to "sukkah" (tabernacle, dwell) with us (John 1:14) and redeem us to God. Parsons notes,

> In light of the work of Yeshua as our *Kohen Gadol* (high priest) of the New Covenant, we now have access to the heavenly Temple of God (Heb 4:16). We are now members of the greater Temple of His body; we are now part of his great Sukkah![10]

We now await His return to establish His kingdom and "tabernacle with us" forever.

Yom Teru'ah (Rosh Hashanah)

Yom Teru'ah (Feast of Trumpets) is celebrated today as the Jewish New Year's Day. It is a time of prayer, self-examination, and repentance lasting ten days. During this time, acts of charity are encouraged, and special prayers are offered for forgiveness.

This holiday is unique among the Torah feasts in that Yahweh provided no specific reason for its observance other than offering sacrifices and resting.[11] After the destruction of the second temple in 70 CE, Judaism was redefined by the rabbis. Yom Teru'ah became associated with the start of the Jewish civil year and was dubbed *Rosh Hashanah*. Interestingly, in Jewish tradition, the Torah portions read on the first two days of Rosh Hashana are about the birth and the binding of Isaac. These passages are a bold prefiguring of Christ.

Yom Teru'ah also commemorates Yahweh's creation of the world. The Hebrew word *teruah* (תְּרוּעָה) means "signal" or "shout of joy," and

---

[9] Isaiah 27:12-13; Jeremiah 23:7-8.
[10] John J. Parsons, The Festival of Sukkot, www.hebrew4christians.com/Holidays/Fall_Holidays/Sukkot/sukkot.html
[11] Leviticus 23:24; Numbers 29:1.

the Israelites marked the first day of the feast by making a joyful noise unto the Lord (Ps 81:1-4). Thus, Yom Teru'ah can also be seen as a foreshadowing of the creation of the new heavens and earth at Yeshua's second coming, when the trumpets will announce the arrival of the Last Days.[12] This is a time of year that sets the tone for the holiest day in the Jewish calendar, Yom Kippur.

Yom Kippur

Yom Kippur, the Day of Atonement, was the only day of the year when the High Priest was allowed to pass beyond the veil into the Most Holy Place, the innermost room of the temple. The High Priest was to take two unblemished male goats and a bull into the temple for an offering. He would sacrifice the bull for his own sin to make atonement for himself and his household. Then he would sacrifice one of the goats as a sin offering for the people. The other goat was presented alive before the Lord. The priest would symbolically pass the sins of Israel onto the animal by placing his hands on it and then sending it out into the wilderness as a scapegoat.[13]

In the New Testament, we learn how Yeshua was so beautifully foreshadowed in this ritual. He was both our atonement—the sacrifice for our sins—*and* the scapegoat (Heb 13:11-12). He is the innocent, unblemished sacrifice,[14] given "once for all" (Heb 10). Upon His death, the temple veil that kept Israel separated from direct access to God's presence was torn down.[15] The final Yom Kippur took place at Calvary. Christ's sacrifice brings forgiveness of sin to all who place their faith in Him. He opened a way for us to be made right with God without priests or temples.

Torahism & The Feasts

Torahism's charges of wrongdoing regarding the feasts are based on the false premise that all Christians are still under the Mosaic Law. While celebrating the Torah feasts can be meaningful for Christians, we are not obligated to observe them as a matter of salvation or obedience. Followers of Jesus today are not made any more righteous in Yahweh's eyes by keeping the feasts He gave to Israel. After describing how God made us alive through Christ, the Apostle Paul wrote:

---

[12] 1 Corinthians 15:51-54; Thessalonians 4:15-18.
[13] See Leviticus 16 for the detailed mitzvot the priests were to follow on the Day of Atonement.
[14] 2 Corinthians 5:21; Hebrews 4:15; 1 Peter 2:22; 1 John 3:5.
[15] Matthew 27:51; Mark 15:38; Luke 23:45; Hebrews 10:20.

> Therefore do not let anyone judge you by what you eat or drink,
> or with regard to a religious festival, a New Moon celebration or
> a Sabbath day. These are a shadow of the things that were to
> come; the reality, however, is found in Christ. (Colossians 2:16-
> 17)

The Mosaic feasts are foreshadows of Christ. The book of Hebrews
teaches that the Law of Moses, with its ceremonial requirements of feasts
and sacrifices, was not the final reality, but rather a shadow of the good
things that were coming in Yeshua (Heb 10). It describes the priestly
gifts and sacrifices of Yom Kippur as "only a matter of food and drink
and various ceremonial washings—external regulations applying until
the time of the new order" (Heb 9:10). By insisting on the observance of
these feasts, Torahism fails to recognize that their fulfillment has already
taken place in Yeshua. Christians worship the Real Thing, not the
"shadows" that pointed to Him. Therefore, in a very real sense, we keep
the feasts today by believing in Yeshua. He is our feast!

A common Torahist rebuttal is to claim that Yeshua and the
Apostles kept the feasts, and we are called to walk as they did. Therefore,
we should be observing the feasts as well. This issue was dealt with in
detail in chapter nine but let me offer one thought on the issue here. At
the start of this chapter, I quoted a man named Brad who claimed that
the apostles taught the first-century believers to keep the feasts of the
Torah. Yet, in the conversation I had with him, Brad could not provide
any scriptural evidence for his claim. There is nothing in the New
Testament to suggest the apostles taught new believers to keep the Torah
feasts. In fact, the teachings we do find in the New Testament—some
cited above, more in the coming chapters—show that the apostles
explicitly taught first-century believers they were *not* required to keep the
feasts.

This issue of keeping the feasts is given additional clarity when
viewed from the vantage point of modern Jewish believers in Yeshua:

> As followers of Yeshua, we want the Jewish people to see and to
> understand the substance of these shadows. And though we are
> no longer under the authority of the Sinai covenant and thus are
> no longer bound to keep the laws concerning the feasts, we still
> seek to find ways to flesh out these fuller realities to the Jewish
> people. For those of us who are Jewish believers in Yeshua,
> particularly in Israel, the celebration of the feast days (Shabbat,

Passover, Sukkot, etc.) affords us a great opportunity to show our people how the Law points to Yeshua.[16]

Feasts in the Last Days

Torah-keepers may also attempt an eschatological argument by citing the prophet Zechariah. He foretells that, in the last days, God will command the faithful among the Gentiles to come to Jerusalem and celebrate the Feast of Booths (Zech 14:16). According to Torahism, this is proof that the feasts are to be kept, even by Gentiles. However, it is quite an unjustified leap to extrapolate a single end-times feast—which will happen when God ultimately brings the Gentile nations into submission to His throne—into a current obligation of Gentile Christ-followers to keep *all* of the Torah feasts every year.

Summary

There is nothing wrong with observing the feasts prescribed by the Torah. They were shadows that pointed to Christ and celebrating them can be a beautiful way to stay connected to the Jewish roots of our faith. However, we are not under the Law of Moses and, therefore, not obligated to observe the feasts as a matter of salvation or obedience. We aren't made right with God by keeping them. We keep the feasts today by believing in Yeshua. He is our feast!

---

[16] Postell, Eitan, Soref, *Reading Moses, Seeing Jesus*, Kindle locations 1620-1627.

12

Keep The Sabbath

*The Sabbath is the day on which we learn
the art of surpassing civilization.*

ABRAHAM JOSHUA HESCHEL

I HAVE ALWAYS THOUGHT SUNDAY was the day Christians were supposed to observe the Sabbath by resting and giving our time to God. And I've felt a little guilty for never fully doing that. I go to church on Sundays to gather in fellowship with other believers, learn about God, read His Word and worship Him. And as a member of my church's music team, I often help lead others in worship. But I can't recall any Sunday where I intentionally avoided work in order to rest and honor God. To be honest, I don't think I know any Christians who observe the Lord's Day to the degree that orthodox Judaism observes Shabbat.[1]

So, I had some trepidation as I dug into this issue. It's a central tenet of Torahism and a pervasive source of its contention with mainstream Christianity. I sensed I would feel convicted about Sabbath observance and might ultimately have to concede the point to Torahism that Christianity is wrong in its practice of the Sunday Sabbath. But I decided I was okay with that because Scripture is my authority, not doctrine, denomination, or tradition. So, I rolled up my sleeves and dug into the Bible to see what it would teach me.

The commandment about the Sabbath appears twice in the Torah, with slightly different wording.

---

[1] Did you know that, in Israel, they have elevators programmed to stop at every floor of the building on Shabbat, so observant Jews do not have to do the "work" of pressing a button?

Exodus 20:8-11	Deuteronomy 5:12-15
Remember the Sabbath day, to keep it holy. Six days you shall labor, and do all your work, but the seventh day is a Sabbath to the Lord your God. On it you shall not do any work, you, or your son, or your daughter, your male servant, or your female servant, or your livestock, or the sojourner who is within your gates. For in six days the Lord made heaven and earth, the sea, and all that is in them, and rested on the seventh day. Therefore the Lord blessed the Sabbath day and made it holy.	Observe the Sabbath day, to keep it holy, as the Lord your God commanded you. Six days you shall labor and do all your work, but the seventh day is a Sabbath to the Lord your God. On it you shall not do any work, you or your son or your daughter or your male servant or your female servant, or your ox or your donkey or any of your livestock, or the sojourner who is within your gates, that your male servant and your female servant may rest as well as you. You shall remember that you were a slave in the land of Egypt, and the Lord your God brought you out from there with a mighty hand and an outstretched arm. Therefore the Lord your God commanded you to keep the Sabbath day.

My Torah-keeping friend Ruth claims, "The early Church Fathers, eager to complete the break with the synagogue, urged the substitution of Sunday for the Jewish Sabbath." Another Torah-keeper said,

> And yes, we were shocked and horrified when we found out that it was the Roman Bishops who separated from the Torah and from Passover and from Sabbath. Then to find out they took the Western congregations with them and then threatened death and excommunication to believers caught practicing what was written in the Torah...yikes! (Greg H.)

The Church of God International (CGI) argues, "There is absolutely no New Testament text stating that God, Jesus, or the apostles changed the Sabbath to Sunday—not a text, not a word, not even a hint or suggestion."[2] Hebrew Roots teacher David Wilber of 119 Ministries

---

[2] Church of God International, "Who Changed the Sabbath to Sunday?" www.cgi.org/who-changed-the-sabbath-to-sunday.

claims that any Christian who does not keep the Torah Sabbath is openly living in sin and deserving of the death penalty prescribed under Moses.[3]

Many Torah-keepers chalk up the Christian abandonment of the weekly Sabbath commands to anti-Jewish sentiment or pagan sun-worship. And while we may disagree with the reasons, we must admit that the New Testament does not teach anywhere that the Sabbath was changed from Saturday to Sunday. The decision to observe Sunday as the Lord's Day was not a biblical directive. And yet every orthodox Christian thinker and theologian from every era and denomination—from the apostle John to Augustine to Anselm to John Calvin to Timothy Keller—has come to the same conclusion: Christ-followers are not required to keep the Mosaic Sabbath commands. How did they arrive there?

The Sabbath is a major point of conflict between Torahism and mainstream Christianity, so we will spend some time examining it from four different perspectives. We will first consider the big picture and biblical themes behind the Sabbath. Then we'll analyze the scriptural data in the Tanakh, and then in the New Testament, and lastly look at Jesus' teachings and relationship to Shabbat.

The Story of the Sabbath

Pulling back from the specific texts and surveying the overall flow of the biblical storyline from the proverbial 30,000-foot view reveals amazing patterns. To uncover the cosmic story of the Sabbath, let's first examine the overarching theme of *rest* in Scripture.

The Bible opens on a scene of amorphous darkness.

> The earth was without form and void, and darkness was over the face of the deep. And the Spirit of God was hovering over the face of the waters. (Genesis 1:2)

The ancient Hebrews were not a sea-faring people and, thus, the sea was associated with chaos. The first chapter of the Bible reveals Yahweh speaking light into the darkness, order into the chaos, life into the void. This happens over six days, each marked by the phrase "there was evening and there was morning."[4] God's creation work then culminated on the seventh day.

---

[3] Wilber made these comments during my debate with him on the question, "Are Christians required to keep the Sabbath?" streamed live on May 2, 2022. He did thankfully acknowledge that the death penalty required by the Mosaic Law is not enforceable today.

[4] Genesis 1:5, 8, 13, 19, 23, 31.

Thus the heavens and the earth were finished, and all the host of them. And on the seventh day God finished his work that he had done, and he rested on the seventh day from all his work that he had done. So God blessed the seventh day and made it holy, because on it God rested from all his work that he had done in creation. (Genesis 2:1-3)

The seventh day was unique. It was not marked with the phrase, "there was evening and there was morning." Yahweh did not go back to His creation work on the eighth day; it was complete. All was as He intended. God's presence filled His creation, and the earth provided everything needed for His creatures. He had appointed human beings—the only one of His creatures made in His image—to partner with Him in ruling over the world. Thus, the never-ending seventh day began with Adam and Eve resting with God and walking in His presence in the Garden.

In Hebrew categories, the number seven (שֶׁבַע *shéva*) is associated with completeness or fullness. And that is exactly what we see in Eden. The seventh day of creation was the true state of peace, contentment, and rest (*shabbat*) we all yearn for. Most of our life is spent striving to impose order on chaos, fighting against disorder and opposition of one kind or another. Unlike Adam and Eve, we have to work daily to satisfy our basic human needs for safety, nourishment, love, and belonging. So we revel in those periods of life where true joy and contentment poke through. They are a primal reminder that there is something better for us. That *shalom* and *shabbat* (peace and rest) are what we were built for. They are baked into the fiber of every human soul.

This sense of shabbat is what the first humans were given in Eden. It was Yahweh's ideal for mankind. And then, disastrously, we were deceived by a dark enemy and forfeited that rest. What happened next to Adam and Eve would later be replayed in the nation of Israel. They were ejected from the sabbath rest of God's presence and sent into exile in the chaos of the wilderness. They had to work as enslaved people, struggling against opposition and disorder.

Because of that first sin, this same tragic storyline of struggle has echoed in the lives of every single human being down through history. Our fundamental longing for completeness is so powerful it causes us to chase after it down the dark alleyways of money, sex, fame, and worldly success. We are all striving for Eden. The apostle Paul elegantly describes this profound yearning for rest.

> For I consider that the sufferings of this present time are not worth comparing with the glory that is to be revealed to us. For the creation waits with eager longing for the revealing of the sons of God. For the creation was subjected to futility, not willingly, but because of him who subjected it, in hope that the creation itself will be set free from its bondage to corruption and obtain the freedom of the glory of the children of God. For we know that the whole creation has been groaning together in the pains of childbirth until now. And not only the creation, but we ourselves, who have the firstfruits of the Spirit, groan inwardly as we wait eagerly for adoption as sons, the redemption of our bodies. (Romans 8:18-23)

The Bible teaches that Yahweh will indeed return all of creation to that seventh-day rest. He will restore His Edenic vision in the end. We are given a prefiguring of that future hope through the nation of Israel. Yahweh rescued them from grueling slavery in Egypt. He led them through chaos and darkness on a journey to the Promised Land, which He called "My rest" (Psalm 95:10-11). But it wasn't a straight shot. In the same way we struggle through life today, Israel struggled through the wilderness. And in the same way God was with them—leading and blessing them amid their tribulations—He is with us today.

Even before the Israelites entered the Promised Land, God gave them a taste of their future rest. He provided the gift of a weekly Shabbat, a day when they were to stop working and striving and rest in Yahweh. Every seventh day, for an entire day, the Israelites could let go and trust God for all their needs.

And here we see the significance of the number seven as indicating completeness or fullness. The weekly Shabbat occurs every seventh day. And each of the seven annual feasts given to Israel by Yahweh in the Mosaic Law (Lev 23) culminates in a seventh-day rest. Moreover, in stark contrast to the nations around her, God commanded that every seventh year Israel was to free her slaves (Ex 21:2), release one another from any outstanding debt (Deut 15:1-2), and let the land rest (Ex 23:10-11). And this culminated in the Sabbath of Sabbaths, the Year of Jubilee. Yahweh commanded Israel,

> You shall count seven weeks of years, seven times seven years, so that the time of the seven weeks of years shall give you forty-nine years. Then you shall sound the loud trumpet on the tenth day of the seventh month. On the Day of Atonement, you shall

sound the trumpet throughout all your land. And you shall consecrate the fiftieth year and proclaim liberty throughout the land to all its inhabitants. It shall be a jubilee for you, when each of you shall return to his property and each of you shall return to his clan. (Leviticus 25:8-10)

All these *sevens* in Scripture point us to the hope of our ultimate, restored rest with Yahweh.

Unfortunately, after finally making it into the Promised Land, the Israelites abandoned God and lost their rest. The storyline repeats. Israel is exiled, tossed back into chaos and turmoil, and enslaved again. But Yahweh did not give up on His people. He sent prophets to let them know that this exile, too, would one day end. He would restore freedom and rest; there was an ultimate Jubilee to come. But, of course, the Hebrew Scriptures end with God's people still waiting for that promised rest.

And then, one Sabbath day early in the first century, a Jewish man from Nazareth stood up in a synagogue and read aloud from the scroll of Isaiah.

The Spirit of the Lord is upon me, because he has anointed me to proclaim good news to the poor. He has sent me to proclaim liberty to the captives and recovering of sight to the blind, to set at liberty those who are oppressed, to proclaim the year of the Lord's favor. (Luke 4:18-19, quoting Isaiah 61:1-2)

This event marked the beginning of Jesus' earthly ministry. And He began by proclaiming the year of the Lord's favor. His Jewish audience would have immediately made the connection. Yeshua was talking about the Jubilee. He was declaring that the ultimate seventh-day rest would come through Him. And He would later claim the title of "Lord of the Sabbath."[5] We see this role play out in His ministry. Yeshua challenged chaos and disorder by casting out demons, freeing people from sickness and disease, and ultimately triumphing in victory over sin and death.

It is certainly no coincidence that Jesus was crucified at the end of the week, and His body rested in the grave on Shabbat. It was the next day, the eighth day, that He was resurrected. Yeshua rose to new life on the first day of the week, inaugurating a new covenant and a new creation. Once again, the life-giving light of Yahweh had pierced the

---

[5] Matthew 12:8; Mark 2:28; Luke 6:5.

chaos and darkness brought about by mankind's sin. And because of the Resurrection, we have an incorruptible hope in a future rest, a future Eden, an ultimate Shabbat. We are not there yet, but Yeshua assures us,

> I have said these things to you, that in me you may have peace. In the world you will have tribulation. But take heart; I have overcome the world. (John 16:33)

Christians today are in a state similar to the ancient Israelites. Yahweh is guiding us toward the Promised Land, but we are still in the wilderness. We still experience tribulation, frustration, and pain. Under the Sinai Covenant, ancient Israel was given the weekly Shabbat to foreshadow the rest that was to come. Under the New Covenant, Christ is our foretaste of God's ultimate Edenic rest in the world to come. He is our Sabbath.

> Come to me, all you who are weary and burdened, and I will give you rest [shabbat]. Take my yoke upon you and learn from me, for I am gentle and humble in heart, and you will find rest [shabbat] for your souls. For my yoke is easy and my burden is light. (Matthew 11:28-30, bracketed comment added)

Shabbat In the Old Testament

With that understanding of the big picture, let's zoom in and look at what the text says. To get a picture of what the word *shabbat* means from a Hebrew perspective, I took an in-depth survey of the Tanakh, reviewing every passage where it is used.[6] *Shabbat* appears 111 times in 89 verses of the Old Testament.[7] And Torahists will invariably point to Genesis 2:2 as its first appearance in Scripture: "And on the seventh day God finished his work that he had done, and he rested on the seventh day from all his work that he had done."

The Hebrew word in Genesis 2:2 translated "He rested" is the verb יִשְׁבֹּת (yisbot), which means "to rest, dwell, sit." It comes from the same root word as the noun shabbat (שׁבת), but it does not refer to the weekly rest commanded by God. Shabbat as a noun does not appear until Exodus 16:23 where we find the Israelites fresh out of Egyptian slavery and wandering in the wilderness. Yahweh had begun providing them with manna, and Moses gave them instructions for collecting it.

---

[6] In the Tanakh, the Hebrew word *shabbat* is used in a generic sense to mean "rest" and as a proper noun to refer to the seventh day of the week given by God as a holy day of rest.

[7] In the ESV translation.

This is what the Lord commanded: "Tomorrow is to be a day of sabbath rest, a holy sabbath to the Lord. So bake what you want to bake and boil what you want to boil. Save whatever is left and keep it until morning." (Exodus 16:23)

Not long after that, the official Shabbat commands were given to Israel at Sinai. And from then on, the Torah—indeed the entire Tanakh—takes the Sabbath very seriously. There is strong and prescriptive teaching about keeping the Sabbath holy and set apart. Phrases such as "remember the Sabbath," "observe my Sabbaths," and "keep my Sabbath Holy" consistently appear throughout the Old Testament. And the Israelites are commanded to "observe the Sabbath, celebrating it for the generations to come as a lasting covenant" (Ex 31:16).[8] The Sabbath is taken so seriously that the death penalty is prescribed for desecrating it, which we see carried out when a man is stoned to death for collecting wood on the Sabbath (Num 15:32-36).

The Torah teaches that God gave Israel the Sabbath to set her apart from every other nation. It was given as a sign of the Mosaic covenant.

Say to the Israelites, "You must observe my Sabbaths. This will be a sign between me and you for the generations to come, so you may know that I am the Lord, who makes you holy" (Exodus 31:13).[9]

And Shabbat is tied to two historical events: God resting on the seventh day of Creation Week (Ex 20:11) and bringing Israel out of slavery in Egypt (Deut 5:15). Many ceremonial dates and practices are tied to the six-to-one ratio of the Sabbath: work six days, rest for one, sow your fields for six years, let the field rest for one, and so on. In the Torah, we get an unmistakable sense of how Shabbat drove the national rhythm of Israel. Her very cadence of life—weekly and annually—was based on it. And then, when we get to the New Testament, everything changes. Dramatically.

Sabbath in the New Testament

The prescriptive teachings about the Sabbath consistently repeated in the Hebrew Scriptures—*keep it holy, do no work, make your offerings, do not desecrate it*, etc.—are nowhere to be found in the New Testament. When

---

[8] This verse, and the permanence of the Sabbath in general, is also discussed in chapter six, *The Torah is Eternal*.
[9] Also see Ezekiel 20:12, 20.

this is pointed out to Torah-keepers, they typically respond by claiming that the Jewish New Testament authors did not need to explicitly teach about keeping the Sabbath because their Jewish readers already knew about it. There would be no need to explain the importance of the Sabbath to a Jew!

Fair enough. But what about the Gentiles? Wouldn't the authors need to teach them about the Sabbath? And why did the authors teach so many other commandments from the Torah that their Jewish audience would not need explained? For example, consider the "Big Ten" of the Mosaic Covenant. The table below shows how each of the Ten Commandments given in the Law of Moses is referenced in the New Testament.

Torah Commandment	Related NT Passages
You shall have no other gods before Me	"Worship the Lord your God and serve him only" (Matthew 4:10; Luke 4:8). "They exchanged the truth about God for a lie and worshiped and served created things rather than the Creator" (Romans 1:25). Also see Acts 7:39-43, 17:16-34; 2 Thessalonians 2:4; Revelation 9:20, 13:4.
You shall not make idols	"Dear children, keep yourselves from idols." (1 John 5:21). "Do not be idolaters" (1 Corinthians 10:7). Also see Acts 17:16; 1 Corinthians 5:11, 6:9, 8:4; Revelation 9:20.
You shall not take the name of the LORD your God in vain	"Our Father in heaven, hallowed be your name" (Matthew 6:9). "Many will come in my name, claiming, 'I am he,' and, 'The time is near.' Do not follow them" (Luke 21:8). Also see Mark 3:29; Luke 12:10; Acts 4:12; Ephesians 5:4; Titus 2:7-8; 2 Thessalonians 1:12; 2 Timothy 2:19; Revelation 13:5-6.

Torah Commandment	Related NT Passages
Remember the Sabbath day, to keep it holy	The New Testament does not directly teach or repeat the commandments about keeping, remembering, or observing the Sabbath or doing no work. Nor is the death penalty for working on it taught or enforced. Jesus did teach, "The Sabbath was made for man, not man for the Sabbath. So the Son of Man is Lord even of the Sabbath" (Mark 2:27-28).
Honor your father and your mother*	"Honor your father and mother" (Matthew 15:4; Mark 7:10; Luke 18:20). Also see Matthew 19:19; Mark 10:19; Ephesians 6:2.
You shall not murder*	"You shall not murder" (Matthew 19:18, Luke 18:20, Romans 13:9). Also see Matthew 15:19.
You shall not commit adultery*	"You have heard that it was said, 'You shall not commit adultery.' But I tell you that anyone who looks at a woman lustfully has already committed adultery with her in his heart." (Matthew 5:27-28) "You shall not commit adultery" (Matthew 19:18) Also see Matthew 5:32, 15:19, 19:9; Mark 7:22, 10:12; Luke 18:20, Romans 13:9; 1 Corinthians 5:11, 6:9; Hebrews 13:4; James 2:11.
You shall not steal*	"You shall not steal" (Matthew 19:18, Romans 13:9). "You must not associate with anyone who claims to be a brother or sister but is . . . a swindler" (1 Corinthians 5:11). Also see Matthew 15:19; Luke 18:20.

Torah Commandment	Related NT Passages
You shall not bear false witness against your neighbor*	"For out of the heart comes . . . false testimony" (Matthew 15:19). "You shall not give false testimony" (Matthew 19:18). Also see Mark 7:22; Luke 18:20; 1 Corinthians 5:11.
You shall not covet*	"Be on your guard against all kinds of greed; life does not consist in an abundance of possessions" (Luke 12:15). "For I would not have known what it is to covet if the law had not said, 'You shall not covet'" (Romans 7:7b). "You shall not covet" (Romans 13:9). Also see Mark 7:22; Romans 1:29, 7:7; 1 Corinthians 6:10; Ephesians 5:5.

* Repeated from the OT verbatim

So the first three commandments, while not repeated directly, are taught and endorsed. The last six commandments are repeated from the Torah verbatim. But the Mosaic commands about the Sabbath are neither repeated, endorsed, nor taught.

It makes one wonder. If the weekly Sabbath held such weight and importance with Jesus and the New Testament authors, why are Christ-followers never taught to keep it? Why don't we see the apostles or disciples instructing anyone to keep Shabbat? And surprisingly, throughout Jesus' most influential and iconic teachings—the Sermon on the Mount, the Greatest Commandment, the Beatitudes, the Lord's Prayer, the Great Commission, the High Priestly Prayer, the Golden Rule, His thirty-or-so parables—the Sabbath is not mentioned.

In fact, more than half of the time any New Testament author mentions the Sabbath, it is as a source of conflict between Yeshua and the Jewish religious leaders. And in one hundred percent of the passages where Jesus teaches about the Sabbath, He is clashing with Jewish leaders over it. While they sought to build fences of man-made rules around the

Sabbath, Yeshua pointed to its original, divine intention. He taught that "The sabbath was made for man, not the man for the Sabbath" (Mark 2:27). This brings up a valid question from our Torah-keeping friends. Why would Jesus bother to correct anyone about the Sabbath if it didn't matter to Him? We have to acknowledge that Yeshua's correction of the Pharisees affirms the ongoing validity of the Sabbath, as does His apocalyptic comment "Pray that your flight may not be in winter or on a Sabbath" (Matt 24:20). As we discussed earlier, Yeshua had every expectation that His Jewish followers would continue to keep Shabbat as a matter of their unique calling as a people. However, to expand this expectation into the teaching that all Christians are required to keep the Mosaic Shabbat commands is simply not justified. And the fact remains: Yeshua never taught or commanded anyone to keep the Sabbath.

Of course, nothing we've looked at explicitly says that the Sabbath has been abolished or that it has been changed to Sunday. Conversely, unlike the rest of the Ten Commandments, the NT does not teach that Shabbat must be kept. Something changed between the Tanakh and the New Testament regarding the Sabbath. In the Law of Moses, it was a commandment carved into stone by God's finger (Ex 31:18) and punishable by death. In the New Testament, the Sabbath regulations do not rise above an assumed tradition for Jewish believers. For those of us who consider Scripture the inspired Word of God, written under the superintendence of the Holy Spirt, this stark contrast cannot be lightly dismissed.

The Sign of the Covenant

Perhaps a telling bit of Scriptural evidence can be found in the fact that God gave the Sabbath as a sign of the Mosaic Covenant. Yahweh told Moses,

> You are to speak to the people of Israel and say, "Above all you shall keep my Sabbaths, for this is a sign between me and you throughout your generations, that you may know that I, the LORD, sanctify you." (Exodus 31:13)

Indeed, the Sabbath was the only sign given of the Sinai Covenant. This makes it unique among the Ten Commandments. And Israel struggled to keep the covenant it represented. God warned them many times through the prophets.

I gave them my statutes and made known to them my rules, by which, if a person does them, he shall live. Moreover, I gave them my Sabbaths, as a sign between me and them, that they might know that I am the LORD who sanctifies them. But the house of Israel rebelled against me in the wilderness. They did not walk in my statutes but rejected my rules, by which, if a person does them, he shall live; and my Sabbaths they greatly profaned. (Ezekiel 20:11-13)

In the end, the Sinai covenant was broken by Israel[10] and replaced by a new and superior covenant in Yeshua.[11] This raises a question. Since the Old Covenant has passed away (Heb 8:13), has the sign of that covenant passed away as well? The old Sabbath rest, which was "a shadow of things to come" (Col 2:16-17) and given only to Israel, has been replaced by a new and superior rest in Yeshua (Heb 4:1-11), which is available to all who believe, Jew and Gentile alike. The Sabbath regulations given in the Mosaic Law, like the Sinai Covenant and the Mosaic Expression, were not intended to last forever. However, the principle of shabbat (rest) in the unchanging Law of God remains. So while the Mosaic legal regulations regarding Shabbat have ended, the sabbath rest continues under the New Expression in a new way.

Shabbat in Hebrews
The book of Hebrews offers a telling insight into the Sabbath under the New Expression. This epistle was written by an anonymous author to an audience primarily made up of Jewish believers in Jesus who were under persecution for their faith in Him. The author directs his reader's attention to their forefathers, the ancient Israelites, fresh out of four centuries of slavery, who'd had second thoughts about their newfound freedom. As they wandered in the wilderness, they began to wonder if God rescuing them out of Egypt had been a big mistake.

"Why is the Lord bringing us into this land, to fall by the sword? Our wives and our little ones will become prey. Would it not be better for us to go back to Egypt?" And they said to one another, "Let us choose a leader and go back to Egypt." (Numbers 14:3-4)

---

[10] Jeremiah 31:32; Hebrews 8:9.
[11] Jeremiah 31:31-34; Hebrews 8:6-13.

In the same way, many first-century Jewish believers in Jesus were having second thoughts. *Wouldn't it be better to return to the temple and the priesthood and the Law we've known all these centuries?* The author of Hebrews encourages them to hold fast to their faith in Christ by demonstrating the many ways that Jesus and the New Covenant are superior to Moses and the Sinai Covenant.[12] Along the way, he offers a profound insight on the Sabbath and its connection to Jesus.

In Hebrews 3, the author quotes directly from Psalm 95, where Yahweh says of the Israelites,

> Therefore I was provoked with that generation, and said, "They always go astray in their heart; they have not known my ways." As I swore in my wrath, "They shall not enter my rest." (Hebrews 3:10-11, quoting Psalm 95:10-11)

In calling the Promised Land "my rest," Scripture casts it as a type or symbol of resting in God. And for forty years, Yahweh refused to let His people enter His rest, the Promised Land.[13] Why did He sentence the Israelites to wander around in the wilderness for so long? It wasn't because they broke the Torah laws. It was their unbelief. The Israelites grumbled against Moses and wanted to return to slavery in Egypt.

> And the Lord said to Moses, "How long will this people despise me? And how long will they *not believe in me*, in spite of all the signs that I have done among them? . . . Your children shall be shepherds in the wilderness forty years and shall suffer *for your faithlessness*, until the last of your dead bodies lies in the wilderness. (Numbers 14:11, 33, e*mphasis added*)

God was angry. But not about a law being broken. His people were not allowed to enter His rest because of their faithlessness. Despite all the signs and miracles He did among them, they did not believe. The author of Hebrews picks up on this detail.

> And to whom did he swear that they would not enter his rest, but to those who were disobedient? So we see that they were unable to enter because of unbelief. (Hebrews 3:18-19)

---

[12] In fact, I would challenge you to work your way through the book of Hebrews and note all the "better than" and "superior to" comparisons. It is quite revealing.

[13] Numbers 26:35, 32:13. See also Deuteronomy 2:14.

Disobedience is defined here not as violating Torah law, but unbelief. Hence the author's strong encouragement to his persecuted Jewish audience to keep believing. Faith is the one requirement for entering God's rest.

> Therefore, while the promise of entering his rest still stands, let us fear lest any of you should seem to have failed to reach it. (Hebrews 4:1)

Guthrie expounds,

> Although the men of the wilderness failed to obtain the "rest," the promise of it still remained for their children. Indeed, the assumption is made that the promise is timeless and is available still to the writer and his readers, hence the further exhortation . . . The writer accepts without question that the promise of entering his rest remains.[14]

The author of Hebrews uses the ancient illustration of the Israelites and the Promised Land to teach his contemporary readers that the promise of entering God's rest still applies to them. They are urged to hold fast to their faith in Christ despite the persecution they've experienced. Their forefathers fell in the desert—they died without entering God's rest—because of their unbelief. And we have a similar opportunity today to enter God's rest if we will continue to believe and not turn away from the gospel we have received.

Notice how Hebrews 4:3 begins. "For we who have believed enter that rest." It doesn't say, "we who have *kept the commandments*." This isn't about behavior. Our membership in God's family is all about having faith in Jesus.

> For we who have believed enter that rest, as he has said, "As I swore in my wrath, 'They shall not enter my rest,'" although his works were finished from the foundation of the world. For he has somewhere spoken of the seventh day in this way: "And God rested on the seventh day from all his works." (Hebrews 4:3-4)

This author is now linking two ideas: God resting on the seventh day of creation and His rest in the Promised Land. Guthrie demonstrates how this passage ties in a third concept: Jesus as our rest.

---

[14] George H. Guthrie, *The NIV Application Commentary*, Hebrews 4.

What believers can now enter is none other than the same kind of rest which the Creator enjoyed when he had completed his works, which means that the rest idea is of completion and not of inactivity . . . It is important to note that the 'rest' is not something new which has not been known in experience until Christ came. It has been available throughout the whole of man's history. This reference back to the creation places the idea on the broadest possible basis and would seem to suggest that it was part of God's intention for man. 'Rest' is a quality which has eluded man's quest, and in fact cannot be attained except through Christ. Jesus himself invited men to come to him to find rest.[15]

The similarity in these concepts becomes evident when viewed side-by-side.

Creation / Eden	Salvation / Redemption
Eden was the culmination of God's plan for creation.	Jesus is the culmination of God's plan for redemption, which began in the Garden (Gen 3:15).
God completed his creation work and then He rested, never to pick it up again. It was finished.	Jesus completed his saving work and then He rested at the right hand of God, never to pick it up again. He declared from the cross, "It is finished."
God rested in Eden, the place He specifically made for His family	God's plan of redemption was specifically made for His family
We had nothing to do with it. Eden wasn't our idea, and it wasn't the result of our efforts.	We had nothing to do with it. Salvation wasn't our idea, and it isn't the result of our efforts.
Eden was a gift freely given by the Father through His power, love, and sovereignty.	Salvation is a gift freely given by the Father through His power, love and sovereignty.

---

[15] George H. Guthrie, *The NIV Application Commentary*, Hebrews 4

How We Enter

If the faith of the Israelites determined whether they would enter God's rest in the form of the Promised Land, what does faith in Christ allow us to enter? In what sense is God's rest available to Christians today? The author of Hebrews says that the promise of rest that God gave Israel via the Promised Land remains available to us today through Christ.

> For if Joshua had given them rest, God would not have spoken of another day later on. So then, there remains a Sabbath rest for the people of God, for whoever has entered God's rest has also rested from his works as God did from his. (Hebrews 4:8-10)

The "rest" the author has been talking about is now explicitly called a "Sabbath rest." That certainly would have gotten the attention of his Jewish readers! He is teaching that Yeshua is our Promised Land, our rest. Jesus said so Himself. "Come to me, all who labor and are heavy laden, and I will give you rest" (Matt 11:28). And in the same way God rested from His creation work on the seventh day because it was completed, those in Christ can rest because He has completed our salvation. Hagner clarifies the connection.

> Following the pattern of exodus typology, the promised rest in the land of Canaan becomes a figure or foreshadowing of the spiritual rest available to the Christian . . . To interpret this rest in terms of a national-political restoration is to miss the author's dramatic shift . . . toward an understanding of Christ as the fulfillment of the promises.[16]

In several places in the New Testament, the apostle Paul defends himself against accusations that he was teaching against the law. And he does so by appealing to a deeper sense of the Mosaic Law.[17] Likewise, there is a deeper sense of the rest hinted at in the weekly Shabbat of the Torah. The rest spoken of in Hebrews comes from trusting in the finished work of Jesus. "For Christ is the end of the law for righteousness to everyone who believes" (Rom 10:4).

There is an eternal principle behind Shabbat, which was expressed differently under Moses than under Christ. And that foundational

---

[16] Donald A. Hagner, *New International Biblical Commentary*, Hebrews.
[17] Romans 3:21-31; Galatians 3:15-22; 1 Timothy 5:17-25.

principle remains valid and in effect even though it is no longer a requirement to express it through ritualistic Sabbath-keeping.

> So then, there remains a Sabbath rest for the people of God, for whoever has entered God's rest has also rested from his works as God did from his. (Hebrews 4:9-10)

The New Covenant Sabbath is much grander and more grace-filled than its Mosaic shadow. It comes into focus when we step back and absorb the staggering truth that Jesus has fulfilled the requirements of righteousness on our behalf. "For our sake he made him to be sin who knew no sin, so that in him we might become the righteousness of God" (2 Cor 5:21). And we enter into this greater Sabbath rest by faith, not by works.

> Then they said to him, "What must we do, to be doing the works of God?" Jesus answered them, "This is the work of God, that you believe in him whom he has sent." (John 6:28-29)

Our job is simply to believe, to place our faith—our believing loyalty—in Christ. "For we who have believed enter that rest" (Heb 4:3). It is a rest from striving to become righteous through our own efforts, from trying to please God through ritual acts of obedience. Jesus said, "Come to me, all who labor and are heavy laden, and I will give you rest" (Matt 11:28). Our rest is in Him. And "whoever has entered God's rest has also rested from his works as God did from his" (Heb 4:10). The Torah Shabbat is a beautiful expression of Yahweh's provision and rest. And that Sabbath ultimately points us to Yeshua (Col 2:16-17), the real Sabbath, Who is our ultimate rest.

The Torah Sabbath was not Prohibited

Sabbath-keeping in the Tanakh was an unearned gift of rest from the Father to His people. The same holds true under the New Covenant. Our rest in Jesus is an unearned gift from the Father. And while keeping the Saturday Shabbat won't contribute anything to that rest or our standing before God, it has also not been it has not been forbidden. If a Christ-follower wants to keep the Mosaic Sabbath regulations, they are free in Christ to do so as a matter of personal preference.[18] Some say it

---

[18] Or in the case of Jewish believers, as a matter of cultural calling or boundary marker of Jewish identity.

helps connect them to the roots of the faith, and that's beautiful. Under the New Covenant, keeping Shabbat is permitted but not required.

Torah-observant teachers who promote the idea that keeping the Sabbath somehow contributes to our righteousness or salvation are completely missing what the New Testament teaches. Christ is our Sabbath. He is the one who said, "Take my yoke upon you, and I will give you rest." I will give you *shabbat*. He is also the one who said, "It is finished." There's nothing we can possibly bring to the table—no weekly rest or other Torah observances—that will add a single thing to what Christ has already accomplished on our behalf.

Jesus and the Sabbath

As we've seen, Shabbat is more than just a commandment given to Israel at Mount Sinai. Scripture ties the Sabbath to the Exodus and to creation itself. It is not an issue to be taken lightly. What our Torah-keeping friends seem to miss, or at least underemphasize, is that Shabbat is under the authority of Christ.[19] So to understand the Sabbath under the New Covenant rightly, we now look to Jesus.

Beginning in the centuries before Christ, the Jewish leaders and teachers of the law began to "build a fence" around the Sabbath. They added man-made rules and regulations intended to help keep their fellow Jews from inadvertently breaking the Shabbat. Babcock recounts some examples.

The Damascus Document, dating to the first century BC, outlines several limits to activity on the Sabbath including,

- walking farther than 1000 cubits
- drinking outside the camp
- drawing water into any vessel
- wearing perfume
- opening a sealed vessel
- assisting an animal to give birth or get out of a pit
- having sexual relations[20]

None of these regulations were given in the Torah. And when Jesus arrived, these man-made additions were the basis of many of His clashes

---

[19] Matthew 12:8, 28:18; Romans 14:5-6; Colossians. 2:16-17.
[20] Bryan C. Babcock, "Sabbath," ed. John D. Barry et al., *The Lexham Bible Dictionary* (Lexham Press, 2016).

with the Pharisees. The majority of His teachings about Shabbat involved the unwinding of man-made regulations that had become wrapped around it. Rather than talking about what cannot be done on the Sabbath, Jesus clarified what is permitted, such as showing acts of compassion,[21] caring for animals,[22] healing others,[23] saving a life,[24] and carrying a bed.[25] What our Torahist friends seem to miss is that, while the Jewish religious leaders strove to put a "fence" around Shabbat out of respect for the authority of Moses, Jesus holds far more authority and deserves far more glory than Moses (Heb 3:3).

> Moses was faithful in all God's house as a *servant*, to testify to the things that were to be spoken later, but Christ is faithful over God's house as a *son*. (Hebrews 3:5-6, *emphasis added*)

Moses was a great prophet and a mediator of Yahweh's law at Sinai. Yeshua, by contrast, is our High Priest of a better ministry and a better covenant enacted on better promises (Heb 8:6). Christ alone reconciles mankind to God and has equal authority with Yahweh.[26] And He came to die for the sins of the world (John 3:16-17), not reform Temple Judaism. This is why Yeshua did not hesitate to interrupt the temple sacrifices by overthrowing the tables of the money-changers. (Mark 11:15-19). And it was on Shabbat that Jesus said,

> "My Father is working until now, and I am working." This was why the Jews were seeking all the more to kill him, because not only was he breaking the Sabbath, but he was even calling God his own Father, making himself equal with God. (John 5:17-18)

Jesus was working on Shabbat? How could that be? We get a glimpse of His reasoning in His response to the Pharisees who criticized Him for letting his disciples pluck grain on the Sabbath.[27] He reminded them that David and his companions ate the bread of the Presence, which was prohibited in the Mosaic Law. And further, Yahweh allowed the priests to work on Shabbat. Jesus was clarifying Shabbat's rightful place and priority in the Mosaic Law. It was not top dog. And then He boldly

---

[21] Matthew 12:1-7; Mark 2:23-28; Luke 6:1-5.
[22] Matthew 12:11; Luke 13:15, 14:5.
[23] Mark 3:1-5; Luke 6:1-10, 13:10–16; John 5:9, 9:14.
[24] Mark 3:4; Luke 6:9.
[25] Matthew 9:6-7; Mark 2:1-12; John 5:8-16.
[26] Mark 2:7, 13:26, Luke 5:21; John 5:18, 5:23; 8:58, 10:30-33, 14:9; Revelation. 1:8, etc.
[27] Matthew 12:1-7; Mark 2:23-28; Luke 6:1-5.

announced, "The Son of Man is the Lord of the Sabbath."[28] That is a title that can only belong to Yahweh, Himself. Jesus is the highest authority.

Indeed, He is the Creator of the universe. The Son co-labored with the Father and the Spirit during the six days of creation and rested with them on the seventh. So He is not only the Lord of Shabbat, He is also Lord of the Torah of Moses. Parsons notes,

> Jewish thinking regards the Sabbath primarily as a testimony that God alone is the Creator of the universe (celebrating His rule over creation, Gen. 2:2-3), and secondarily as a memorial of the redemption from Egypt (Deut. 5:15). The Sabbath is a day of blessing wherein a "double portion" of heavenly food is provided as a foretaste of *olam haba* (the world to come). In all of these aspects Yeshua shows Himself to be Lord. His miracles reveal His authority and rule over creation, His sacrificial death as the Lamb of God (שֵׂה הָאֱלֹהִים) redeems the whole world from slavery to sin (John 1:29; 1 Cor. 15:3-4; 2 Cor. 5:21), He provides heavenly food as our Bread of Life (John 6:35), and His ministry on our behalf provides an everlasting rest from attempting to find acceptance before God through ritual acts of righteousness (Titus 3:5-6; Heb. 4:9-10; Eph. 2:8-10). In Yeshua we don't work toward a place of victory, but rather work from it (1 Cor. 15:57).[29]

Christians, as a whole, are not bound by the Mosaic Law. Followers of Jesus are not required to offer sacrifices in the temple (Deut 12:11), put a mezuzah on our doorposts (Deut 6:9), or circumcise our males on the eighth day after birth (Lev 12:3). And we are no more required to keep the Mosaic regulations regarding Shabbat[30] than we are to mete out the Mosaic death penalty for *not* keeping it.[31]

Paul teaches that followers in Christ have a new relationship to the Law. Under the New Covenant, we are now "married" to Christ, the Lord of the Sabbath (Rom 7:1-6). And under the New Expression, it is not the one who keeps Shabbat who fulfills the law. Rather, "the one who loves another has fulfilled the law" (Rom 13:8-10).

---

[28] Matthew 12:8; Mark 2:28; Luke 6:5.
[29] John J. Parsons, "Yeshua our Sabbath Rest," Hebrew4Christians.com.
[30] Exodus 20:8-11; Deuteronomy 5:12-15.
[31] Exodus 31:14-15, 35:2.

For the whole law is fulfilled in one word: "You shall love your neighbor as yourself." (Galatians 5:14)[32]

Even Jewish followers of Yeshua who choose to keep Shabbat do not do so as a matter of legal obligation or a condition of righteousness. Rather they keep Shabbat as a response to God's grace toward them as a people. All Christians are made complete by our faith in Yeshua (Eph. 1:3-14). And therefore, the rest He gives us is complete as well. His grace is sufficient for us (2 Cor 12:9). So ironically, when our Torah-keeping friends advocate for legalistic Sabbath observance, rather than honoring the commands of Yahweh, they are undermining His grace.

The Lord's Day

From a Christ-centered perspective, there is something bigger and even more important than the Sabbath, and it occurred on the first day of the week. The Resurrection was a cosmic event that split history in two. It is by far the most critical fact in all of Christendom.

And if Christ has not been raised, our preaching is useless and so is your faith. More than that, we are then found to be false witnesses about God, for we have testified about God that he raised Christ from the dead . . . And if Christ has not been raised, your faith is futile; you are still in your sins. Then those also who have fallen asleep in Christ are lost. If only for this life we have hope in Christ, we are of all people most to be pitied. (1 Corinthians 15:14, 17-19)

If all of Scripture points to Christ and all of Christ's work rests on His Resurrection, it is no exaggeration to say that the Resurrection is the single most important event in human history. It is more important than the Sabbath by far. And it is no accident that Yeshua rose on the first day of the week, rather than Shabbat.[33]

God's appointed times in the Torah are holy, and His appointed times in the New Testament are no less so. Not only did Yahweh ordain that Yeshua's resurrection should occur on the first day of the week, He also chose the first day of the week to officially birth His Church. Fifty days after the Resurrection, on the Torah date for Shavu'ot, Yahweh sent

---

[32] See also Galatians 6:2 and James 2:8
[33] Many Torah-keepers claim that Jesus was actually resurrected on Shabbat but wasn't discovered until the following morning. That claim is addressed in the discussion of Easter in chapter seventeen.

the Holy Spirit to anoint believers and baptize them just as Jesus had promised.

> And I will ask the Father, and he will give you another Helper, to be with you forever, even the Spirit of truth, whom the world cannot receive, because it neither sees him nor knows him. You know him, for he dwells with you and will be in you . . . But the Helper, the Holy Spirit, whom the Father will send in my name, he will teach you all things and bring to your remembrance all that I have said to you. (John 14:16-17, 26)

The arrival of the Holy Spirit is recorded in Acts 2.

> When the day of Pentecost arrived, they were all together in one place. And suddenly there came from heaven a sound like a mighty rushing wind, and it filled the entire house where they were sitting. And divided tongues as of fire appeared to them and rested on each one of them. And they were all filled with the Holy Spirit and began to speak in other tongues as the Spirit gave them utterance . . . Peter, standing with the eleven, lifted up his voice and addressed them . . . So those who received his word were baptized, and there were added that day about three thousand souls. (Acts 2:1-4, 14, 41)

The arrival of the Holy Spirit on Pentecost was the spark that ignited the Church and inaugurated the spread of the Gospel. And it happened on the first day of the week. It makes sense that the early Church, understanding the staggering importance of the Resurrection and Pentecost, chose to endorse Sunday as *The Lord's Day* (Rev 1:10). Even the Jewish believers who continued to keep Shabbat regularly gathered with the church on Sundays, as well.[34]

For Christians, the Lord's Day is not observed as a legal requirement but rather a gift, a God-ordained rhythm for our lives. This was the original intention for Shabbat before mankind got its hands on it. Howell notes, "the original divine purposes for the Sabbath were rest for man's body and nurture of man's soul in undistracted worship of God."[35] And that rest is no longer bound to a specific day of the week. Colossians

---

[34] Acts 20:7; 1 Corinthians 16:2.
[35] Don N. Howell, Jr., *Servants of the Servant: A Biblical Theology of Leadership*, (Wipf & Stock Publishers, 2003), p. 164.

teaches we should not let anyone judge us by a Sabbath day because it was a foreshadow of the Real Thing, Yeshua (Col 2:16-17).

Summary

Torahism has a major problem with Christians not celebrating the Sabbath on the last day of the week. Shabbat was given as a sign of the Sinai Covenant and, as such, has never been expected of Gentiles. And even Jewish believers in Jesus keep Shabbat for different reasons under the New Covenant. It is not required of anyone as a matter of salvation or righteousness. Many Christians wisely choose to set aside one day a week as the Lord's Day for worship and rest. However, it is not observed as a legal obligation. Instead, it is a gift, a God-given rhythm for our lives. And because the specific day of the week no longer matters, most Christians have chosen Sunday in honor of Christ's death-defeating resurrection.

13

Eat Kosher

There are never too many napkins or too many potatoes.

JEWISH PROVERB

F OR MANY TORAH-KEEPERS, the issue of unclean food carries quite a bit of emotion. Torahism subscribes to the dietary restrictions given in the Law of Moses and believes it is vital that believers today maintain those restrictions. There are several arguments we are likely to encounter on this issue. Many Torahists argue that God gave the kosher food laws to keep His people healthy. For instance, one Torah-keeping teacher argued:

> When Paul told Timothy that the "food" was "sanctified" by the Word and prayer, he was not telling believers they can go ahead and eat dog now as if it's sanctified as long as you bless it first. That is disgusting! And that goes for pork and all its parasites and worms, and shellfish and it's flesh-eating, bacteria-carrying nastiness. It is time believers return to understanding the foundational truth of the faith they *think* they are practicing. The Father designed and created the world and designed each animal to do its job. He gave His Word and established it forever. Then sent his Son to live it out. He came and obeyed, and we should follow His example. Yet the Roman Religion would have us believe our Father wants us to stuff our faces with the feces-eating, garbage disposal system of the earth? Crows, possums, turkey vultures, and roadkill are all on the menu, just pray for it first?! Not only is that disgusting, preposterous and ridiculous but it's a tragic disregard for our Father's love that informs us in

Leviticus that He designed them not haphazardly but quite intelligently. (Ben H.)

Another Torah-keeping teacher claims,

> All commands given in the Torah are for our protection from hurt, harm and danger. For instance, don't eat anything unclean like pork. If you obey that command, it's your protection from getting the trichinosis worm that can harm you. (Rocky S.)

This theory may be common, but it is not biblical. The Torah nowhere links the kosher food laws to health. In fact, the language used in the Bible confirms that the intent of the commandments is not to protect us from parasites or bacteria. Leviticus says of dead animals,

> And by these you shall become unclean. Whoever touches their carcass shall be unclean until the evening, and whoever carries any part of their carcass shall wash his clothes and be unclean until the evening. (Leviticus 11:24-25)[1]

Are Torah-keepers suggesting God thought parasites and bacteria went away when the sun went down? The fact that the uncleanness only lasted until evening shows these were commands of ritual purity, not public health concerns. The animals forbidden in the Torah (Lev 11) could not have been unclean in and of themselves for two reasons.

First, because God made them all and saw that they were good (Gen 1:20-25). God does not create unclean things. Pigs, camels, rabbits, ostrich, shellfish, and all the rest are part of God's creation, and He called them "good." And the fact that "The earth is the Lord's and the fullness thereof" (Psalm 24:1) is precisely why the apostle Paul told Christians they could,

> Eat whatever is sold in the meat market without raising any question on the ground of conscience. For "the earth is the Lord's, and the fullness thereof." (1 Corinthians 10:25-26)

"Yes," our Torah-keeping friends will reply, "but God did not make all things good for *eating*." Which brings us to the second reason we know non-kosher animals are not inherently unclean. After the Flood,

---

[1] See also Leviticus 11:27-28, 31:32, 39-40.

God blessed Noah and his sons and said to them, "Be fruitful and multiply and fill the earth. The fear of you and the dread of you shall be upon every beast of the earth and upon every bird of the heavens, upon everything that creeps on the ground and all the fish of the sea. Into your hand they are delivered. Every moving thing that lives shall be food for you. And as I gave you the green plants, I give you everything. (Genesis 9:1-3)

God told Noah he could eat *anything*. Torahists will respond by pointing to Genesis 7, where Yahweh commanded Noah, "Take with you seven pairs of all clean animals, the male and his mate, and a pair of the animals that are not clean, the male and his mate" (Gen 7:2). The distinction between clean and unclean animals is offered as evidence that God had declared certain animals unclean even before the Law of Moses. Yet, the fact that Noah brought both clean and unclean animals onboard before the Flood does not change the fact that *after* the Flood, God told Noah he could eat anything (Gen 9:3). In Hebrew, the phrase *kol remes* (כָּל־רֶמֶשׂ) literally means "the whole of, or all, creeping or moving things." It would refer to *all* the animals on the ark, clean and unclean, as acceptable to Yahweh as food.

Why the Kosher Food Laws?

If not for health reasons, why were the Mosaic food laws given? The dietary restrictions were one of several identity markers that distinguished Israel as Yahweh's "treasured possession among all peoples . . . a kingdom of priests and a holy nation." (Ex 19:5-6). God declared certain animals unclean in a ritual sense. They were given at Sinai to set the descendants of Abraham apart from the other nations, the Gentiles.

The Torah inextricably links unclean people and unclean food. Yahweh commanded Israel,

You shall therefore separate the clean beast from the unclean, and the unclean bird from the clean. You shall not make yourselves detestable by beast or by bird or by anything with which the ground crawls, which I have set apart for you to hold unclean. You shall be holy to me, for I the Lord am holy and have separated you from the peoples, that you should be mine. (Leviticus 20:25-26)

One of the ways given under the Mosaic Law to distinguish the Israelites from all the other nations was the kosher food laws. As we just saw, food is not inherently unclean. But in the Mosaic Law, God, in His sovereignty, pronounced a set of foods ritually unclean for Israel (Lev 11). Gentiles, however, were not forbidden from eating these foods. For example, Israel was told,

> You shall not eat anything that has died naturally. You may give it to the sojourner who is within your towns, that he may eat it, or you may sell it to a foreigner. For you are a people holy to the Lord your God. (Deuteronomy 14:21)

The food God prohibited for Israel was allowed for the Gentiles. The Torah explicitly teaches that Jews are not allowed to eat certain foods that non-Jews are free to eat. Under the Mosaic Covenant, what you ate revealed who you were. And that remained true until Christ came and everything changed. In Christ, there is no "Jew and Gentile."

> For there is no distinction between Jew and Greek;[2] for the same Lord is Lord of all, bestowing his riches on all who call on him. (Romans 10:12)[3]

Under Yahweh's New Covenant, the People of God are defined solely by their faith in Yeshua. "And if you belong to Christ, then you are Abraham's descendants, heirs according to promise" (Gal 3:29, NASB). Thus, there is no further need to distinguish between Jews and Gentiles. The legal food restrictions served their purpose and were fulfilled in Christ, Who,

> has broken down in his flesh the dividing wall of hostility by abolishing the law of commandments expressed in ordinances, that he might create in himself one new man in place of the two [Jew and Gentile], so making peace, and might reconcile us both to God in one body through the cross, thereby killing the hostility. (Ephesians 2:14-16)

---

[2] In his writings, Paul often referred to non-Jews (Gentiles) as the "uncircumcised" or "Greeks." Circumcision was an identity marker for Israel. And thanks to Alexander the Great, the world Paul lived in was dominated by Greek thought and the Greek language. Thus "Greek" became a sort of shorthand for referring to non-Jews.

[3] See also Acts 20:21; Romans 1:16, 3:30; 1 Corinthians 12:13; Galatians 3:14, 3:28-29, 5:6, 6:15; Colossians 3:11.

That Which Defiles: Mark 7

Ironically, when our Torah-keeping friends press the topic of unclean food, it leads to a wealth of scriptural evidence that demonstrates Christians are no longer required to keep the Law of Moses. A standard text for this discussion is Mark 7:1-23, where Yeshua clashes with the Pharisees. Torahists often cite the following passage:

> And he said to them, "Then are you also without understanding? Do you not see that whatever goes into a person from outside cannot defile him, since it enters not his heart but his stomach, and is expelled?" (Thus he declared all foods clean.) (Mark 7:18-19)

The Parenthetical Text

Ruth, a Torah-keeping acquaintance, claimed the parenthetical text "Thus he declared all foods clean" in verse 19 was not included in the original manuscripts. It was added later by translators. She provided a link to the Codex Sinaiticus Manuscript (CSM) to prove her point. This fourth-century manuscript contains the earliest complete copy of the New Testament.[4] I looked up the passage in that translation and confirmed Ruth was correct. There is no parenthetical statement at the end of verse 19. However, the text Ruth challenged is still there. It is just not placed inside parentheses.

> And he said to them: "So even you are without understanding? Do you not perceive that nothing from without by entering into a man can defile him? because it goes not into his heart, but into his belly, and is cast out into the sink, *making all meats clean.*" (Mark 7:18-19 CSM, *emphasis added*)

The Traditions of Men

When I pointed this out to Ruth, she pivoted and claimed Jesus is not teaching about eating unclean foods but rather about ceremonial washing before a meal. He is teaching against the traditions of men. So I reviewed the larger passage in Mark 7. It starts with the Jewish leaders asking why Jesus' disciples were not following the traditions of the elders and washing their hands before taking food.

---

[4] You can find the Codex Sinaiticus online at www.codexsinaiticus.org.

And the Pharisees and the scribes asked him, "Why do your disciples not walk according to the tradition of the elders, but eat with defiled hands?" (Mark 7:5)

Ruth had a point. The initial question was about ritual hand washing before a meal, which is not a Mosaic command but a tradition from the Talmud. Yeshua often rebuked His fellow Jews for following their traditions at the expense of the commandments of God. And here in Mark 7, Jesus responded to the Pharisees a few verses later.

And he called the people to him again and said to them, "Hear me, all of you, and understand: There is nothing outside a person that by going into him can defile him, but the things that come out of a person are what defile him." (Mark 7:14-15)

The Jewish leaders had asked about a specific, external issue—ritual hand washing—but Jesus responded by addressing a more significant, internal concern: that which defiles. What does His response mean exactly? The disciples wondered that very thing and asked Him about it in private.

And when he had entered the house and left the people, his disciples asked him about the parable. And he said to them, "Then are you also without understanding? Do you not see that whatever goes into a person from outside cannot defile him, since it enters not his heart but his stomach, and is expelled?" (Thus he declared all foods clean.) And he said, "What comes out of a person is what defiles him. For from within, out of the heart of man, come evil thoughts, sexual immorality, theft, murder, adultery, coveting, wickedness, deceit, sensuality, envy, slander, pride, foolishness. All these evil things come from within, and they defile a person." (Mark 7:17-23)

Yeshua twice repeats what would have been a shocking statement to a first-century Jew: *whatever goes into a person from outside cannot defile him* (v. 15, 18). The Pharisees had asked why Jesus' disciples were not following the traditions of the elders (v. 1-5), and He responded with a broader lesson. It is not what goes into a man's body that makes him unclean, but what comes out of his heart (v. 18-19).

By enforcing the "commandments of men," the Pharisees were missing the point and erroneously looking for purity and righteousness in outward physical signs and behaviors. The commands of Yahweh, on the other hand, are concerned with the inward purity and righteousness of our hearts. Whether it is from unwashed hands or unclean meat, Yeshua taught that eating food is not what defiles a man. Because food "enters not his heart but his stomach and is expelled" (Mark 7:19).

The Definition of Food

Another common Torahist argument regarding Mark 7 (and other passages relating to food) is that *not everything is food*. When a passage mentions food, Torah-keepers often suggest that where the text says "food" or "meat," it is actually referring to clean or kosher food.

> When a Jewish person says to another Jewish person "let's eat some food," both parties intrinsically understand the statement to be about kosher food. It's just like when an American says to another American "let's eat some food." They both naturally understand that dog meat will not be on the menu. (Luke S.)

> Mark chapter 7 is about eating *bread* with unwashed hands. It's not about meat at all. You better read it again because it is the key to understanding the New Testament. (Kevin M.)

Let's take a look at the two objections above in order. First, the idea that all food comments in the New Testament should automatically be understood as speaking of kosher food is a recipe for disaster. Under that assumption, we are far more likely to be led astray than get it right. For example, if that is what Mark meant to convey in v. 19, then he was informing his readers that Jesus declared *all clean foods clean.* And why would He need to declare clean foods clean? They are already clean. Under that assumption, v. 19 becomes a non sequitur unrelated to the verses before and after it. Context is king, and the context of this passage doesn't support the notion that Jesus was sharing the redundant fact with his Jewish disciples that clean food is clean.

In the second argument, we find the same pattern we saw with Ruth's argument. The Pharisees asked about a specific issue—eating bread[5] with unwashed hands—and Yeshua responded by addressing a larger concern. In verse 19, Mark says that Jesus declared πάντα βρώματα (*panta bromata*, lit. "all, every food") clean. He wasn't making

---

[5] The Greek word ἄρτος (artos) found in some translations of Mark 7:2 and 7:5 means "bread, loaf, or food." Some translations render it "food," some use "bread," and some leave the word out altogether.

the nonsensical statement that Jesus declared all bread clean. Bread was already clean. Instead, Mark was making the profound claim that Jesus proclaimed *all foods* clean.

Peter's Vision

Another telling passage regarding food and cleanliness comes from Acts 10, where the apostle Peter was given a vision.

> The next day, as they were on their journey and approaching the city, Peter went up on the housetop about the sixth hour to pray. And he became hungry and wanted something to eat, but while they were preparing it, he fell into a trance and saw the heavens opened and something like a great sheet descending, being let down by its four corners upon the earth. In it were all kinds of animals and reptiles and birds of the air. And there came a voice to him: "Rise, Peter; kill and eat." But Peter said, "By no means, Lord; for I have never eaten anything that is common or unclean." And the voice came to him again a second time, "What God has made clean, do not call common." This happened three times, and the thing was taken up at once to heaven. (Acts 10:9-16)

Torahists argue that Peter's vision was not actually about food but rather allowing the unclean Gentiles into the nation of Israel. And the rest of the story in Acts 10-11 supports their claim about Gentiles. The vision of the sheet compelled Peter to share the Gospel with a man named Cornelius, who then became the first Gentile convert recorded in the Bible (Acts 10:23-48). However, as we saw earlier, the Torah directly links unclean food to unclean people. And I believe this is why in Acts 10, God used a vision of food to indicate a change in the status of people. Peter's vision taught a change in both the Gentiles *and* the food laws.

Torah-keepers strongly disagree, of course. They insist Peter's vision was solely a message about the Gentiles. However, if that were true, it would present three significant problems. First, on what basis is Torahism willing to allow for a change in the Law on the issue of people, but not food? It is an arbitrary standard based on a precommitment to keeping the kosher food laws.

Second, if the vision were solely a metaphor for the Gentiles, the commands "kill and eat" (v. 13) and "What God has made clean, do not call common" (v. 15) would be based on a falsehood. God would be communicating to Peter that formerly unclean people are now clean by falsely declaring that previously unclean food is now clean. And God does not engage in false advertising. "It is impossible for God to lie" (Heb 6:18).

Third, "God is not a God of confusion" (1 Cor 14:33). Imagine Peter trying to explain Torahism's version of his vision to other Jews.

"Wow, Peter! God showed you that all food is now clean?"

"Well, no. The vision was about eating unclean food, but it only meant that the Gentiles are now welcomed into the People of God."

"Oh! So, in the vision, God said the Gentiles are now welcome?"

"Not exactly. He just showed me a bunch of unclean food and told me to eat it. But I knew He meant that the Gentiles are now welcome."

"Wait. So exactly what did God say in this vision?"

"He said, 'Rise, Peter, kill and eat.'"

"Kill and eat the Gentiles?!"

"No! He was talking about the animals."

"Yahweh commanded you to eat unclean animals?"

"Yes."

"But you're saying the vision does *not* teach that all food is now clean?"

"Right. It was just an analogy."

"So you didn't actually eat unclean animals in the vision?"

"No! I told God I had never eaten anything common or unclean."

"He must have been proud of you for keeping the kosher food laws!"

"Actually, He said, 'What God has made clean, do not call common.'"

"But He said that about the food, not the Gentiles, right?"

"Right."

"Let me get this straight. In the vision, God said He made all food clean and you were not to call it common. But He didn't really mean all food is clean?"

"Right."

"So…God lied in the vision?"

"No! Not really. He was just using food as an example."

"So even though God declared all food clean, all food is *not* clean?"

"Now you're getting it."

Food & The Tabernacle

There is one additional aspect to the food laws that Torahism misses. Namely, the connection between the food laws and the tabernacle. Torahists often point to Leviticus 11 without realizing that it is part of a larger passage known as the Laws of Purity which run from Leviticus 11-15. In Leviticus 16, these Purity Laws are tied to the purity of the tabernacle. Postell, Eitan, and Soref explain the connection:

> Beyond the fact that there is no longer a functioning tabernacle/temple, followers of Yeshua now are themselves the temple of the Holy Spirit (1 Cor. 3:16), the purity of which is no longer contingent upon following the Laws of Purity in Leviticus 11–15, but upon the final and perfect sacrifice of the Messiah Yeshua. Yeshua has fulfilled all the Laws of Purity for us, including the food laws! For this reason, both Paul and the writer of Hebrews are able to declare to Yeshua's followers, both Jewish and Gentile, that all foods are clean (Heb. 9:8–10, 13:9; 1 Tim. 4:1–5).[6]

The Big Picture

The passages examined above are not the only places where the New Testament teaches that all food is now clean. For example,

> Do not, for the sake of food, destroy the work of God. Everything is indeed clean, but it is wrong for anyone to make another stumble by what he eats. (Rom 14:20)

> Eat everything that is sold in the meat market, without raising questions for the sake of conscience, since the earth is the Lord's, and all that is in it. If any of the unbelievers invites you over and you want to go, eat everything that is set before you, without raising questions for the sake of conscience. (1 Cor 10:25-27)

The New Testament also teaches we should not let anyone judge us regarding food and drink (Col 2:16-17) and that the kingdom of God is not a matter of eating and drinking but of righteousness and peace and joy in the Holy Spirit (Rom 14:17). Paul, who is "persuaded in the Lord Jesus that nothing is unclean in itself" (Rom 14:14), teaches that food

---

[6] Postell, Eitan, Soref, *Reading Moses, Seeing Jesus*, Kindle location 1612-1615.

will not bring us closer to God. "We are not worse off if we don't eat, and we are not better if we do eat" (1 Cor 8:8).

Lastly, we can't ignore that the decision rendered by the apostles and elders—and confirmed by the Holy Spirit—at the Jerusalem Council was not to enforce the Mosaic dietary laws on new believers.[7] That said, it is important to remember that just because we have freedom in Christ to eat all food, it does not mean that we *should* eat all food. The New Testament teaches us to forego any food or tradition that might cause a brother to stumble or lead to discord in the body of Christ.[8] "You, my brothers and sisters, were called to be free. But do not use your freedom to indulge the flesh; rather, serve one another humbly in love" (Gal 5:13).

And here again, we have to acknowledge that eating kosher, while not required, has not been forbidden. Thus, Jewish followers of Jesus are not only allowed to keep the kashrut laws, a case could be made that the New Testament expects they will do so as a matter of their Jewish identity. Likewise, Gentiles who feel led by God to eat kosher can do so with a clean conscience. There is great freedom in Christ.

The line gets crossed when Torahism teaches that not keeping the Mosaic dietary restrictions is wrong, sinful, and lawless. That is just not the case. Where is all this unbiblical Torahist teaching about abstaining from food coming from? I'm not going to suggest that the following passage specifically targets Torahism, but if the shoe fits.

> Now the Spirit expressly says that in later times some will depart from the faith by devoting themselves to deceitful spirits and teachings of demons, through the insincerity of liars whose consciences are seared, who forbid marriage and require abstinence from foods that God created to be received with thanksgiving by those who believe and know the truth. For everything created by God is good, and nothing is to be rejected if it is received with thanksgiving, for it is made holy by the word of God and prayer. (1 Timothy 4:1-5)

Summary

Noah was allowed to eat every moving thing. Centuries later, the Law of Moses established specific dietary restrictions. Centuries after that, Jesus declared all foods clean, and the epistles teach the same thing in multiple places. How are we to understand Yahweh's changing directives

---

[7] We looked at that decision in detail in chapter seven, "The Torah Is for All Nations."
[8] Romans 14:19-21; 1 Corinthians 8:13, 10:25-30.

regarding food? The Principle & Expression framework says that the unchanging Law of God is expressed to His people differently at different times. The kosher food laws of the Mosaic Expression were not intended to last forever. They were given to set God's People, the Jews, apart from the Gentile nations. But under Christ, there is no more distinction between Jew and Gentile in that sense. Therefore, the kosher laws given to Israel as an outward expression of ritual purity are no longer required. They can, however, be kept as a matter of personal preference or, in the case of Jewish believers, cultural calling.

14

The Temple, Priests, Sacrifices & Worship

You ought to let the Jews have Jerusalem;
it was they who made it famous.

WINSTON CHURCHILL

I N THE LAW OF MOSES, God ordained a detailed and beautiful set
of commandments for a system of priests, sacrifices, and worship
to set Israel apart from every other nation on earth. These
mitzvot—which cover religious ceremonies, worship, the temple,
atonement, sacrifices, offerings, and more—are so interwoven that they
need to be examined as a single, connected system. Our Torah-keeping
friends concede that if we were to discover that even one commandment
in the Mosaic Law was removed or added to, it would mean the entire
Law has been broken. And in this chapter alone we will see how, because
of the work of Christ, over 150 mitzvot from the Law of Moses have
become fulfilled or are no longer binding.

Priests
Through His death and resurrection, Yeshua ushered in a New
Covenant that brought about a seismic shift in God's holy priesthood.
To understand this change, we need first to understand
the *kohanim* (priesthood) established under the Mosaic Law. Out of the
twelve tribes of Israel, God appointed the tribe of Levi alone to serve
Him as priests. He commanded that all priests be Levites, hence the
term *Levitical Priesthood.*

Then you shall bring Aaron (*the first High Priest under the Law of Moses*) and his sons to the entrance of the tent of meeting and shall wash them with water and put on Aaron the holy garments. And you shall anoint him and consecrate him, that he may serve me as priest. You shall bring his sons also and put coats on them, and anoint them, as you anointed their father, that they may serve me as priests. And their anointing shall admit them to a perpetual priesthood throughout their generations. (40:12-15, *comment added*)

The Levitical priests, all the tribe of Levi, shall have no portion or inheritance with Israel. They shall eat the Lord's food offerings as their inheritance. They shall have no inheritance among their brothers; the Lord is their inheritance, as he promised them . . . For the Lord your God has chosen him out of all your tribes to stand and minister in the name of the Lord, him and his sons for all time. (Deuteronomy 18:1-2, 5)

Aaron and his descendants were called to be God's priests. Yahweh put the Levitical priesthood in a position of spiritual leadership over Israel. They were given the responsibility and privilege of doing service in the temple[1] and officiating at the sacrifices, ceremonies, feasts, and daily services. According to Machon HaMikdash,[2] by doing so, the priests would,

serve as a conduit to bring down God's radiant blessing and influence into this world. In fact, it is on this account that [the priests] are commanded to deliver God's blessing of peace and love to the people."[3]

This was established in the Torah under the Law of Moses. And it is what the Jewish people today still try to do as best they can without a temple or a Levitical priesthood.

And here's where things get interesting. In chapter six, we looked at the Hebrew terms used to describe the nature of the Levitical priesthood, such as *perpetual, everlasting, for all time,* and *throughout their*

---

[1] It started as a tabernacle (tent) in the wilderness which the Israelites would carry around with them. Later Solomon built a permanent temple in Jerusalem.

[2] Machon HaMikdash (in English: "The Temple Institute") is a non-profit educational and religious organization located in the Jewish quarter of Jerusalem's Old City.

[3] The Temple Institute, "The Levitical Priests: Their Function and Role in the Holy Temple," *Machon HaMikdash*, www.templeinstitute.org.

generations. These are the terms and phrases Torahism leans on when trying to convince us that the Mosaic Law is still in effect. They point to the Torah and say, "See? It says right here that the Law of Moses is perpetual, forever, everlasting." Yet, if the Mosaic Law is still in effect, the descendants of the tribe of Levi should be the only people allowed to function as God's priests today. That's what the Law of Moses requires. But the New Testament teaches something quite different.

There is an illuminating passage in Hebrews that explicitly addresses the changes to the Levitical priesthood because of the work of Christ. Let's read through it and then break it down.

> Now if perfection had been attainable through the Levitical priesthood (for under it the people received the law), what further need would there have been for another priest to arise after the order of Melchizedek, rather than one named after the order of Aaron? For when there is a change in the priesthood, there is necessarily a change in the law as well. For the one of whom these things are spoken belonged to another tribe, from which no one has ever served at the altar. For it is evident that our Lord was descended from Judah, and in connection with that tribe Moses said nothing about priests.
>
> This becomes even more evident when another priest arises in the likeness of Melchizedek, who has become a priest, not on the basis of a legal requirement concerning bodily descent, but by the power of an indestructible life. For it is witnessed of him, "You are a priest forever, after the order of Melchizedek." For on the one hand, a former commandment is set aside because of its weakness and uselessness (for the law made nothing perfect); but on the other hand, a better hope is introduced, through which we draw near to God. (Hebrews 7:11-19)

This passage is explicit and unambiguous. And did you catch the last line? The Levitical regulations given under the Law of Moses have been *set aside.* They are no longer in effect. And why were they set aside? They had become *weak and useless.*

This passage explains that the priestly regulations were weak in comparison to Christ because they were of the flesh. The Levitical priests were appointed based on their physical lineage. Moreover, the priests had to offer sacrifices not just for God's People but also for their own sins. The priests were sinful human beings, and their sacrifices couldn't truly forgive sin (Heb 10). The priestly regulations had become useless because they were only shadows (Heb 10:1), which pointed to the Real Thing (Col 2:16-17). And now that the Real Thing, Jesus, has come and fulfilled them, there is no longer a need for a Levitical priesthood. The book of Hebrews was written to Jewish Christians who were under persecution for their faith in Yeshua. They were feeling insecure, and some wanted to return to the Levitical priesthood they knew so well. The author of Hebrews warned them against doing so.

The writer kept in mind the temptation his readers were facing to go back into the old temple system. This is why he reminded them (Heb. 7:19) that Jesus Christ has accomplished what the Law could never accomplish: He brought in a better hope, and He enables us to draw near to God. To go back to Judaism would mean losing the enjoyment of their fellowship with God through Christ. The only hope Judaism had was the coming of Christ, and that blessing these believers already had.[4]

The author of Hebrews builds this case by showing how the priesthood of Jesus was not in the order of Aaron, as required under the Law of Moses. Instead, our attention is directed to a time four centuries before the Law was given and an enigmatic priest named Melchizedek. Who was Melchizedek? We don't know a lot about him. But what we do know is fascinating. Strobel offers some helpful insight.

During Abraham's meeting with the king of Sodom, Melchizedek made a brief appearance (see Genesis 14:18–20). He was both a king and a priest of God, a rare combination that prefigures Jesus. Melchizedek's priesthood was superior to the traditional Levitical priesthood because while the Levitical priests received tithes from Israelites who benefited from God's promise, Melchizedek received a tithe from the very one to whom the promise was made (see Hebrews 7:4–7). The Levitical priesthood, which operated under the Law of Moses, was inferior to that of Melchizedek's priesthood, which did not operate under the regulations of the law (see Hebrews 7:11–12).[5]

---

[4] Wiersbe, W. W., *The Bible Exposition Commentary* (Victor Books, 1996), p. 301.
[5] Lee Strobel, *Case for Christ Study Bible* (Zondervan, 2009), p. 981.

In other words, Yeshua, like Melchizedek, supersedes the Law and its Levitical priesthood. Why? Let's look at Hebrews 7:1-7 and let the New Testament interpret the Old Testament for us.

For this Melchizedek, king of Salem, priest of the Most High God, met Abraham returning from the slaughter of the kings and blessed him, and to him Abraham apportioned a tenth part of everything. He is first, by translation of his name, king of righteousness, (*the name "Melchizedek" means "king of righteousness" in Hebrew*), and then he is also king of Salem, that is, king of peace. (*The word "Salem"—or in Hebrew, "Shalom"— means peace*).

He is without father or mother or genealogy, having neither beginning of days nor end of life (*Unlike other figures in Scripture, we're not given Melchizedek's genealogy or family line. He just mysteriously appears without qualification*) but resembling the Son of God he continues a priest forever. (*The author of Hebrews links Yeshua to Melchizedek on the basis of eternality.*)

See how great this man was to whom Abraham the patriarch gave a tenth of the spoils! And those descendants of Levi who receive the priestly office have a commandment in the law to take tithes from the people, that is, from their brothers, though these also are descended from Abraham. But this man who does not have his descent from them received tithes from Abraham and blessed him who had the promises. It is beyond dispute that the inferior is blessed by the superior. (Hebrews 7:1-7, *comments added*)

The Levitical priests received tithes from their fellow Israelites who were also beneficiaries of God's promise. But Melchizedek received a tithe from Abraham himself, the very man to whom God had given the promise in the first place. And Melchizedek's blessing of Abraham indicates that Melchizedek's priesthood was superior to the priesthood of Abraham and his descendants, the Levites. The Levitical priesthood was grounded in the Law of Moses and the order of Aaron. By contrast, the priesthood of *Yeshua* is grounded in the order of Melchizedek. Jesus, like Melchizedek, stands outside the Law and its Levitical priesthood. And Jesus introduced a better hope than the Mosaic Law.

In addition to Genesis 14 and Hebrews 5-7, Melchizedek is mentioned one other place in Scripture. And it is a text that has caused Jewish sages and rabbis to spill a lot of ink over the centuries. Psalm 110 is a messianic book containing prophecies about the coming Messiah.[6] There King David wrote,

> The Lord has sworn and will not change his mind, "You are a priest forever after the order of Melchizedek." (Psalm 110:4)

When David wrote of the coming Messiah, why did he say, "in the order of Melchizedek" rather than "in the order of Aaron," as the Mosaic Law required? This would have been a burning question to first-century Jewish believers in Yeshua. And it is a question Torahism should be asking itself today. A "need for another priest to come" (Heb 7:11) reveals that the Levitical priesthood of the Mosaic Law was not intended as the final state of God's priesthood. That's why Melchizedek was mentioned in Genesis 14 and linked to the Messiah in Psalm 110. It was God's plan all along that the Mosaic priesthood would end.

But that's not all. Let's return to Hebrews 7, picking up at verse 23.

> The former (*Levitical*) priests were many in number, because they were prevented by death from continuing in office, but [Jesus] holds his priesthood permanently, because he continues forever. (*i.e., Appointing new priests when the old one dies—which was required under the Law of Moses—has ended. Jesus' victory over death means there will be no more changes in the priesthood.*) Consequently, he is able to save to the uttermost those who draw near to God through him since he always lives to make intercession for them. (*The salvation Jesus offers is superior to anything the Levitical priesthood could provide.*)

> For it was indeed fitting that we should have such a high priest, holy, innocent, unstained, separated from sinners, and exalted above the heavens. (*The Levitical priests were certainly not unstained or innocent or exalted above the heavens!*) He has no need, like those high priests, to offer sacrifices daily, first for his own sins and then for those of the people, since he did this once for all when he offered up himself. For the law appoints men in their weakness as high priests, but the word of the oath, which

---

[6] Psalm 110 is the most quoted psalm in the New Testament.

came later than the law, appoints a Son who has been made perfect forever. (Hebrews 7:23:-28, *comments added*)

In a break with Mosaic Law, our new High Priest was not chosen based on His tribal ancestry. Yeshua does not even meet the priestly requirements of the Law! Instead, His priesthood is based on His victory over death (Heb 7:16). By referencing Melchizedek, the author of Hebrews shows us that Christians are heirs of God's covenant with Abraham,[7] which was ultimately realized through Yeshua.[8] With the advent of Christ and His atoning work on the cross, we have graduated to the greater priesthood foreshadowed by Melchizedek. Jesus is now our high priest.

A Torah-keeping Theory

Hebrews 7 puts our Torah-keeping friends in a bit of a pickle. How can Jesus be our high priest if He doesn't meet the Torah's qualifications? It would seem there are two ways to resolve that. We can either conclude that Jesus is not a priest or that the Torah's priestly qualifications have changed. Hebrews 7:12 suggests the correct answer is the latter. "For when there is a change in the priesthood, there is necessarily a change in the law as well" (Heb 7:12). However, Torahism has a third option to offer. David Wilber of 119 Ministries suggests,

> The way that the author of Hebrews solves this issue is that Jesus is a priest in the heavenly realm, which is not subject to the laws that govern the earthly priesthood. When the author says that there is a change to the law, he means that the laws of the earthly priesthood do not apply to the heavenly priesthood . . . The law "changes" when it comes to the heavenly priesthood. But there is no change to the law that governs the earthly priesthood . . . . These two realms—the earthly, where the Levitical priesthood functions, and the heavenly where Messiah's priesthood functions—coexist in our present age.[9]

Wilber does not offer any scriptural support for this claim. Although Hebrews talks about things in the heavenly realms, such as the tabernacle, it says nothing of a heavenly priesthood or a heavenly law. It speaks only of the Levitical priesthood. And I find no passages in the

---

[7] Also see Galatians 3:29-29.
[8] Genesis 12:7; 13:15, 24:7; Galatians 3:16.
[9] David Wilber, "Matthew 5:18 and the Torah: A Response to R. L. Solberg" YouTube.

New Testament where laws that govern the heavenly priesthood are discussed, much less said to have changed.[10]

There is no doubt that Jesus is a heavenly high priest. Hebrews describes Him as a high priest "who is seated at the right hand of the throne of the Majesty in heaven" (8:1). And it teaches that "Christ has entered, not into holy places made with hands, which are copies of the true things, but into heaven itself, now to appear in the presence of God on our behalf" (9:24). But Wilber's argument comes up short in its unfounded claim that when the author of Hebrews wrote about changes in the priesthood and the law (7:12), he meant, as Wilber put it, "the laws of the earthly priesthood do not apply to the heavenly priesthood." That idea is foreign to the text of Hebrews 7 and the teaching of the New Testament.

More Priestly Changes

Under the New Covenant, not only is the priesthood no longer constrained to the tribe of Levi, it is not even limited to Israel. *All* believers in Jesus—whether Jew or Gentile—are now priests.

> As you come to him, the living Stone—rejected by humans but chosen by God and precious to him—you also, like living stones, are being built into a spiritual house to be a *holy priesthood*, offering spiritual sacrifices acceptable to God through Jesus Christ . . . You are a chosen people, a *royal priesthood*, a holy nation, God's special possession, that you may declare the praises of him who called you out of darkness into his wonderful light. (1 Peter 2:4-5, 9, *emphasis added*)

Under the Sinai Covenant, offering sacrifices to God was the responsibility of the Levitical priests. Under the New Covenant, we each offer our own "spiritual sacrifices acceptable to God through Jesus Christ" (1 Pet 2:5). And don't miss the significance of Peter's description of those who follow Yeshua. It comes directly from the Torah. At Sinai, as the LORD was about to give the Law, He told Israel,

> Now therefore, if you will indeed obey my voice and keep my covenant, you shall be my *treasured possession* among all peoples, for all the earth is mine; and you shall be to me a *kingdom of*

---

[10] The heavenly priesthood is, however, an oft-discussed topic for Jehovah's Witnesses.

priests and a *holy nation.* These are the words that you shall speak to the people of Israel. (Exodus 19:5-6, *emphasis added*)

Under the Law of Moses, the Levites were priests with special access to God. Under the New Covenant, *all believers* are priests able to approach God's throne of grace with confidence (Heb 4:16). Those in Christ, both Jew and Gentile, are called "a chosen people, a royal priesthood, a holy nation, God's special possession" (1 Peter 2:9).

This teaching is as explosive for the theology of Torahism today as it was for Judaism in the first century. The Torah continually speaks of the Levitical priesthood,[11] through whom the Mosaic Law was applied to the Israelites. That priesthood drove the national and spiritual identity of Israel. Imagine how much of the Law of Moses had to change to accommodate this new order of priests under the New Covenant. To suggest that the priestly Mosaic laws are still in effect is to undermine the priesthood of the New Covenant under Jesus.

Sacrifices

While researching Torahism, I began to wonder what it sees for the future of mankind. Most Torah-keepers claim, along with Judaism, that the Law of Moses is to last until the end of time. If that's true, it would mean the commandments about sacrifices are to be kept literally forever. Could that be right? Will there be no end to the sacrificing of animals for our sin?

Most Torah-keepers hold the Jewish position that a third temple will be built one day, and at that time, all the temple laws—including blood sacrifices—will resume. There are Orthodox Jews in Israel today who still practice the techniques of ritual sacrifice so that the knowledge will not be lost.[12] Judaism teaches that when the "real" Mashiach comes, the temple will be rebuilt, if it is not already rebuilt by then. And from then on, the sacrifices and offerings will continue until the very end of time.[13] This is why Judaism's daily services include prayers for the restoration of the temple and the resumption of its rituals, including the sacrifices.

---

[11] See especially the books of Numbers and Deuteronomy.

[12] In fact, a Pesach (Passover) sacrifice was made in the year 2000 within sight of the temple Mount. See www.mechon-mamre.org/jewfaq/qorbanot.htm.

[13] Personal correspondence with Shlomo of Mechon Mamre (Jerusalem, Israel) on April 13, 2019. Shlomo wrote, "This might seem strange, but all of the commandments of the Torah are permanent, in effect from the time they were given till the very end of time. So, while we have not had the temple sacrifices since 70 C.E., we do need to eventually rebuild the temple and renew the sacrifices as they were done originally. If we have not renewed the temple before the Mashiach comes, then the temple will be renewed in his time."

This is not an unreasonable position for orthodox Jews who reject Yeshua as the Mashiach and do not believe the New Testament. But what about Torahism, which *does* accept the New Testament and Jesus as Messiah? I've spent a good amount of time discussing this point with my Torah-keeping friends. While many agree that Christ died for our sins, they also paradoxically believe that the temple must be rebuilt and blood sacrifices for sin renewed. One Torah-keeper told me,

> The Torah will be valid when the Messiah reigns from Jerusalem for 1000 years! And he will participate in the temple worship prescribed in the Torah. The scriptures reveal even animal sacrifices will resume: Ezekiel 43:20, 26, 45:15-20; Isaiah 56:7; Jeremiah 33:18; Zechariah 14:20-21; Malachi 3:3-4. (Rachel E.)

Rachel believes the Law of Moses will still be binding after Jesus' return. And here is an excerpt from a discussion with my friend Sue.

Me: I'm a little confused. If the animal sacrifices are to be renewed one day, what do you believe was the point of Yeshua's sacrifice on the cross?

Sue: Every sacrifice was for sin, bro? And if every sacrifice was NOT for sin, then why shouldn't the temple be rebuilt and the sacrificial system be revived for all believers to enjoy?[14] If there were offerings given for thanksgiving, for festival, peace, and vows, why wouldn't someone who says they follow the God of the Hebrew Bible willingly go to Jerusalem and give such offerings? Those who believe Yeshua died on the cross and that his death satisfied a debt that the guilty could not pay, then they would not need to bring that type of sacrifice, correct?

Me: I'm not quite following. Are you saying that when the sacrificial system is restored, it will not include sacrifices for sin? Just the offerings for thanksgiving and peace, etc.?

Sue: The scriptures answer your question and I am under no obligation to. Especially since you appear to struggle with accepting what they clearly state about the return of the temple and Yahweh's acceptance of the worship that will go on there!

---

[14] I found this a surprising comment. The sin sacrifices were given in the Law of Moses as a bloody reminder that our sin leads to death. Hardly a ceremony to "enjoy."

The animal sacrifices *will* be restored. The Torah was, is, and remains binding and is a huge blessing to all who join themselves to the house of Israel. Like Psalm 19 says, "The Law of Yahweh is perfect refreshing the soul!" If the Christian religion you hold to requires you to think that the clearly stated return of the temple and its sacrifices make what Yeshua did meaningless, that is your problem!

<u>Me</u>: But that brings us back to the original question. If the blood sacrifices for sin *are* to one day be renewed, what do you believe was the point of Yeshua's blood sacrifice on the cross? I'm asking because if the blood sacrifices for sin are to be renewed, as you say they are, then Yeshua's sacrifice was not "once for all" (Heb 10:10) and does not seem to have accomplished anything. And on the other hand, if they are *not* to be renewed, then the Law of Moses has changed.

Sue never responded.

What Did Yeshua's Sacrifice Accomplish?

After dialoguing with hundreds of people on this topic, I have yet to find a clear answer. If the blood sacrifices for sin are to be required of us forever, what did Jesus' blood sacrifice accomplish? A Torah-keeping teacher named Tim Hegg offers a curious theory in his commentary on Hebrews. In response to the line "there is no longer any offering for sin" (Heb 10:18), Hegg wrote,

It is not uncommon to find among the Christian commentators the viewpoint that by this statement, our author is declaring the abolishment of the sacrificial system set forth in the Torah. But our author is not referring to the animal sacrifices of the Levitical system when he writes "there is no longer any offering for sin." His primary point in the immediate context is that Yeshua offered himself once for all time and thus stands in direct contrast to the sacrifices which were offered daily, weekly, monthly, as well as in connection with the yearly festivals.

What is more, these sacrifices were a continual "reminder" of sin, whereas, by the sacrifice of Yeshua for those he would save, their sins are no longer charged against them by God himself. Thus, in declaring that "there is no longer any offering for sin," our author is reinforcing his earlier statement that Yeshua died once, never to die again. If in the New Covenant promised by Jeremiah God is stated to remember sin "no more," and if the sacrifices of bulls and goats never took away sin, then the only conclusion one could reach is that Yeshua's self-sacrifice is eternally efficacious and there is therefore no need for Him to offer Himself again and again. The statement "there is no longer any offering for sin" is in regard to Yeshua's offering for sin, not the animal sacrifices which pointed forward to his atoning work.[15]

Hegg argues that 10:18 is "not referring to the animal sacrifices of the Levitical system." Rather, it teaches that Jesus' sacrifice was "eternally efficacious" and there is no need for Him to "offer Himself again and again." But that is not what this text teaches at all. Verse 18 is the final verse of a passage that spans verses 1-18, the topic of which is Christ's sacrifice once for all. This section can be summarized as follows.[16]

The Law was a shadow of the good things to come, but it cannot truly cleanse us from sin (v. 1), so its annual sacrifices had to be continually offered (v. 2-4). But Jesus' death and resurrection did away with the first covenant and established the second (v. 5-9)[17] and, therefore, "we have been sanctified through the offering of the body of Jesus Christ once for all" (Heb 10:10). The author then repeats the same idea for emphasis: The Levitical priests repeatedly offered the same animal sacrifices, which can never take away sins (v. 11), but, by contrast, Jesus made a single offering of Himself that perfected us "for all time" (v. 12-14). When Yahweh promised the New Covenant through Jeremiah, He said He would remember His people's "sins and their lawless deeds no more" (v. 15-17). And where there is forgiveness of these sins, "there is no longer any offering for sin" (v. 18).

The pervasive, recurring theme of the book of Hebrews is the superiority of Christ over Moses. His ministry is better (8:6), His covenant is better (7:22; 8:6), His sacrifice was better (9:23; 12:24), He is a better high priest (10:11-13), with a better temple (9:11), and He is worthy of more glory than Moses (3:3). And in chapter 10, the author is contrasting the Mosaic sacrifices and priesthood with that of Yeshua.

---

[15] Tim Hegg, *A Commentary on the Book of Hebrews Chapters 9–13*, TorahResource, 2016, pp. 115-116.

[16] Please don't take my word for it! Read Hebrews 10 for yourself.

[17] The text of 10:9 simply says, "does away with the first in order to establish the second." The first and second what? It does not directly say. But the context indicates it must either be referring to the covenants or the priesthoods.

And every priest stands daily at his service, offering repeatedly the same sacrifices, which can never take away sins. But when Christ had offered for all time a single sacrifice for sins, he sat down at the right hand of God (Hebrews 10:11-12)

This is evidently a point of great importance to the author of Hebrews because he makes it three different times. Earlier, he wrote,

[Jesus] has no need, like those high priests, to offer sacrifices daily, first for his own sins and then for those of the people, since he did this once for all when he offered up himself. (Heb 7:27)

Nor was it to offer himself repeatedly, as the high priest enters the holy places every year with blood not his own, for then he would have had to suffer repeatedly since the foundation of the world. But as it is, he has appeared once for all at the end of the ages to put away sin by the sacrifice of himself. (Hebrews 9:25-26)

The Levitical priests offered continual sacrifices that could never take away sin (10:4). Christ offered a single sacrifice "once for all" (10:10) that was so eternally effective that "there is no longer any offering for sin" (10:18). In fact, it was so powerful it retroactively redeemed all the sins committed under the first covenant (Heb 9:15)! And then Jesus sat down at the right hand of God because He was finished (Heb 10:12). The animal sacrifices were a "shadow" (10:1) that prefigured the real sacrifice to come. And when our superior High Priest offered His superior sacrifice—which was the "true form" of sacrifice required for sin (10:1)—He fulfilled and brought to an end the recurring requirement of animal sacrifices required under the Law.

Hegg holds the paradoxical position that Jesus' sacrifice was "eternally efficacious," yet the Mosaic requirement of animal sacrifices for sin remains. Which begs the question, *eternally efficacious for what?* Jesus is the sacrificed "Lamb of God, who takes away the sin of the world" (John 1:29). And now that He has made such a great offering once and for all, why would we ever return to the inferior sacrifices of bulls and goats? To suggest such a thing is an affront to the sufficiency of Christ's atoning blood.

Why the Animal Sacrifices?

At this point, some Torahists will protest that blood sacrifices for sin must have been prescribed in the Law of Moses for a reason. Bates provides an excellent explanation in an article on Leviticus,

> Because God is holy, and the average person is not, a means to be made pure was necessary. Enter the sacrificial system. Sin results in consequences and nothing made this more evident than the sacrifice. So prevalent was the need for sacrifice that unintentional sins required the life of an animal. Logically, this resulted in the realization that sin brings death, and the only way to forgive this sin was for something else to take the sinner's place. This is most clearly stated in Leviticus 17:11, "For the life of a creature is in the blood, and I have given it to you to make atonement for yourselves on the altar; it is the blood that makes atonement for one's life." Sacrifice is expected for sins you didn't even consciously commit! How is this fair? How is this just? You might even respond that it is impossible to remain clean and holy under such conditions. And you'd be right. Because that's the point.
>
> The sacrifice is required because God is holy. It applies to every part of daily life because every part of our humanity is unholy. This is the message of Paul (Rom 5:12-21; 8:5) and John (1 John 2:2; 3:5). It is why Jesus came to be sin on our behalf (2 Cor 5:21), the just for the unjust (1 Pet. 3:18). He did this because it is impossible for any human being to keep himself holy or be able to approach God through his or her own efforts. The message of Leviticus is the message of the cross . . . Without Leviticus, the resurrection becomes meaningless. Without all that had been foreshadowed in the Old Testament, the action of Christ in the New becomes nothing more than an interesting historical event.[18]

In chapter four, we saw how God has expressed His unchanging principle of blood atonement for sin (Lev 17:11) differently over time. It was first revealed in the Garden through the skins of animals. This was a "shadow" of Christ's sacrifice. Later, under the Law of Moses, the shadow took on more detail as the expression changed to the ritual

---

[18] Clark Bates, "What's a Christian to do With Leviticus?" *Exe-Jesus*, www.exejesus.com.

sacrifice of bulls and goats. And finally, under the New Covenant, the shadow became the real thing. Yahweh's final expression of His blood atonement principle was through Christ, "whom God put forward as a sacrifice of atonement by his blood, effective through faith" (Rom 3:25).

Christ's death is the ultimate fulfillment of the picture portrayed in the Mosaic sacrifices. Before then, God's people sought atonement through sacrifices given in anticipation of what Christ would ultimately achieve. Through faith, they could rightly rejoice in the forgiveness of sins promised to them in Jesus. This is why the temple requirement of blood sacrifice for sin atonement ended at Yeshua's resurrection. He defeated sin and death. When the Real Thing arrives, the shadows that point to it are no longer necessary.

Worship

To a first-century Jew, the highest expression of worship was under the Levitical priesthood at the temple in Jerusalem. This was the Holy Place, the central sanctuary where Yahweh was to be worshipped. The *anan* (עָנָן, cloud or mist) of Yahweh's presence that led Israel through the wilderness (Ex 13:21-22) and engulfed Mount Sinai at the giving of the Law (Ex 24:15-18) also filled the tabernacle.

> Then the cloud (*anan*) covered the tent of meeting, and the glory of the LORD filled the tabernacle. And Moses was not able to enter the tent of meeting because the cloud (*anan*) settled on it, and the glory of the LORD filled the tabernacle. (Exodus 40:34-35, *comments added*)

After the tabernacle became a permanent temple, the *anan* of Yahweh dwelled there, as well (1 Kings 8:10–11). Israelites knew that true worship happens in Yahweh's presence. Given this history, it is not hard to imagine how difficult it would have been for first-century Jewish followers of Jesus to embrace a different way of worshiping. Yet, a new kind of worship is exactly what Yeshua taught.

In a conversation at the well of Jacob, a Samaritan woman said to Jesus, "Our ancestors worshiped on this mountain, but you Jews claim that the place where we must worship is in Jerusalem" (John 4:20). She was referring to the temple, which is what the Torah commands.[19] Indeed, the Torah requires every able Jew to travel to Jerusalem three

---

[19] As the rightful place of worship, many Jewish synagogues at the time were oriented toward Jerusalem for this very reason.

times a year for feasts.[20] Yet, Yeshua's reply to the woman revealed that a change in worship was upon them.

> "Woman," Jesus replied, "believe me, a time is coming when you will worship the Father neither on this mountain nor in Jerusalem [at the temple]. You Samaritans worship what you do not know; we worship what we do know, for salvation is from the Jews. Yet a time is coming and has now come when the true worshipers will worship the Father in the Spirit and in truth, for they are the kind of worshipers the Father seeks. God is spirit, and his worshipers must worship in the Spirit and in truth." (John 4:21-24, bracketed comment added)

Jesus inaugurated a new standard for worship. It is no longer about a physical location but rather worshipping "in the Spirit and in truth" (John 4:24). Under the New Covenant, there is no longer a geographic "holy place." Yeshua prophesied that the temple would be destroyed,[21] and His prophecy came to pass in 70 CE. A new temple has displaced the physical temple prescribed in the Torah. We believers in Yeshua, individually and collectively as the body of Christ, are the new temple.

> Don't you know that you yourselves are God's temple and that God's Spirit dwells in your midst? If anyone destroys God's temple, God will destroy that person; for God's temple is sacred, and you together are that temple. (1 Cor 3:16-17)[22]

The apostle Peter describes Christians as "living stones" built up as a new living temple (1 Pet 2:4-10). Paul says we are "a holy temple in the Lord" (Eph 2:21). And again, "Or do you not know that your body is a temple of the Holy Spirit within you, whom you have from God?" (1 Cor 6:19). And in an unambiguous statement of change, Second Corinthians quotes the declaration Yahweh made in the Torah to describe His presence in the temple [23] and applies it to Christ-followers today:

---

[20] These are known as the Pilgrimage Feasts. They include Passover, Shavuot, Sukkot. See Deuteronomy 16:16.

[21] Matthew 24:1-2; Mark 13:1-4; Luke 21:5-7.

[22] Also see 1 Corinthians 6:19-20; 2 Corinthians 6:14-18; Ephesians 2:19-22.

[23] Exodus 29:45; Leviticus 26:12.

For we are the temple of the living God; as God said, "I will make my dwelling among them and walk among them, and I will be their God, and they shall be my people." (2 Corinthians 6:16)

Even if the temple was still standing today, believers in God are no longer required to make a pilgrimage to Jerusalem. Instead, we have been sent *from* Jerusalem, so to speak, to make disciples of all nations (Matt 28:16-20, Acts 1:8). Meanwhile, Jews and many Torahists—both of whom keep the Law of Moses—cling to the idea that the proper worship of Yahweh is bound to Jerusalem and, therefore, the temple needs to be rebuilt. My friends Bob and Sue travel to Israel regularly as part of their perceived obligation under Torah Law. And I personally know an American Torah-keeper who plans to leave his wife and kids and relocate to the Middle East so that he can keep these Mosaic pilgrimages. He considers his wife disobedient and lawless for not joining him. This is what I mean when I say that Torah-keeping tends to elevate Moses above Jesus.

The Presence of God

In the Law of Moses, there is a proximal aspect to holiness. The closer you are to the presence of God, the closer you are to His blessing. Conversely, the further you are from His presence, the closer you are to the place of the curse, so to speak. In the Garden, after Adam and Eve sinned, mankind lost its direct access to God's presence. Later, through the family of Abraham and the giving of the Torah on Mount Sinai, Yahweh began restoring access to His presence, starting with the Tabernacle. "Then have them make a sanctuary for me, and I will dwell among them" (Ex 25:8).

Under Mosaic Law, God's presence was housed in the tabernacle as He would "tabernacle" or camp with His people. Thus, the Torah instructed the Israelites to set up the tabernacle in the center of the camp and organize the twelve tribes around it in such a way that they had equal access to it.[24]

---

[24] See Numbers 2. Note that the Levites camped in the middle with the tabernacle. They did not have their own camp (nor any land in Israel after the temple was built) because the Lord was their inheritance (Deuteronomy 10:8-19; Numbers 2:17).

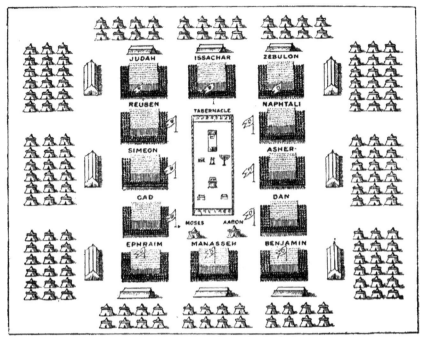

The Wilderness Camp, from a drawing in the
Biblia Sacra Polyglotta (London, 1657).

Notice the sense of hierarchy present in this arrangement. Holiness radiated from the tabernacle in the center. Under Mosaic Law, access to Yahweh's presence was highly regulated. One didn't just wander haphazardly into the Holy Place. If you were outside the camp altogether (outside the edges of the map above), you were in the "unholy place," so to speak. Once you entered the camp, there would be greater holiness. As you crossed into the outer courtyard of the tabernacle in the center of camp, the holiness increased. Stepping inside the tabernacle brought more holiness; only priests were allowed there. And finally, inside the tabernacle was a room called the Most Holy Place where only one person in all of Israel, the High Priest, was allowed inside, just once a year.

This whole system kept believers at a distance. The hierarchy of holiness sent a clear message to Israel that the direct access we had to God's presence in the Garden was not yet restored. It was unthinkable for a Jew under the Mosaic Law to consider approaching God's throne of grace with confidence and freedom. Not even the high priest did that!

Yet this is just what Christians are now able to do under the New Covenant.[25]

The hierarchy prescribed in the Torah was literally torn down by God when, upon Christ's death, the veil in the temple was split in two from top to bottom (Matt 27:51).[26] His sacrifice removed the temporary boundary established by the Law of Moses and restored direct access to Yahweh's presence. Notice how the author of Hebrews ties in themes of temple worship and proximal holiness as he calls the early Jewish believers—and by extension, the modern-day Christian—to persevere in faith.

> Therefore, brothers and sisters, since we have confidence to enter the Most Holy Place by the blood of Jesus, by a new and living way opened for us through the curtain, that is, his body, and since we have a great priest over the house of God, let us draw near to God with a sincere heart and with the full assurance that faith brings, having our hearts sprinkled to cleanse us from a guilty conscience and having our bodies washed with pure water. (Hebrews 10:19-22)

The believer's relationship to God has changed dramatically under the New Covenant. The hierarchy of holiness prescribed in the Law of Moses has been fulfilled through Christ and is no longer in effect.

Rebuilding the Temple

What of Torahism's claims regarding the biblical prophecies about rebuilding the temple, as seen in Isaiah, Jeremiah, Ezekiel, Zechariah, and Malachi? Is the temple to be physically rebuilt one day and all its duties and responsibilities under the Torah renewed? A detailed examination of biblical prophecy is beyond the scope of this book. And, truthfully, I have yet to fully develop my eschatological position on the end times. But that won't be necessary in order to gain a sufficient answer to these questions.

Most Torah-keepers agree with orthodox Judaism that the temple is to be rebuilt in Jerusalem and that God will renew the Torah commandments regarding temple services at that time. But as we've seen, a full renewing of the Mosaic temple laws would not make sense under

---

[25] Hebrews 4:16, Ephesians 3:12; 1 John 5:14. Special thanks to Bruce Gore for the insights on the proximal aspect to holiness under the Mosaic Law.
[26] See also Mark 15:38 and Luke 23:45.

Christ. This does not necessarily mean there won't be a new temple built under the New Covenant. There are Jews and Christians who believe the visions of the prophets contain the blueprints of a new physical temple that will be built at the second coming of Christ. Others see these temple prophecies as true but symbolic; they depict the reality of God's presence returning to His people in the Messianic Kingdom, but not necessarily in the form of a physical building. Which, if true, would agree with the book of Revelation, which prophesies, "I did not see a temple in the city, because the Lord God Almighty and the Lamb are its temple" (Rev 21:22).

The biblical prophecies about rebuilding the temple are mysterious and enigmatic, which is why the debate over whether they are literal has been going on for millennia. And it certainly won't be solved here. Whichever position we take must be considered in the context of the whole story of Scripture. New temple or not, we know that God will not renew those Torah temple laws that were fulfilled by the work of Yeshua. Postell, Bar, and Soref note,

> The continuous operation of the tabernacle with its sacrificial system, the Levitical priesthood, the ceremonial washings, etc. (i.e., the Sinai covenant), was specifically designed not to last. And as we meditate on the description of the tabernacle and its significance as found in Scripture for all believers today, its symbolism and built-in limitations are designed to point us to a better high priest, a better sacrifice, and a better temple to which we now have direct access in Yeshua.[27]

Ferguson adds an interesting insight.

> In John 2, Jesus cleansed the temple. Presumably there was anger in the voices that demanded to know his credentials. On what authority did He do this? He answered by a prophetic appeal to His own death and resurrection couched in terms of the destruction and raising again of another temple (John 2:19-22). Could any more daring way have been found to express the old order's inadequacy? To a Jew, the temple was the most important building on earth. To Jesus, however, it was but a shadow, a temporary context for entering the presence of God. Christ was the reality to which such shadows pointed. He was God the Son

---

[27] Postell, Eitan, Soref, *Reading Moses, Seeing Jesus*, Kindle location 1615-1619.

come to 'tabernacle among us' (John 1:14). Jesus Himself is the
new temple.[28]

Summary

When Torahism calls for a return to the old system, it not only turns its
back on what Jesus has accomplished; it rejects the Torah itself, which
ultimately points us to Christ. Under the New Covenant, more than 150
mitzvot of the Law of Moses—those dealing with priests, sacrifices, and
the temple—were fulfilled by Jesus and have come to an end. We no
longer need the Levitical priests to mediate between man and God
because Yeshua is now our High Priest and has opened the way to God.
Blood sacrifices are no longer required for atonement because Yeshua
sacrificed Himself for our sins "once for all." God's presence is not bound
to a physical temple. Instead, we, the body of Christ, are now His temple.

---

[28] Sinclair B. Ferguson, *In Christ Alone: Living the Gospel Centered Life* (Reformation Trust, 2007),
p. 60.

PART FOUR
Historical Claims

15

Christianity Was Corrupted

But as for you, teach what accords with sound doctrine.

TITUS 2:1

I N THE COURSE OF MY PUBLIC DISCUSSIONS with Torah-keeping friends I started seeing some bizarre comments. For example, a woman I will call Mary posted about me, "He's heard the truth. Now it is on him what he will do with it. Either accept it or reject it and go on his merry Roman way." *Roman way?* What was she talking about? Did she think I was Italian? Catholic? I quickly learned it wasn't just Mary saying things like this. Other Torah-keepers offered similar comments.

You're a Roman, lawless Christian who thinks the Roman-rooted religion that the catholic religion started is the true gospel. (Ben G.)

If you want to agree with the Roman emperor and the Greeks and the church fathers and say God and Jesus violated their own prohibitions (given multiple times) that is totally your prerogative. And you would be with roughly two billion people who are doing the same. (Jodie S.)

I have proven repeatedly the Roman Bishops separated from Torah. But it really doesn't matter what I write because you are honestly within your right and free will to practice Romanised Christianity. I refuse to do it. (Isaac T.)

A belief common to most of Torahism is that theological corruption was introduced in the early centuries of the Christian faith, which led to Christianity breaking away from its Jewish roots, and this corruption remains intact to this day. The belief in an ancient, uncorrected theological pollution motivates many Torah-keepers to re-examine Scripture, free from the "false bias" of Christianity. In doing so, they claim to have uncovered what the Bible "really" teaches. And it turns out that what Christians hear on Sunday mornings are false teachings passed down through the centuries.

The theology of Torahism is held by various sects, so there is no single source text that sums up this corruption theory. Therefore, like the creed of general beliefs presented in chapter three, I've compiled a general statement of Torah-keeper's views on historical corruption. The following creed was assembled from multiple sources, so every Torah-keeper may not agree with every point. But it does a good job of capturing the prevailing beliefs within Torahism regarding the corrupted roots of Christianity.

During the first few centuries after Christ, anti-Jewish sentiment was rampant throughout the Roman empire. As a result, many Christians began distancing themselves from practices that might have appeared to be Jewish to avoid persecution. Since the beliefs and practices of the original Christian Church had much in common with the Jews, this rejection of Jewishness led to significant misunderstandings in Christian theology. Some Christians even retained some of their former pagan traditions and began blending those beliefs and practices with their newly acquired faith in Yeshua.

As Christian doctrine formed, the church fathers and leaders began to exert their anti-Jewish influence. Judaism was maligned, and the validity of the Hebrew Scriptures was brought into question. This polluted version of Christian theology crystallized at the Council of Nicaea. This assembly represented a significant shift in the thinking and development of the Christian church as it broke away from the Apostles' teachings. Christian doctrine began to hack away at the Jewish roots of the faith. Theological corruption calcified into creeds and dogma. From there, Christianity continued to grow, brick by brick, like a tower built on a faulty foundation.

Over the centuries, the Christian Church became a monolithic religious and political force that fostered false doctrine and knowingly lied to its followers, keeping them illiterate and in the dark about the truth of Scripture. However, over the past couple of centuries, the worldwide literacy rate has increased dramatically, and the "common man" finally has direct access to read Scripture for himself. He has been discovering the truth about what Scripture says, realizing that modern Christianity is a lie and the Bible teaches something very different from what the contemporary church would have us believe. Thus, the Torah-observant movement is gaining momentum.

This statement is a perfect example of why engaging with Torahism can be a difficult undertaking. Doing so requires a good amount of historical and theological parsing. Many of the claims underlying their theories are correct. But just like doing our sums in arithmetic, one wrong calculation along the way can send the whole equation veering off track. The charges of historical corruption are the "root of the tree," so to speak; the source from which all of Torahism's theology and teachings have grown.[1] Let's examine this corruption theory and see how it aligns with history and Scripture.

Defining what "Jewish" Means

Torahism's theory of corruption starts with the claim that during the first few centuries after Christ, anti-Jewish sentiment was rampant throughout the Roman empire, including among the early Church fathers. Before examining this claim in detail, we need to understand what is meant by the term "Jewish" and consider the unique relationship between Judaism and Christianity.

The word "Jewish" can apply to one's ethnicity or faith, and the two do not always align. Even within the global Jewish community, the majority of Jews say "Jewishness" is determined by multiple factors, including ancestry, culture, and personal perception.[2] There are millions of non-observant Jews in the world today; people of Jewish ancestry who do not practice the Jewish faith. Conversely, many who are not of Jewish

---

[1] You will find a comprehensive, scholarly examination of this issue in my book, *Divergence: Examining Jewish-Christian Relations in the Early Church* (Williamson College Press, 2021).
[2] See *Pew Research 2016*, "A Closer Look at Jewish Identity in Israel and the US" and The *Jerusalem Post*, "Poll Many Israelis see Jewish Identity as Being Self-Identified."

ethnicity have converted to Judaism.[3] So there is a difference between the Jewish *people* and Jewish *theology*.

From a Christian perspective, this has several outworkings. First, mainstream Christianity should affirm that as an ethnic group, Jews are to be loved and valued and are rightly called God's "Chosen People." Yahweh sent our Savior into the world through the Jewish race and the nation of Israel. Indeed, Jesus explicitly declared that "salvation is from the Jews" (John 4:22). Moreover, the apostles and New Testament authors—whom Christians love and revere—were all Jews with the lone exception of Luke. Therefore, Christians must condemn anti-Semitism and the persecution of the Jewish people in the strongest possible terms. Anyone who calls themselves a Christian and attacks, oppresses, or discriminates against Jews is directly disobeying the teachings of their own Jewish Savior, Yeshua HaMashiach.

Second, Christianity can be seen as a continuation or evolution of the Jewish faith from a theological perspective. Our faith did not suddenly begin when Jesus arrived on the scene. He was revealed as far back as the first book of the Torah![4] In fact, all of the Hebrew Bible points toward Christ. Yeshua Himself taught this. "And beginning with Moses and all the Prophets, he explained to them what was said in all the Scriptures concerning himself" (Luke 24:27).[5] The unbroken storyline of the Bible reveals that Jesus fulfilled the Jewish prophecies and Yahweh's promises to Israel. Make no mistake, Christianity stands on the shoulders of the patriarchs of the Jewish faith.

And therein lies the rub. Since the first century, the Jewish faith has been at odds with Christianity on what both sides rightly claim are critical issues. Christians believe that those Jews who rejected Jesus in the first century took a wrong turn. (Or maybe it is more accurate to say they missed the turn and kept going straight.) Modern Judaism teaches that if *Yeshua haNotzri* (Jesus the Nazarene) really existed, He was neither divine nor the Jewish Messiah. Judaism also rejects the New Testament as Holy Scripture. It is in this sense that Judaism as a religious belief system must be rejected, along with any other belief system that denies Jesus and our Scriptures.

Christians must live in the tension of accepting and loving the Jewish people and the Jewish roots of our faith, while at the same time rejecting

---

[3] Notable modern examples of non-Jewish converts to Judaism include Sammy Davis, Jr., Marilyn Monroe, and Ivanka Trump.

[4] See Genesis 3:15, and maybe even Genesis 1:3. See chapter nineteen, "There is No Trinity," for further discussion.

[5] See also Luke 24:44-49; Colossians 2:16-17; Hebrews 10:1-18.

those tenets of Judaism that oppose Yeshua. This is the same posture we adopt for all belief systems and worldviews. We should love Atheists, Muslims, Hindus, Pagans, B'haists, Zoroastrians, and all the rest. But at the same time, we must reject their belief systems where they contradict Yeshua. Maintaining this balance, however, is most difficult with Judaism since we are "brothers from the same Father," so to speak.

Anti-Jewish Sentiment in the Church

As to the allegation of anti-Jewish sentiment leveled by Torahism, sadly, there is truth to this claim. Throughout history, there have been Christians who have persecuted Jews, often on the specious basis that "they killed Jesus." These Christian bigots point to biblical passages where some of the first-century Jewish religious leaders played a role in the crucifixion of Yeshua[6] and conveniently ignore the fact that many other Jews loved and followed Him.[7] The Jewish New Testament authors were not condemning all Jews as a nation or a race.

Sadly, some Christians have twisted these passages into the disparagement of an entire race of people. F. F. Bruce described it as an "indiscriminate anti-Jewish polemic" that mirrored the Greco-Roman pagan attitudes to the Jews.[8] The early church father Augustine wrote, "Jews have been scattered throughout all nations as witnesses to their own sin and to our truth…Scatter them abroad, take away their strength. And bring them down O lord."[9] Even if it is true that the Jewish people were scattered as a punishment for rejecting their own Messiah, it does not merit their persecution or abuse at the hands of Christians. Our Lord taught us to love our enemies and pray for those who persecute us (Matt 5:44). Yet the Jewish rejection of Christ has grievously served as justification for decidedly un-Christian atrocities against the Jewish people, including persecution and murder.[10]

There is no denying Torahism's claims that anti-Semitism has reared its ugly head in the history of the Christian church. However, we cannot accurately judge a belief system based on those who abuse it. And the teachings of Yeshua are diametrically opposed to these sorts of atrocities against any people group. Those who carry out heinous acts like this in

---

[6] Matthew 23:31-33; Mark 11:8, 14:1; Luke 19:47; John 5:18, 7:1, 8:44.
[7] In fact, in the New Testament, we find several instances of these two groups of Jews opposed on this issue: Acts 2:23, 3:13; 1 Thessalonians 2:14-15.
[8] F. F. Bruce, *1 and 2 Thessalonians*, (Zondervan, 1982), p. 45.
[9] Robert Michael, *A History of Catholic Antisemitism: The Dark Side of the Church*, (Palgrave MacMillan, 2008), p. 29.
[10] Stan Meyer, "Why Do Most Jews Not Believe in Jesus?" www.jewsforjesus.org.

the name of Christ are operating in open defiance of His teachings. Nothing in the New Testament advocates violence, much less calls for lesser treatment of the Jewish people. It is not what Jesus taught, nor what the Jewish New Testament authors believed.

> I ask then: Did God reject his people? By no means! I am an Israelite myself, a descendant of Abraham, from the tribe of Benjamin. God did not reject his people, whom he foreknew. (Rom 11:1-2a).

God did not reject the Jewish people, and neither should we. The behavior of those who call themselves Christians yet carry out anti-Semitic atrocities is rightly denounced by Christian and Torahist alike. But the question we want to ask is this. Did this anti-Semitism lead to a corruption of Christian theology? Let's examine a few events in the early church.

Marcion

Marcion of Sinope (85-160) was a controversial figure in early Christianity who can uniquely shed light on the charge of historical corruption leveled by Torahism. His views are precisely the kind of anti-Jewish sentiment that our Torah-keeping friends claim held sway in the early centuries. Marcion believed Jesus was the savior sent by God, but he rejected the God of Israel and the Hebrew Bible. In fact, his study of the Hebrew scriptures led him to conclude that most of the teachings of Yeshua were incompatible with the hostile and aggressive God of the Old Testament.

Marcion believed the Bible refers to two different gods: the benevolent God of love and mercy Jesus proclaimed and the "finite, imperfect, angry Jehovah of the Jews."[11] In his work *Antitheses* (~144), Marcion outlined this contrast, describing the God of the Old Testament as a *Demiurge*—a lesser god who created the physical universe. He considered this deity a harsh Jewish tribal god as severe and unmerciful as his Law. This Old Testament God commanded us to love our neighbor but hate our enemies and taught vengeance, saying, "An eye for an eye, and a tooth for a tooth." By contrast, the Supreme God of the New Testament commands us to love our enemy and "turn the other cheek."[12]

---

[11] Phillip Schaff, *History of the Christian Church, Volume II: Ante-Nicene Christianity. AD 100-325* (Christian Classics Ethereal Library, 1882), p. 300.
[12] Ibid.

Because of the stark contrast he saw between the Old and New Testaments, Marcion concluded that Christianity was wholly unconnected to Judaism. He compiled a version of the Bible that rejected all the books of the Tanakh and included just eleven New Testament books. And even from these, he removed or edited passages that did not align with his theology. For example, Marcion twisted the words of Jesus in Matthew 5:17 to say the exact opposite of what they meant: "I am come not to fulfill the law and the prophets, but to destroy them."[13]

This is precisely the kind of early anti-Jewish sentiment our Torah-keeping friends decry. So how did the Church fathers receive Marcion's anti-Jewish theology? They rejected it as utter heresy! The Church wanted nothing to do with Marcion's corrupt teachings and excommunicated him. In fact, he was opposed with such vigor that when Marcion met Polycarp in Rome and asked, "Dost thou know me?" Polycarp responded, "I know the first-born of Satan."[14]

Marcion's teachings were written against at great length in the early centuries of the Christian faith, most notably Tertullian's five-book commentary *Against Marcion* (~208 CE). A century after that, Constantine ordered the Marcionites' meeting-houses be handed over to the Church and forbid them from worshipping in public or in private.[15] The Church fathers were agreed. Marcion's teachings should be allowed no place in Christian doctrine. Indeed, their urgent desire to set the record straight before Marcion's anti-Jewish heresy spread any further is what hastened the establishment of our biblical canon.

The Council of Nicaea

The Council of Nicaea was an ecumenical church meeting convened by the Roman emperor Constantine in 325 CE. Many Torahists point to this council as "ground zero" for the corruption of Christianity. They claim this is where the various anti-Semitic sentiments and teachings circulating among early Christian leaders solidified into an anti-Jewish doctrine agreed on by the whole Church. This, claims Torahism, is where Christianity officially left the Torah behind.

Some Torah-keepers believe the effort to remove the "Jewishness" from Christian doctrine at this council was motivated by a desire to make it more palatable to Gentile believers. And that the Council of Nicaea is

[13] Schaff, *History of the Christian Church*, p. 300.
[14] Irenaeus, *Against Heresies* (Adv. Haer.) iil.c. 3.
[15] Eusebius, *De Vita Constantini* (Life of Constantine), III. 64.

where the church began to develop the idea that the Jewish scriptures were no longer is valid.[16] One Torahist author describes it this way:

> Believers were taught over 1,700 years ago to forsake their Hebraic roots to take on the mantle of pagan sun god worship through the practice that started in the days of Constantine. This is where the Saturday Sabbath was made illegal and all believers were bound by law to forsake the biblical Sabbaths, Feast Days of the Lord, eating biblically as God outlined in His instruction manual, separating what was clean from what is unclean . . . We cannot be separated out, a Holy nation unto (God), if we are still partaking of the abominations of Babylon.[17]

The detailed historical ins and outs of this council, while fascinating, are outside the scope of our current discussion. What matters as we look back over the centuries is the ultimate outcome of the council. What was decided, and how did it impact the trajectory of Christianity?

The council discussed many issues, including the Sabbath and Easter, which are examined in chapters twelve and seventeen of this book. But their primary focus was the Arian controversy which concerned the deity of Christ. This is what motivated the statement we know today as the *Nicene Creed*. And despite whatever ignoble biases may have existed among the council members, the creed it generated for posterity contains no hint of anti-Jewish sentiment. While there are no statements in the creed that directly affirm the Jewish roots of the Christian faith, there are a few telling acknowledgments. The opening statement clearly references the opening verses of the Torah (Gen 1). And the phrase "in accordance with the Scriptures" is significant because the term *Scripture* as understood by the Council included the entirety of the Hebrew Bible. There is also a reference to the Jewish "Prophets." As Oden explains,

> Nicaea was a milestone not because it presented something new, but because it held to that same faith that had been received directly from the apostles through the Spirit and with minimal perversion."[18]

---

[16] Jim Busch video "Following G-d out of Christianity, Step 1."

[17] Steve Gustine, *What is the Hebrew Roots Movement? A Response to Common Misconceptions* (Steve Gustine, 2013), p. 2.

[18] Oden, "The Faith Once Delivered," p. 39.

And don't miss what is perhaps the most significant historical fact of all on this topic. The Christian canon, as accepted by the early Church fathers and unchallenged at Nicaea, has always included the whole of the Hebrew Bible. If anti-Semitism had risen to the level of removing or reducing the "Jewishness" of the faith, we would expect sections of the Hebrew Bible (if not all of it) to have been edited or left out entirely. But that did not happen. The Christian Old Testament contains the same body of text as the Jewish Tanakh.[19]

Interestingly, Augustine, whose anti-Jewish quote I shared above, was present at several church councils and exerted a decisive influence in including the complete Hebrew Bible as part of the Christian canon.[20] Despite the presence of anti-Jewish sentiment, when it comes to Christian doctrine and the Bible itself, we find little evidence that the church fathers sought to remove the "Jewishness" from the Christian faith.

The People of God

There is one last aspect of Torahism's accusation of corruption to consider. Torah-keepers often accuse mainstream Christians of promoting *replacement theology*.[21] This is a belief that the Christian Church has replaced Israel in God's plan of redemption and, therefore, the Jews are no longer God's chosen people. It claims the promises made to Israel in the Tanakh are (or will be) fulfilled in the Christian church rather than the nation of Israel. Here are a few of the comments I've received from Torahists on this issue.

> The earth will be governed by the Torah! (Isaiah 2:3) And the Torah is what will be taught and kept! (Isaiah 66, Zech 8 and 14). Replacement theology or supersessionism must blatantly abolish the words of the prophets and of Rabbi Yeshua Himself to get around the approaching literal fulfillment of these passages (while Jerusalem's construction cranes are *literally everywhere* across the land of Israel and Jerusalem.) (Jodie S.)

---

[19] The order of books and verse numbers differ, but the text of the Old Testament is the same as the Tanakh.

[20] Schaff, *History of the Christian Church*, p. 324.

[21] Also known as *supersessionism* or *fulfillment theology*.

Why does the church always come up with the same doctrine of "replacement theology"? That is absolutely one of the most evil doctrines of demons out there! (Roger C.)

We receive wonderful benefits, blessings and deliverance from harm that comes to people who obey the Torah! The Torah will be practiced in the 1000-year reign of Messiah according to the prophecies in scripture. Unless you don't believe those scriptures anymore, which is classic replacement theology. (Kim K.)

When it comes to the question "who are God's people?" replacement theology does not reflect a biblical view. Scripture does not teach the Christian Church "replaces" Israel. Rather it says the People of God are no longer defined by their national identity but by their faith in Yeshua. Galatians teaches "it is those of faith who are the sons of Abraham" (Gal 3:7), and, "If you belong to Christ, then you are Abraham's seed, and heirs according to the promise" (Gal 3:29). Ephesians says,

Through the gospel the Gentiles are heirs together with Israel, members together of one body, and sharers together in the promise in Christ Jesus. (Ephesians 3:6)

In the New Testament, Gentile believers are described as having been grafted into the People of God, like wild shoot grafted in among the natural branches of an olive tree, sharing in its nourishing root (Rom 11:11-24). This idea is echoed in Ephesians, where we read,

But now in Christ Jesus you who once were far off (Gentiles) have been brought near by the blood of Christ. For he himself is our peace, who has made us both one (Jews and Gentiles) and has broken down in his flesh the dividing wall of hostility by abolishing the law of commandments expressed in ordinances, that he might create in himself one new man in place of the two, so making peace, and might reconcile us both to God in one body through the cross, thereby killing the hostility . . . For through him we both have access in one Spirit to the Father. (Ephesians 2:13-16, 18)

Under the New Covenant, God's People are "one body," made up of Jews and Gentiles, whom the Bible refers to as the "Israel of God" (Gal 6:16). This doesn't mean that there are no more Jews or Gentiles. But rather that we are "sharers together in the promise in Christ Jesus" (Eph 3:6).

Summary

While Torahism's claims about the existence of anti-Jewish sentiment in the early centuries of the Christian church are true, it did not ultimately corrupt church theology. Indeed, the early church fathers rejected the anti-Jewish theology of heretics like Marcion and agreed that all of the Hebrew Scriptures should be included in the Christian Bible. The final work of the Council of Nicaea, including the Nicene Creed, does not contain anti-Jewish teachings or theology.

16

Why Has No One Realized
This Until Now?

*Life is like riding a bicycle: to keep your
balance you must keep moving.*

ALBERT EINSTEIN

I N A VIDEO PUT OUT BY an organization called *New2Torah*, the winsome host Zachary Bauer explains that one of the most common questions a Torahist hears while sharing their newfound faith with their Christian friends is this: "If what you're saying is true, why, in all these thousands of years, has no one has figured that out?"[1]

This was one of the big questions I had when I first stumbled across Torahism. It appears to be a newer theological movement that claims to have finally discovered the ancient truth that we should still be living under the Law of Moses.[2] Yet there are thousands of brilliant minds— highly educated scholars and thinkers from various cultures and eras, many of whom were fluent in multiple languages, including Hebrew and Greek—who have spent a collective two thousand years studying the same Scriptures and come to the opposite conclusion. Ignatius, Polycarp, Augustine, Anselm, Aquinas, Luther, Calvin, Edwards, Wesley, Chesterton, Spurgeon, Billy Graham, C.S. Lewis, et al. These men were not infallible or flawless by any stretch of the imagination. But they were brilliant thinkers with a passion for God. So why should we believe Torahism over this illustrious panel? Bauer offers two reasons.

---

[1] Zachary Bauer, New2Torah video "The Church Lied to Us."
[2] As discussed in chapter three, Torahism is nothing new. It can be traced back to the earliest days of Christianity.

First is the issue of literacy. Bauer claims that most people throughout history have been illiterate and that literacy rates have grown exponentially over time. The further you go back in time, Bauer says, the less literate people there were. "The biggest reason this hasn't been discovered until now is because just in the last hundred years . . . literacy has gone off the charts."[3]

The worldwide literacy rates have undoubtedly increased in the last century or two. However, "literacy" merely refers to one's ability to read, not their ability to reason. Thus, an increase in global literacy rates does not necessarily correspond to a rise in *biblical literacy*, the ability to read and rightly understand the Bible. An uneducated yet literate reader can understand the basic truths of the Bible. But we wouldn't look to them to develop a comprehensive, biblically accurate theology or discover the myriad cultural, historical, linguistic, philosophical, and theological insights hidden in Scripture. In fact, one could argue that the more literate the world becomes, the more likely errant interpretations of Scripture will pop up. Indeed, an increase in the number of people who can read but are not interested in spending years of their life studying one book seems a fertile environment for errant theology.

That said, even if 99% of the general population were illiterate, it would have little bearing on the state of Christian theology. Christian doctrine was developed by well-trained, highly literate theologians and scholars. This does not guarantee their work is accurate, of course. But it does suggest that Christian theology was not impacted by world literacy rates.

The second reason Bauer says Christians are just now discovering Torah-observance is that we have such easy access to the Bible. He claims the Church kept the written Word from the average believer so they could lie to us. And he has a point. For a period, the Church did try to keep the laity in the dark. It was a power play. They did not want the unwashed masses interpreting Scripture for themselves because they wanted to maintain control. Restricting access to Scripture allowed the Church to fabricate doctrines and amass power and wealth. This led to abuses like collecting indulgences (money) from believers who wanted to get their dead relatives out of purgatory. At that time, the average citizen didn't have access to a Bible and couldn't read one if they did, so they just believed what the Church told them and paid up.

---

[3] Ibid.

The Church Lied to Us

In one sense, Bauer's allegation that the Church lied is a bit kind. At times in history, the Church not only lied but also manipulated, abused, murdered, and exerted enormous amounts of political pressure to keep the masses in the dark. Consider the lengths the Church of England went to in an attempt to keep the written Word of God out of the hands of the common folk.

In the Middle Ages, the Latin Vulgate was the Bible of the Church, and most people in England couldn't read or write Latin. In 1382, John Wycliffe translated the Latin Vulgate Bible into English. His handwritten translation allowed the average person to read the Bible for the first time and led to a public outcry against the clergy. The masses discovered disturbing inconsistencies between the practices and character of their Church leaders and what the Bible taught. In 1526, William Tyndale published the first printed version of the New Testament in English. The masses read the translation voraciously, which, again, caused no small uproar. The Crown began collecting illegal Tyndale New Testaments and burning piles of them in the streets. Which led Cardinal Wolsey to famously proclaim, "No burnt offering could be more pleasing to Almighty God than the burning of a Tyndale New Testament."[4] In the end, the full weight of the Church of England was brought to bear, and God's Word still got out.

The fact is that there have been learned men in every generation since Jesus who have had access to God's Word and could read it in the original Hebrew, Aramaic, and Greek. They studied it intensely, understood what it taught, and knew that the Church had gone astray. This culminated in Martin Luther's 95 Theses and the Reformation. But there were many forerunners of Luther who knew this as well; Nicholas of Lyra, Valla, Erasmus, the Brethren of the Common Life, Savonarola, Hus, Waldo and his Waldensians, Wycliffe, and so on. It is not as if the whole world was in the dark about the truth of Scripture until Torahism arrived on the scene in recent years. In fact, we see from the story of Tyndale that even the "common man" has had access to the Word of God and the ability to read it for more than seven centuries.

Summary

Many Torah-keepers claim that because of the relatively recent increase in global literacy and access to the Bible, believers are finally starting to

---

[4] Ibid.

free themselves from the lies taught by the Christian Church. They are beginning to learn for themselves what Scripture "really" says. But Torahism has been around since the first century when the Apostles and the Holy Spirit roundly rejected it. And although the Church tried to keep the Bible from the "unwashed masses" for a time, they were not ultimately successful. There have been learned men in every generation who have had access to God's Word and understood what it taught. (Hence the Reformation.) The average believer has had access to the Word of God and the ability to read it for centuries. This is why Torahism has never been widely accepted as true. It simply does not align with what Scripture teaches.

17

Christmas & Easter
Are Pagan Holidays

My secret to a happy, stress-free Christmas? I'm Jewish.

UNKNOWN

A VERY COMMON ARGUMENT FROM TORAHISM—in fact, it's
the first argument I heard and was the catalyst for this book—
is that Christmas and Easter are pagan, man-made holidays
and should not be observed. This is an argument that often carries a lot
of emotion. My friend Bob wrote,

> Okay, let's say I'm wrong about *X-mess* being pagan. Why
> wouldn't I just go back to the original feast of the Lord (in this
> case, the Feast of Tabernacles) and celebrate it then? I'll tell you
> why, because tradition is held in higher regard than the truth,
> and that is exactly what was going on in Yeshua's day with the
> Pharisees. That's why Yeshua told them they disregard God's
> word for the traditions of men.
>
> You can't find anywhere in the scriptures where Yeshua, or Paul,
> or any of the disciples celebrated *X-mess*. But I can find them
> keeping the Feast of Tabernacles. Aren't we supposed to strive
> to be like Yeshua and do the things he did and walk in the same
> way he walked? He never walked in the ways of the pagans, he
> kept Yahweh's feasts (holy days)! So thanks, but no thanks! I'll
> stick to what Yeshua kept. Merry pagan X-catholic-*mass* to you.
> (Bob S.)

First, we have to grant Torahism's point that Christmas and Easter are not mandated in the Bible. They are, in fact, man-made holidays established by the church. Torahism correctly points out that at the Council of Nicaea, the Christian church decided not to celebrate Easter on the same day that the Jews celebrated Passover. Which raises the question, why is this a problem?

The Bible certainly forbids keeping the feasts of the pagans (Deut 12:29-31). But it nowhere teaches that we cannot keep man-made holidays of remembrance to God. In fact, Yeshua celebrated a man-made festival not given in the Torah.

> At that time the Feast of Dedication took place at Jerusalem. It was winter, and Jesus was walking in the temple, in the colonnade of Solomon. (John 10:22-23)

The Feast of Dedication, which we know today as Hannukah, is a man-made festival that commemorates an event that occurred centuries long after the Hebrew Bible was completed. Namely, the rededication of the temple in the Maccabean revolt against the Seleucid Empire (167 BCE).

Our Torah-keeping friends will argue that this verse does not expressly say that Jesus *kept* this feast, only that He was walking in the temple in Jerusalem when it occurred. This is a pretty big stretch. Are we to imagine Jesus engaged with his fellow Jews in the temple as they observed the feast but did not celebrate it Himself? Notice He did not rebuke the Jews for keeping a man-made feast. In fact, John treats His attendance as a non-issue, a background fact offered in passing. The apostle makes no effort to distance Jesus from the keeping of a supposed Torah-breaking feast. To what extent Jesus participated in the festival is not mentioned. But unlike the moneychangers in the temple or the Pharisees' hypocritical teachings, Jesus did not oppose the Feast of Dedication.

In truth, formally remembering what God has done for us is a very biblical thing to do. The Hebrew word *zakar* (זכר, to remember) appears over 200 times in Scripture. The practice of remembering saturates the Psalms, is at the heart of the Torah feasts, and is the entire point of celebrating the Last Supper.

> And when he had given thanks, he broke it, and said, "This is my body, which is for you. *Do this in remembrance of me.*" In the same way also he took the cup, after supper, saying, "This cup is

the new covenant in my blood. Do this, as often as you drink it, *in remembrance of me*." (1 Corinthians 11:24-25, *emphasis added*)

So there is nothing wrong with celebrating the birth or resurrection of Yeshua. In fact, I would argue that doing so in a God-honoring way is a very biblical, very *Hebrew* thing to do. The Torah does not mandate many of the feasts that Jews celebrate today, such as *Hanukkah, Purim, Tisha B'Av, Tu Bishvat,* etc. But it is not wrong to celebrate them. The same is true of Christmas and Easter. And since they are not biblically mandated events, there is no "wrong" day to observe them. What is meaningful and God-honoring is that we regularly and intentionally remember and celebrate what He has done for us.

Secular v. Religious

Many Torahists claim that both Christmas and Easter are rooted in paganism. And before we examine those allegations, an important distinction must be made between the religious and secular observance of those holidays. Santa Claus, elves, the Easter bunny, colored eggs, and so on are obviously not part of the biblical story of Jesus' birth and resurrection. These and other cultural traditions are not found in the Bible. And we can be just as opposed to the godless secular versions of these holidays as any Torah-keeper.

However, when placed in their proper context—as man-made, cultural accoutrements to the celebration of world-changing biblical events—these traditions are harmless. In the same way that King Solomon used pagan labor and materials to build a temple to the Lord (1 Kings 5), Christians today can appropriate cultural traditions in their celebration of what Yahweh has done in history. As long as our hearts and minds are focused on our Savior as the reason for the celebration, we are free in Christ to decorate, put up Christmas trees, dye eggs, and so on.

Pagan Roots of Christmas

Torah-keepers who decry the pagan roots of Christmas typically point to the traditions of ancient Rome, especially Saturnalia, the month-long celebration in honor of Saturn, the god of agriculture. Around that same time of year, the Romans also observed a pagan feast honoring the children of Rome called Juvenalia. And on December 25th, many upper-class Romans celebrated the birthday of Mithra, the god of the sun and war.[1] So there is plenty of historical precedent for pagan winter celebrations. The question is how those celebrations relate to the Christian celebration of Christmas.

The date of Jesus' birth is not mentioned in the Bible, but it probably occurred in the spring because shepherds wouldn't likely be herding in the middle of winter. Historians are uncertain how the particular date of December 25th was arrived at for Christmas. Tradition holds that Pope Julius I officially chose the date in an effort to capitalize on the traditions of the pagan Saturnalia festival.[2] By observing Christmas at the same time as traditional winter solstice festivals, the theory goes, church leaders believed the chances would be greater that the celebration of Christ's birth would be widely embraced. And it seems to have worked. By the Middle Ages, Christianity had, for the most part, replaced pagan religions.[3] Does this make Christmas a pagan holiday? There are three reasons I say no.

First, Christians started Christmas as the Feast of the Nativity to celebrate the birth of Jesus Christ. It did not evolve out of pagan celebrations of Mithra or Saturn or any winter gods. In fact, the historical roots of Christmas were decidedly anti-pagan. Second, pagan gods and idols are not worshipped (or even mentioned) during the religious observation of Christmas. Rather, the focal point is God coming to earth to save the world. Churches hold services in which the Christmas story is read aloud from Scripture, Yahweh is glorified through hymns and carols, and the gospel is preached. This is the antithesis of pagan worship. Lastly, pagans do not participate in the religious observation of Christmas nor recognize it as a holiday.

Don't get me wrong. Christmas has certainly (and sadly) been secularized and commercialized. But are Christians today unknowingly participating in pagan rituals when we celebrate Christmas? Absolutely not. What you set your heart and mind on is what you worship. And the Christian celebration of Christmas is focused on the birth of Christ.

Pagan Roots of Easter

Many of the cultural traditions attached to the secular version of Easter can be linked to pagan springtime fertility rituals. And I am not going to defend the secular, commercialized version of Easter. But Torahists

---

[1] "History of Christmas," www.history.com.
[2] New Advent, *Catholic Encyclopedia*, Christmas.
[3] "History of Christmas."

often claim that even the Christian religious observance of the Resurrection has pagan roots. Let's take a look.

Ishtar

Torahists often repeat the popular atheist claim that Easter has its roots in Ishtar because the words are so similar. And there are at least two glaring flaws with this claim. First, the celebration of Christ's Resurrection has not always been called "Easter." In fact, the celebration of the Resurrection began centuries before the English word "Easter" came into existence.[4] Even today, Easter is not called "Easter" everywhere. Most languages refer to the holiday using some form of the word *Pascha*, which comes to us from the Hebrew word for Passover, *Pesach* (פֶּסַח). For example, in Albanian, Easter is called *Pashke*. In Italian, it is *Pasqua*. In French, *Pâques*, in Norwegian, *Påske*, in Spanish, *Pascua*.

Second, the Christian celebration of Easter has no historical connection to Ishtar. Ishtar wasn't a feast or celebration; she was a mythical Mesopotamian deity, a goddess of war and sexual love. Ishtar was the protector of temple prostitutes and the patroness of the alehouse. What does a mythical, Mesopotamian warrior-sex goddess have to do with the resurrection of a historical Jewish man in the first century? The answer, of course, is nothing. Ishtar and Easter do not align in religion, symbols, type, or timeframe.

- The Mesopotamian religion was polytheistic, worshipping several primary gods and thousands of lesser gods. This is the antithesis of the monotheism of Judeo-Christianity.

- Ishtar's symbols were not eggs and bunnies, as Torah-keepers often assert, but rather the lion, the storehouse gate, and the eight-pointed star.

- Ishtar was a goddess (entity, deity). Easter is a feast (celebration, remembrance). There was no ancient "Ishtar" that evolved into Easter.

- Ishtar worship dates to ~3,000 BCE and had almost entirely died out by 400 BCE. The annual commemoration of the resurrection of Yeshua did not begin until at least 500 years later with the early Christian church.

---

[4] No one knows exactly where or how the English word "Easter" was landed on. Most linguists trace its origin back to Old English, which would place it somewhere between AD 500-1100.

The only connection between Ishtar and Easter is that the two words sound similar.

Paganism and Christianity

Other Torahists will claim that the English word *Easter* was derived from *Eostre*, the Anglo-Saxon goddess of spring and fertility; hence the connection with bunnies and eggs, both of which were seen as symbols of fertility. However, bunnies and eggs have nothing to do with the Christian celebration of Easter. In fact, nowhere in Scripture are eggs or bunnies used as symbols of anything. They are just a modern cultural tradition, not a part of the religious observation of Easter. More importantly, Easter has nothing to do with fertility.

This claim about the pagan roots of Easter is based on a superficial understanding of both paganism and Christianity. In the pagan worldview, a spring feast was a repeated annual attempt to appease the gods and goddesses in the hope they would bless the people with an abundant crop of food in the next season. That entire enterprise is foreign to the Christian celebration of Easter in which Christ-followers gather annually to remember and commemorate the Resurrection of Christ. Easter is not a forward-looking event full of hope for agricultural success. It is a remembrance, a look back at the most significant event in human history, when God raised His Son from the dead.

Unlike pagan rites, Christians do not make sacrifices to God in the hope of earning His blessings. It is just the opposite. At Easter, Christians gather to remember the sacrifice God made for us! We celebrate the resurrection of Jesus of Nazareth; the eternal Passover Lamb sacrificed for the sins of the world, Who, three days later, was resurrected, defeating sin and death. Therefore, like Christmas, there are three reasons I say Easter is not a pagan holiday.

First, Christians started Easter to commemorate the resurrection of Christ. It did not evolve from pagan spring or fertility rituals. Its historical motivation is decidedly anti-pagan. Second, pagan gods and idols are not worshipped (or even mentioned) during the Christian observation of Easter. Instead, the focus is on the death and resurrection of Yeshua. Churches hold services in which His passion story is read aloud from Scripture, God is glorified by the singing of hymns, and the Gospel is preached. This is the antithesis of pagan theology. Lastly, pagans may participate in spring fertility rituals, but they do not participate in the Christian observation of Easter, nor even recognize it as a holiday.

Passover and Easter

There is a great deal of confusion and controversy surrounding Passover and Easter in Torahism. It stems from the historical era scholars refer to as "the parting of the ways," which spans the first three centuries of Christianity as it emerged out of Jewish theology and culture. The era began with Jesus' earthly ministry, and the New Testament authors do not shy away from the importance of the Passover to His story.

Yeshua's family made the journey to Jerusalem every year for Passover (Luke 2:41-43). And though Scripture does not explicitly say so, it is reasonable to conclude that, as an obedient Jew who kept the Law perfectly, Jesus continued observing it every year. The feast of Passover was also an essential part of Yeshua's crucifixion narrative. All four Gospels expressly mention it.[5] At the Last Supper, Jesus said, "I have earnestly desired to eat this Passover with you before I suffer" (Luke 22:15).

The book of Acts reveals that Jewish believers in Yeshua continued to observe Passover even after His ascension. But they recognized a new, deeper meaning in the feast, acknowledging Jesus as the ultimate lamb to which it pointed: "Christ our Passover lamb has been sacrificed" (1 Cor 5:7); He is "the Lamb of God, who takes away the sin of the world" (John 1:29); we are redeemed by "the precious blood of Christ, a lamb without blemish or defect" (1 Pet 1:19); those in Him triumph "by the blood of the Lamb" (Rev 12:11).

In the century or so after the temple's destruction, a conflict concerning the date of the Passover feast began to emerge. The Torah declared Passover was to begin on the 14th day of the Jewish month of Nisan.[6] A group of mostly Jewish believers in Jesus called *Quartodecimans* ("fouteenthers") argued that Passover must continue to be observed on 14 Nisan as the Law of Moses required. On the other hand, a growing faction of Christians—largely made up of Gentile believers who, not being under the Mosaic Law, felt no obligation to its calendar—contended that, because Jesus rose on a Sunday, Christians should observe Passover on the Sunday after the Paschal Moon.

As the Church grew and became more Gentile, the conflict over Passover eventually grew to such a state that it was threatening unity and had to be addressed. Enter the Council of Nicaea in 325 CE. In Torah-keeping circles, this assembly is often viewed as the boogeyman of

---

[5] Matthew 26:17; Mark 14:12; Luke 22:15; John 19:14.
[6] Exodus 12:18; Leviticus 23:5.

ancient Christianity. Conspiracy theorists advance many claims: *Nicaea replaced Shabbat with Sunday gatherings! The council invented the Trinity!* Many theories, such as the two just mentioned, are simply untrue. But on the issue of Easter, our Torah-keeping friends are not entirely off-base.

While the council did not determine the specific date the Church should observe Easter, it did decide that all Christians should keep it on the same date. And further, they should keep it on a Sunday, the day the Lord rose from the grave.[7] What was ultimately established at Nicaea was independence from the Jewish calendar for the sake of church-wide uniformity.

Eusebius records a letter from Constantine regarding the Easter decision.[8] In the letter, Constantine takes offense at the religious Jews who denied Jesus and His resurrection. And sadly, he moved beyond a theological disagreement into a disparaging personal opinion of the Jews as a people. His negative comments were damaging and contributed to a shameful rise in anti-Jewish sentiment within the Church over the following centuries. These un-Christ-like sentiments were expressed in the form of Christian attitudes and behavior but, interestingly, had little impact on Christian theology. The entire unedited Jewish Bible remained part of the Christian canon, and Jesus was understood and taught to be the Jewish Messiah it foretold.

However, Passover had begun taking on a new meaning for followers of Yeshua long before Constantine. As early as the second century, the observance of Passover by Gentile Christians began to look dramatically different from the Jewish feast. Yahweh gave Pesach to Israel to commemorate her Exodus out of Egypt. But the focus of the early Christians had naturally shifted to the resurrection of Christ. And while Passover contains a powerful foreshadowing of His sacrifice and death, it says nothing of His Resurrection.

Don't get me wrong. It is no coincidence Jesus celebrated His Last Supper as a Passover Seder. His death and resurrection occurred during the very Pesach holiday that had been foretelling His passion for over a

---

[7] In the centuries following Nicaea, numerous attempts were made at calculating a date for Easter that all of Christendom could affirm. It was not until the early ninth century under Charles the Great that a calculation was unanimously adopted. Schaff & Wace (1997) note, "It is curious that after all the attempts that have been made to get this matter settled, the Church is still separated into East and West—the latter having accepted the Gregorian Calendar from which the Eastern Church, still using the Julian Calendar, differs in being twelve days behind. And even in the West we have succeeded in breaking the spirit of the Nicene decree, for in 1825 the Christian Easter coincided with the Jewish Passover!"

[8] *On the Keeping of Easter*, Found in Eusebius, Vita Const., Lib. iii., 18–20.

millennium. But Passover is not Easter, and we should not conflate the two. Pesach today involves eating unleavened bread and bitter herbs and recounting Israel's deliverance from Egypt. By contrast, the Christian celebration of Easter commemorates the story of Yeshua's glorious victory over sin and death. So, while Torahism may decry celebrating Easter on a date other than 14 Nisan, the decision of the Nicene Council was neither unbiblical nor illogical. As the Gateway Center for Israel notes,

> In modern parlance, Easter and Passover represent two entirely separate holidays and faith traditions, despite their shared origins . . . When Christians collapse both Easter and Communion into Passover, they lose a proper honoring of the uniqueness of all three events, and they also commit the historical error of assuming the Passover Jesus observed is identical to the Passover the Jewish community observes today.[9]

In the end, Scripture does not mandate a celebration of the Resurrection, so being dogmatic on the date of Easter seems neither wise nor profitable. The particular date of observance is far eclipsed by the importance of the event being celebrated. Our focus that time of year should be on the victorious work of Christ, our Messiah, Who walked out of His grave that historical Sunday morning, defeating death and sin and reconciling mankind to God.

Three Days and Three Nights

There is another allegation of corruption popular in Torahism that, in all honesty, I find puzzling. Some Torah-keepers see a deceptive miscalculation regarding the amount of time Jesus spent in the grave. They point to Matthew 12, where the Pharisees and teachers of the Law asked Yeshua for a sign.

> He answered, "A wicked and adulterous generation asks for a sign! But none will be given it except the sign of the prophet Jonah. For as Jonah was three days and three nights in the belly of a huge fish, so the Son of Man will be three days and three nights in the heart of the earth." (Matthew 12:39-40)

---

[9] Gateway Center for Israel, "A Christian Guide to Passover," www.centerforisrael.com/papers/a-christian-guide-to-passover.

When asked for proof that He was the Messiah, Jesus gave just one sign: He would be in the grave for three days and three nights. However, if He died and was buried on a Friday and rose on Sunday—as "Roman-corrupted" theology teaches—He was only in the grave for two days and two nights. Thus, our Torahist friends cry "foul" and argue that something doesn't add up. And I'll be honest. I cannot figure out what this theory supposedly proves. The Bible is clear that He rose on the first day of the week. So, working backwards using the Hebrew calculation of time, a literal "three days and three nights" in the grave would place Jesus' death on a Wednesday. Which would mean what, exactly? Whatever the point, the claim is widespread enough to need addressing.

Pastor Charles Dowell of StraitwayTruth Deliverance Ministries explains that we need to view this issue of "three days" from a Hebrew perspective, remembering that the Bible is an Eastern book written in an Eastern culture. "The Jewish day starts at sundown," he explains. "So Yeshua was actually crucified on a Wednesday afternoon. That way, when Mary went to the tomb before sunrise on the first day of the week, we now have the 'three days and three nights' Yeshua predicted."[10] He has even generated a graphic to explain this theory.

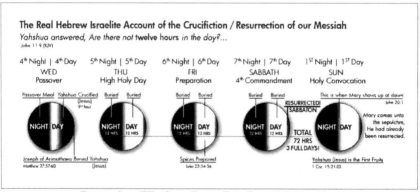

Excerpt from "The Great Easter Fraud" poster designed by Pastor Charles Dowell Jr. and illustrated by Steve Lesperance.

How do we reconcile the apparent discrepancy between the number of days Jesus predicted and the actual amount of days between Good Friday and Easter Sunday? Well, a little Scriptural research shows that this is not a math issue; it is a language issue. In the New Testament, several Hebraic idioms are used interchangeably to refer to the third day. For example,

---

[10] Charles Dowell, *Pagan Holidays*, www.straitwaytruth.com/straitwaytruth-resources.htm.

The next day, the one after Preparation Day, the chief priests and the Pharisees went to Pilate. "Sir," they said, "we remember that while he was still alive that deceiver said, '*After three days* I will rise again.' So give the order for the tomb to be made secure *until the third day*." (Matthew 27:62-63a)

The Jewish officials used the phrases "after three days" and "until the third day" synonymously; they understood them to mean the same thing. Yeshua understood them that way, as well. Consider the various ways He worded His predications about rising.

As they were gathering in Galilee, Jesus said to them, "The Son of Man is about to be delivered into the hands of men, and they will kill him, and he will be raised *on the third day*." And they were greatly distressed. (Matthew 17:22-23, *emphasis added*)[11]

Jesus answered them, "Destroy this temple, and *in three days* I will raise it up." The Jews then said, "It has taken forty-six years to build this temple, and will you raise it up *in three days*?" But he was speaking about the temple of his body. (John 2:19-21, *emphasis added*)

And he began to teach them that the Son of Man must suffer many things and be rejected by the elders and the chief priests and the scribes and be killed, and *after three days* rise again. (Mark 8:31, *emphasis added*)

Jesus used four different phrases to describe the same length of time: "three days and three nights," "on the third day," "in three days," and "after three days." A broader survey of the New Testament reveals a wealth of references to Yeshua's resurrection occurring "on the third day" and "in three days."[12] How are we to explain these discrepancies? Were the New Testament writers confused? Was Jesus continually changing His mind? Surely not!

In modern English these phrases indicate different lengths of time. But in first-century Hebrew categories, they were idioms that could be used interchangeably to refer to the same amount of time. And interestingly, of all the phrases Jesus used, the one our Torah-keeping

---

[11] See also Matthew 16:21, 20:18-19.
[12] Matthew 26:61, 27:40; Mark 8:31, 9:31, 10:34, 14:58, 15:29; Luke 9:22, 13:32, 18:33, 24:7, 24:21, 24:46; John 2:19-20; Acts 10:40; 1 Corinthians 15:4.

friends hang their hat on—"three days and three nights"—is the only one He used just once. And He chose that phrase because, in that instance, he was quoting directly from the Tanakh: "And Jonah was in the belly of the fish three days and three nights" (Jonah 1:17b).

If Torahism wants to press for a literal interpretation of "three days and three nights," which is only found in Matthew 12:40, they have their work cut out for them. Because in eighteen other verses, Jesus referred to His time in the grave using phrases that, if taken literally, contradict Matthew 12:40.[13] Which brings us back to the original question: what is the point of this Torah-keeping claim?

Yeshua Rose on Shabbat

Another common claim from our Torah-keeping friends is that Jesus rose from the dead on the Sabbath, but his tomb wasn't discovered empty until the next day.

> Brother, I keep showing you scripture after scripture. Yeshua was gone from the tomb on Sunday. Meaning he already arose on the Sabbath. These are Yah's sacred times. (Jay M.)

Jay is correct, of course, that the tomb was found empty on the first day of the week. All four Gospels confirm this.

> Now after the Sabbath, toward the dawn of the first day of the week, Mary Magdalene and the other Mary went to see the tomb. (Matthew 28:1).

> And very early on the first day of the week, when the sun had risen, they went to the tomb. (Mark 16:2)

> But on the first day of the week, at early dawn, they went to the tomb, taking the spices they had prepared. (Luke 24:1)

> Now on the first day of the week Mary Magdalene came to the tomb early, while it was still dark, and saw that the stone had been taken away from the tomb. (John 20:1)

The Bible says the tomb was discovered empty after Shabbat, early on a Sunday morning. But does it offer any reason to think Jesus had

---

[13] Matthew 16:21, 17:23, 20:19, 26:61, 27:40, 27:63; Mark 8:31, 9:31, 10:34, 14:58, 15:29; Luke 9:22, 13:32, 18:33, 24:7, 24:46; John 2:19-20.

actually been raised from the dead the previous day? Not even a hint. If Yeshua rose on Shabbat but wasn't discovered until the next day, it would introduce a great deal of confusion into His prophecies about rising again. For example, Jesus told His disciples,

> The Son of Man must suffer many things and be rejected by the elders and chief priests and scribes, and be killed, and on the third day be raised. (Luke 9:22)[14]

When Yeshua spoke of being raised "on the third day," was He referring to the day He would rise or the day His disciples would *learn* that He had risen? If He was raised on Shabbat, and that was the third day, then His followers did not learn of it until the fourth day. And the New Testament says nothing about a fourth day. In fact, the apostle Peter expressly teaches that Jesus was raised on the third day.

> They put him to death by hanging him on a tree, but God raised him *on the third day* and made him to appear, not to all the people but to us who had been chosen by God as witnesses, who ate and drank with him after he rose from the dead. (Acts 10:39-41, *emphasis added*)

Alternately, if "the third day" was intended to refer to the day Jesus would be discovered alive, He was actually resurrected on the second day. And the New Testament says nothing about a second day, either. In fact, it says,

> From that time Jesus began to show his disciples that he must go to Jerusalem and suffer many things from the elders and chief priests and scribes, and be killed, and *on the third day* be raised. (Matthew 16:21, *emphasis added*)

This brings us to the larger point of the Torahist objection regarding "three days." Torah-keepers raise the "three days" problem in the context of the Easter/Passover debate. But exactly what they are trying to prove or disprove with this argument is unclear. Even if we were to agree that Jesus was crucified on a Wednesday instead of a Friday, it would have no bearing on whether He was raised from the dead on the first day of the week or if Christians should celebrate His resurrection on Easter Sunday.

---

[14] See also Matthew 16:21, 17:23, 20:19; Mark 8:31; Luke 18:33, 24:7, 24:46; Acts 10:40; 1 Corinthians 15:4.

Summary

Torahism is correct that Christmas and Easter are man-made holidays not mandated in Scripture. But there is nothing wrong with man-made remembrances of God moving among His people. Jesus observed the man-made Feast of Dedication. Historically speaking, the motivation for the Christian holidays of Christmas and Easter was the commemoration of the work of Christ, not pagan gods or rituals. The Christian version of these holidays includes reading Scripture, remembering what Jesus did for us, and praising the One True God. On these holidays, Christians are not worshipping nature or the earth but the Creator of nature and earth. This makes these holidays decidedly anti-pagan celebrations. What's more, pagans do not participate in the religious observation of Christmas or Easter, nor even recognize them as holidays in their religion.

PART FIVE

Claims About God & Salvation

18

Yeshua Was Not Divine

*The master said: Jesus the Nazarene practiced
magic and deceived and led Israel astray.*

TALMUD

O N THE CONTINUUM OF BELIEFS ABOUT JESUS, from Judaism
to Christianity, Torahism holds a unique position. On one end
of the spectrum is Judaism, which rejects Yeshua as both
Messiah and God incarnate. The Orthodox Jewish view says,

> Assuming he existed, and assuming that the Christian scriptures
> are accurate in describing him (both of which are debatable), he
> simply did not fulfill the mission of the Mashiach as Jews have
> always understood it."[1]

On the other end of the continuum is Christianity and Messianic
Judaism, which proclaim Jesus as Savior, Messiah, and God incarnate.
Torahism falls somewhere in the middle, depending on who you ask.
The majority of Torah-keeping Christians accept Jesus as divine.
However, there are Torahists on the extreme end of the belief system
who deny His deity, and in this chapter, we will deal with their claims.

As evidence, divinity-denying Torahists typically point to the many
New Testament passages in which Jesus submits to—and is seen as
separate from—the Father. In these verses, He directs others to the
Father, speaks to the Father, and prays to the Father, not Himself. For
instance,

---

[1] *Mechon Mamre*, "Mashiach," www.mechon-mamre.org.

- Jesus answered, "My teaching is not my own. It comes from the one who sent me." (John 7:16)
- Not everyone who says to me, "Lord, Lord," will enter the kingdom of heaven, but only the one who does the will of my Father who is in heaven. (Matthew 7:21)
- For I did not speak on my own, but the Father who sent me commanded me to say all that I have spoken. (John 12:49)
- By myself I can do nothing; I judge only as I hear, and my judgment is just, for I seek not to please myself but him who sent me. (John 5:30)
- So Jesus said, "I do nothing on my own but speak just what the Father has taught me." (John 8:28b)

Torah-keepers who hold this position will invariably challenge us to find any verse where Jesus says, "I am God" or "Worship me."[2]

Can you show me any place in the Bible where Yeshua said to worship him? He always said to worship the Father! He said he is the door to the Father, so why do Christians stop and worship the door that gets them to the Father?! (Rocky S.)

Where did Yeshua ever refer to Himself as God? He always pointed to the Father, spoke to the Father, prayed to the Father, not Himself. (John H.)

Based on arguments like this, they reason that worshipping Jesus, a mere human being, is the height of idolatry and a grievous sin. And we have to agree that Jesus is separate from and submissive to His Father. But we can't stop there and ignore the rest of what Scripture teaches. To do so would be to commit the fallacy of cherry-picking on which Torahists claim modern Christianity is built. To truly understand who Yeshua is, we have to look at what the entirety of Scripture says about Him.

Scriptural Data

While the specific phrases our Torahist friends ask to see are not found in Scripture, the presentation of Jesus as divine is unavoidable. In fact, one would have to work pretty hard to miss the many ways Scripture

[2] This is a standard line of argumentation used by atheists and Muslims to undermine Yeshua's divinity.

asserts His divinity. Yeshua's deity is the foundational belief from which the New Testament authors wrote, and it is the only way to make sense of His own words. Frame puts it this way,

> The deity of Christ . . . is not to be found only in a handful of controversial verses. It is found in one way or another on nearly every page of the New Testament. Even a book-length treatment is scarcely sufficient to do justice to the evidence. Christians do injustice to the subject when they focus exclusively on the relatively few (but very significant) passages in the New Testament where Jesus is called *theos*, "God." These passages are only the tip of the iceberg . . . The doctrines of the deity of Christ and the deity of the Spirit were not controversial among first-century Christians. The New Testament writers rarely, if ever, try to prove them. But they mention and imply them again and again. They presuppose them—and, as Cornelius Van Til used to say . . . presupposition is often the best proof.[3]

The divinity of Yeshua is a consistent thread not just in the Gospels and the New Testament, but throughout the entire Bible. Consider how the Torah would answer the following questions.

- Who has all authority in heaven?
- Who has no beginning or end?
- Whose words represent the foundation of life?
- Through Whom were all things made?
- Whose name is I AM?
- Who is able to inaugurate God's covenants?
- Who can bring salvation to mankind?
- Who has the right to pass judgment on humanity?
- Who determines who will enter the kingdom of heaven?
- Who is able to fulfill God's promises?
- Who can inaugurate the Kingdom of God?
- Who has the authority to offer the full forgiveness of sins?

The answer to all of these questions, of course, is Yahweh. God alone can do these things. On that point, we find agreement between Jews, Torahists, and Christians alike. Yet, we see Yeshua doing all these divine, God-only things in the New Testament. How can that be? A

---

[3] Frame, *The Doctrine of God*, p. 654.

mere human could not do them. Either the New Testament is full of false teachings and therefore not the Word of God, or Jesus is God incarnate. Consider the following Scriptural evidence.

Yeshua's God-only attributes and activities	Scriptural Sources
Jesus was given all authority in heaven and on earth	Matthew 11:27, 28:18; John 17:2; Ephesians 1:22-23; Colossians 2:10; 1 Peter 3:22; John 3:35; Philippians 2:10
Jesus has no beginning or end	Matthew 28:20; John 1:1, 8:58, 17:5; Hebrews 7:3, 7:16, 7:24, 13:8; Colossians 1:17; Revelation 1:8, 1:17
Jesus' words represent the foundation of life	Matthew 7:24, 11:28-29; John 8:31-32
Through Jesus all things were made	John 1:3; Colossians 1:16; 1 Corinthians 8:6; Hebrews 2:10
Jesus claims the title "I AM"	John 8:58. (See also John 4:26, 6:35, 9:5, 10:7, 11:25, 13:13, 14:6, 15:1; Revelation 1:8.)
Jesus inaugurated God's New Covenant	Jeremiah 31:31-34; Matthew 26:28; Mark 14:24; Luke 22:20; 1 Corinthians 11:25; 2 Corinthians 3:6; Hebrews 7:22; 8:6, 9:15, 12:24, 13:20
Jesus brings salvation to mankind	Matthew 19:29; John 3:16-18, 6:47; Romans 10:9; 2 Corinthians 5:21; Acts 4:12, 16:30-31; Hebrews 7:2
Jesus judges man and decides who will enter the kingdom of heaven	Matthew 25:31-31; John 5:22, 27, 30, 8:16; Acts 17:31; Romans 2:16
Jesus fulfilled God's promises	Genesis 3:15, 15:1-15; Deuteronomy 18:15-18; Isaiah 9; Jeremiah 31:31-34

Yeshua's God-only attributes and activities	Scriptural Sources
Jesus inaugurated the Kingdom of God	Mark 1:15, 4:11, 9:1, 12:34; Luke 4:43, 8:1, 10, 16:16, 17:21; John 3:3 Acts 8:12
Jesus offered the full forgiveness of sins	Matthew 9:1-8; Mark 2:1-12

Jesus' Self Identity

In addition to these God-only attributes and abilities, we can also look to Yeshua's own words as evidence of His deity. Many of His sayings and teachings only make sense if spoken by someone divine. For example, during His Sermon on the Mount, Jesus said, "Blessed are you when people insult you, persecute you and falsely say all kinds of evil against you because of me" (Matt 5:11). If a mere man told his Jewish followers they would be blessed by God for being persecuted "because of me," they would have been stoned to death as a false prophet! The Old Testament prophets taught nothing of the sort. They always pointed away from themselves and toward God in reverence and fear.

Yeshua also said He was the bread of life (John 6:35), the light of the world (John 8:12), the resurrection (John 11:25-26), the way, the truth, and the life (John 14:6), and greater than the temple (Matt 12:6). And He made many enigmatic, divine claims such as, "No one comes to the Father except through Me" (John 14:6), "without Me you can do nothing" (John 15:5), and "whoever lives and believes in Me shall never die" (John 11:26). He also taught, "I, when I am lifted up from the earth, will draw all people to myself" (John 12:32). Teachings like this from the mouth of a mere human prophet would render them either a charlatan or a lunatic.

Follow Me

Another staple of Yeshua's earthly ministry was His commands for people to follow Him.[4] A merely human prophet or teacher would teach his hearers to follow *God*, not "follow me." For example, when the young man asked Jesus, "Teacher, what good thing must I do to get eternal life?" His ultimate answer was,

[4] Matthew 4:19, 16:24, 19:28; Mark 1:17, 10:21; Luke 5:27, 18:22; John 1:43, 8:12, 21:19.

If you want to be perfect, go, sell your possessions and give to the poor, and you will have treasure in heaven. Then come, follow me. (Matthew 19:21)[5]

Yeshua did not tell the man that to be perfect he should keep the Torah. He said, "follow me." And not just follow Him, but Jesus demanded that we be willing to lose everything to follow Him. His teaching in Luke 14:25-33 is about counting the cost of being His disciple. He requires us to put loyalty to Him above loyalty to our own families (a huge issue in first-century Middle Eastern culture) and "take up our cross" and follow Him.[6]

The Great Commission

Yeshua's presupposition of divinity is also apparent in the following passage in Matthew.

Now the eleven disciples went to Galilee, to the mountain to which Jesus had directed them. And when they saw him they worshiped him, but some doubted. And Jesus came and said to them, "All authority in heaven and on earth has been given to me. Go therefore and make disciples of all nations, baptizing them in the name of the Father and of the Son and of the Holy Spirit, teaching them to observe all that I have commanded you. And behold, I am with you always, to the end of the age." (Matthew 28:16-20)

There are at least seven ways Jesus presupposes His own divinity in this short passage. (1.) His disciples worshiped Him and He did not rebuke them for the idolatry of worshipping someone other than God, (2.) He claimed all authority in heaven and earth was His, (3.) He commanded new disciples to be baptized in *His* name rather than God's name, (4.) He made Himself (the Son) equal to the Father and the Holy Spirit, (5.) He said that new disciples must be taught to obey *His* commandments rather than God or the Torah, (6.) He spoke as if the things He taught His disciples were "commandments," not merely the teachings of a human rabbi, and (7.) He claimed to be omnipresent and everlasting.

---

[5] Matthew 19:21; Luke 18:22.
[6] Matthew 16:24; Luke 14:27.

Can you imagine the same things being said by a mere human being? To illustrate the absurdity, imagine the same passage written about a fellow named Gary.

Gary's eleven disciples went to Galilee, and when they saw Gary, they worshiped him. Then Gary came to them and said, "All authority in heaven and on earth has been given to me. Therefore, go and make disciples of all nations, baptizing them in the name of the Father and of Gary and of the Holy Spirit." Then Gary taught them to obey everything he had commanded them. And he told them that surely Gary will be with them always, to the very end of the age.

The truth is that Jesus said and did so many things that only God can say and do that the Pharisees and the teachers of Law wanted to kill him for it.

For this reason, they tried all the more to kill him; not only was he breaking the Sabbath, but he was even calling God his own Father, making himself equal with God. (John 5:18)[7]

Notice that in the many New Testament passages cited above, Yeshua never uttered the phrase "I am God" nor expressly taught His divinity. He simply assumed divine status and behaved and spoke accordingly. If Jesus is not God, His own words cast Him as a deranged cult leader on par with Jim Jones or Charles Manson. We could only consider Yeshua's teachings pure and admirable if He indeed were divine. As C.S. Lewis famously wrote,

I am trying here to prevent anyone saying the really foolish thing that people often say about Him: I'm ready to accept Jesus as a great moral teacher, but I don't accept his claim to be God. That is the one thing we must not say. A man who was merely a man and said the sort of things Jesus said would not be a great moral teacher. He would either be a lunatic — on the level with the man who says he is a poached egg — or else he would be the Devil of Hell. You must make your choice. Either this man was, and is, the Son of God, or else a madman or something worse. You can shut him up for a fool, you can spit at him and kill him as a demon or you can fall at his feet and call him Lord and God,

---

[7] Also see Matthew 26:4; Mark 11:18, 14:1; Luke 19:47; John 7:1.

but let us not come with any patronizing nonsense about his being a great human teacher. He has not left that open to us. He did not intend to.[8]

There is much more to say regarding the Scriptural evidence for the divinity of Jesus. We could point to the divine titles used for Him in the New Testament.[9] We could examine the New Testament passages that directly identify Yeshua as God.[10] We could look at the many salutations of the New Testament epistles, which refer to Jesus as equal to God. However, such an exhaustive exploration of His divinity is beyond the scope of this book, and the point has been made.

The New Testament authors plainly taught that Yeshua was divine. The only logically consistent way to deny the deity of Christ would be to deny the New Testament, which Judaism does. On the other hand, if we accept the New Testament as the inspired Word of God (as Torahism does), it is absurd to deny the deity of Jesus. Without His divinity, we're left with nothing more than Lewis' madman.

Also a Man

Yeshua was divine, and yet, at the same time, He was also a human man. He slept,[11] ate and drank,[12] wept,[13] suffered physical death,[14] and so on. This is another area where Torahists who deny the deity of Christ borrow atheist arguments. They claim Jesus could not have been God because God does not get tired or hungry or thirsty, and God cannot be killed. Some will even share mocking memes—such as a picture of Yeshua praying with the text, "Are you there, dad? It's me, you." My friend Bob challenged, "If Yeshua was God, why did he not know some things, like when he told his disciples that only the Father knows the hour?"

This is a valid line of questioning. The idea that Jesus had two natures—one human, one divine—is a mystery, to be sure. But it is not a contradiction, and further, it is precisely what Scripture teaches.

---

[8] C. S. Lewis, *Mere Christianity* (HarperCollins, 1952, 1980), p. 52.

[9] Divine titles used for Yeshua in Scripture include Son of God, Son of Man, Christ, Messiah, Savior, Holy One, Redeemer, The Alpha and the Omega, Righteous One, and more.

[10] These include the Greek phrases *theos*, *morphē theou*, and *theotēs*. See Frame, *Doctrine of God*, p. 672.

[11] Mark 4:38; 8:24.

[12] Matthew 9:10; Luke 7:34.

[13] John 11:35.

[14] Matthew 27:50; Mark 15:37; Luke 23:46; John 19:30.

Yeshua is God who became flesh and dwelled among us.[15] He has existed eternally,[16] and yet He was also born of a woman.[17]

The Bible does not say how this is possible, other than that it was God's will. Our finite human minds are left to ponder the riddle. It is one of the many miracles of God testified to in Scripture, but it is far from the biggest. The Torah opens with the greatest miracle of all: "In the beginning, God created the heavens and the earth" (Gen 1:1). Ancient Hebrew did not have a word for "universe." They used the phrase "the heavens and the earth" to mean everything that exists. If we accept the miracle that Yahweh created literally everything that exists— all matter, space, time, and life itself—out of literally nothing, then all the other miracles in the Bible are child's play for Him. While we may never know exactly *how* Jesus could have both divine and human natures, the author of Hebrews helps us understand *why*.

> Since the children have flesh and blood, he too shared in their humanity so that by his death he might break the power of him who holds the power of death—that is, the devil—and free those who all their lives were held in slavery by their fear of death. (Hebrews 2:14-15)

While the idea of "God incarnate" is a difficult concept to get our minds around, determining whether it is true is a simple matter of deciding if you believe the Bible. Like Yeshua's divinity, if we accept the New Testament as the inspired Word of God, we have no other choice than to accept that He had two natures.

Summary

While specific phrases like "I am God" or "worship Me" are not uttered by Jesus, the teaching that He is divine cannot be avoided. Yeshua does things that only God can do, such as creating the universe, determining who will enter Heaven, and fulfilling God's promises. He self-identifies as divine by claiming to be the Bread of Life, the Way, the Truth, the Life, and the Light of the World. He also repeatedly taught His disciples to "follow Me" (rather than follow God) and accepted their worship without protest. Jesus said and did so many things that only God is supposed to say and do that the Pharisees and the teachers of Law

---

[15] John 1:14; Romans 1:3, 8:3; 1 Timothy 3:16; Colossians 1:15; Hebrews 1:2-3.

[16] John 1:1-3, 8:56; 1 John 1:1-2; 1 Corinthians 8:6; Colossians 1:16; Hebrews 2:10.

[17] Isaiah 7:14, 9:6; Matthew 1:18; Luke 1:35; Galatians 4:4.

wanted to kill Him for it. If Yeshua is not God, His own words reduce Him to nothing more than a cult leader on par with Jim Jones or Charles Manson.

19

There Is No Trinity

Hear, O Israel: The Lord our God, the Lord is one.

DETERONOMY 6:4

B OTH JUDAISM AND TORAHISM TEACH there is one God, the
Lord, Yahweh.[1] Christians believe the same thing.[2] Even the
demons believe "God is one," and they shudder (James 2:19).
So what is the issue? Those Torah-keepers who deny the divinity of
Christ naturally also reject the Trinity. In the words of my friend Rocky,
they believe "the Trinity doctrine is a corrupt, Romanized theology."
Although the majority of Torah-keeping Christians accept the Trinity,
there are enough who reject it that we need to spend a short chapter
refuting their claims.

I will be honest. The Trinity is a concept I have trouble fully
understanding. It is taught in Scripture and is a logically coherent
concept, so I accept it as true. But, like the dual natures of Yeshua, how
it is possible is a mystery. And I don't think we should be surprised that
an infinite creator God who spoke the very universe into being is an
entity our finite human minds cannot completely comprehend. The best
and brightest scientists of our age cannot figure out how gravity works
or how wild animals know precisely where to go every year when they
migrate across hundreds of miles. So how can we expect to understand
everything about God, the Creator of gravity and migratory animals?

The word trinity means "tri-unity," and it is not a word you will find
in the Bible. However, the concept of the Trinity is taught in many
passages. It is something God revealed progressively over time. While

---

[1] Deuteronomy 6:4; Zechariah 14:9.
[2] Mark 12:29; 1 Corinthians 8:6.

the Trinity does not come into full focus until the advent of Jesus, it's hinted at in various ways throughout the Torah. In fact, one could argue that we get a glimpse of the Trinity in the opening verses of the very first book.

> Now the earth was formless and empty, darkness was over the surface of the deep, and the Spirit of God was hovering over the waters. And God said, "Let there be light," and there was light. (Gen 1:2-3)

This passage suggests a plurality in Yahweh. He is the Father speaking and the Holy Spirit hovering over the waters. What about the Son? In John 1, which is patterned after Genesis 1, Jesus (the Son) is the Word through whom all things were made (John 1:1-3). Colossians 1:16 teaches, "For by [Jesus] all things were created, in heaven and on earth, visible and invisible, whether thrones or dominions or rulers or authorities—all things were created through him and for him." So perhaps in this verse in Genesis, when we read the phrase "and God said," we are seeing the Son manifest as the Word of God. This does not prove the Trinity, of course, but it is a compelling picture of the plurality of God.

A few verses later, God says, "Let us make man in our image, after our likeness" (Gen 1:26). Why is this passage written in the plural? One Torahist proposed it is the use of the "royal we." However, there are no instances of a monarch using plural verbs or plural pronouns of himself in all of Old Testament Hebrew.[3] Others have suggested God is speaking of Himself and the angels. However, Scripture does not teach that man was made in the image of angels, nor that angels participated in the creation of man. Something else is at play here. While this verse is a long way from a formal doctrine of the Trinity, it suggests another intriguing picture of it.

There is also the mysterious story in Genesis 18, where three visitors visit Abraham bearing prophetic news. Throughout the passage, the author interchangeably refers to these three visitors using plural pronouns (them, they) and as "Yahweh." In other words, the passage portrays Yahweh appearing to Abraham as three men. Proof of the Trinity? No. Another intriguing picture of the plurality of God? Perhaps.

---

[3] Wayne Grudem, *Systematic Theology, An Introduction to Biblical Doctrine* (Grand Rapids, MI: Zondervan, 1994), p. 227.

Interestingly, some Jewish scholars reluctantly admit that the theological idea of the Trinity can be found in the Hebrew Bible. For example, Benjamin Sommer, a Jewish Professor of Bible and Ancient Semitic Languages at the Jewish Theological Seminary of America, said:

> We Jews for centuries have objected to the Trinity, have labeled it pagan, have said, "Well, it's clear the core of Christianity doesn't come out of the Hebrew Bible, the Tanakh. (Christians) are being disloyal to the Old Testament." Actually, I think that's not true. To my surprise, I came to the conclusion—somewhat to my dismay—that we Jews have no theological right to object to the Trinity . . . Fundamentally the theological model used by Christianity is a model that shows up in our own sacred literature.
>
> If you read some of the church fathers on the story of Abraham and the three visitors, they make a linkage between that story and the doctrine of the Trinity . . . Those three visitors become a harbinger of, a hint at, the later idea of the Trinity . . . And they're really correct that there is a linkage between the theological intuition that's behind the idea of the Trinity and the theological intuition that's behind the story in Genesis 18.[4]

Why Does It Matter?

Why is any of this important? Because to deny any part of the Trinity is to deny a part of Holy Scripture. The doctrine of the Trinity is a foundational teaching of the Bible that has long been held as a litmus test for heresy. Scripture teaches five truths that we must hold in tension. Consider the following small sampling of scriptural data that supports each of these five facts, which are all true at the same time.

Biblical Truths	Scriptural Data
The Father is God	Deuteronomy 32:6; Isaiah 63:16, 64:8; Jeremiah 3:19; Matthew 6:26; Luke 12:30; John 20:17; Romans 15:6; 1 Corinthians 8:6; 2 Corinthians 1:3

---

[4] Benjamin D. Sommer, "The Bodies of God and The World of Ancient Israel," *Lecture Series Video.*

Biblical Truths	Scriptural Data
The Son is God	Matthew 11:27, 28:18, 25:31-33; John 5:22, 27, 30, 8:16, 17:2; Acts 17:31; Romans 2:16; Ephesians 1:22-23; Colossians 2:10; 1 Peter 3:22; Philippians 2:10
The Holy Spirit is God	Mark 3:28-29; Acts 5:3-4, 9:31; Romans 15:30; 1 Corinthians 6:11; Philippians 2:1; Hebrews 10:15-17; Revelation 2:18, 29
The Father, Son and the Holy Spirit are distinct from one another	Matthew 3:16-17, 12:32, 17:5; Luke 3:21-22; John 15:26; Romans 15:19; 2 Corinthians 13:14; Ephesians 2:21-22, 4:4-6; Philippians 3:3; Revelation 1:4-5, 2:7
God is one	Deuteronomy 6:4; Zechariah 14:9; Mark 12:29; 1 Corinthians 8:6; James 2:19

It may be hard for our finite minds to grasp what this entirely means, but the amount of scriptural data supporting each of the five statements above is overwhelming. And they are harmonized logically in the Christian teaching that "God is one in essence, and three in persons." Let's take a brief look at some examples from God's Word.

First, there are many passages in which the Father, Son, and Holy Spirit are mentioned together and share divine status. For example, in Matthew 28:19, Jesus says, "Therefore go and make disciples of all nations, baptizing them in the name of the Father and of the Son and of the Holy Spirit."[5] And He teaches, "But when the Helper comes, whom I will send to you from the Father, the Spirit of truth, who proceeds from the Father, he will bear witness about me" (John 15:26).

Second, if the concept of the Trinity is not true, then many of Yeshua's teachings are rendered illogical. For instance, He tells His disciples: "But the Advocate, the Holy Spirit, whom the Father will send in my name, will teach you all things and will remind you of everything I have said to you" (John 14:26). In this passage, Jesus asserts three

[5] Also see Romans 15:19; 2 Corinthians 13:14; Ephesians 2:21-22, 4:4-6; Philippians 3:3; and Revelations 1:4-5, 2:7.

distinct, divine entities: (1.) The Son tells us that (2.) the Father will send (3.) the Holy Spirit. He did not say, "When I send myself in my own name, I will remind you of everything I said." Our Lord chose His words to indicate that, in addition to Himself, there is Another who will send, and yet Another who will *be* sent. Further, it is clear that each of these three entities or "persons" must be divine based on their functions.

Perhaps the most explicit example is found in Matthew.

> As soon as Jesus was baptized, he went up out of the water. At that moment heaven was opened, and he saw the Spirit of God descending like a dove and alighting on him. And a voice from heaven said, "This is my Son, whom I love; with him I am well pleased." (Matthew 3:16-17)

Again, this passage indicates three distinct persons. The Father speaks from heaven, the Son is baptized on earth, and the Holy Spirit descends from Father to Son. And at the same time, we know that God is one. Without the concept of the Trinity, this passage becomes nonsensical. With the Trinity, it is a beautiful picture of a triune God at work in His universe. It is in these passages (and the many others like them) that we get a clear picture of the New Testament authors who,

> fully endorsed the three key theological strands that would later be woven into a tight doctrinal cord: only one God exists; the Father, Son, and Holy Spirit are three distinct persons; and the title 'God' befits each of them."[6]

The Necessity of the Trinity

When it comes to the Trinity, even more stirring than the mystery of *how* is the majesty of *why*. Zacharias notes,

> There is unity and diversity in the community of the Trinity; there is both majesty and mystery. If God ever says He loves, who was He loving before creation? If God says He speaks, who was He speaking to before creation? Both communication and love are contained in the Godhead right from the beginning . . . It's only in the Christian faith that love precedes life. In every other belief system, life precedes love.[7]

---

[6] John Y. Kwak and Douglas Geivett, "Trinity: A Historical and Theological Analysis."
[7] Ravi Zacharias, "Unity in Diversity, the Majesty & Mystery of the Trinity" video.

The ramifications of this statement are staggering. In non-Christian worldviews—rather than being past-eternal and grounded in God—love is merely a human concept that came about after mankind arrived on the scene. If love did not exist prior to humanity, then God existed without love for a past eternity. And further, humans can define love however they wish. That is not the biblical concept of love.

> Dear friends, let us love one another, for love comes from God. Everyone who loves has been born of God and knows God. Whoever does not love does not know God, because God is love . . . And so we know and rely on the love God has for us. God is love. Whoever lives in love lives in God, and God in them. (1 John 4:7-8, 16)

Scripture teaches that God is eternal, and God is love. Therefore, love is eternal. Said another way, God has always existed, so love has always existed. However, love can only exist in a relationship between persons. Thus, for love to be past-eternal, there must be past-eternal persons in a relationship. The Christian doctrine of the Trinity says that love has existed eternally in the triune relationship within the Godhead.

Moreover, God made mankind in His image,[8] which is why we hunger for relationships and love. The core of what it means to be human is to be in relationship with others. Yahweh, the triune God, modeled that before Creation, and He models it for us in the pages of Scripture. Coleman puts it this way:

> Looking through John 5:19-27; 16:13-15 is just fascinating. The Father entrusts all things to the Son: his authority, his power over life and judgment. But the Son will not do anything by himself; he will only do what he sees the Father doing. The Spirit will not speak of himself nor seek his own glory. He will bring glory to Jesus by taking what belongs to Jesus and showing it to us. Three self-giving, self-effacing persons constitute the amazing God whom Christians worship![9]

This is what those Torah-keepers who deny the Trinity turn their backs on. They deny the very nature of God and undermine the true, biblical meaning of love.

---

[8] Genesis 1:26-27, 9:6; 1 Corinthians 11:7.
[9] R. G. Coleman, "Is 'Trinity' an Unwarranted Complication on the Christian Message?", *SimplyChrist Ministries.*

Summary

A minority of Torah-keepers deny the Trinity, which is an overtly heretical position to take. Although it is hard for our finite minds to grasp what it fully means, the amount of scriptural data supporting the concept of a triune God is overwhelming. The only logically coherent way to deny the Trinity is to deny the New Testament, which Judaism does. But if we accept the New Testament as the inspired Word of God, as Torahism does, it becomes incoherent to deny the Trinity. Those who deny the triune God deny the complete nature of God and undermine the true, biblical meaning of love.

20

Salvation & the Torah

I will never forget your precepts,
for by them you have given me life.

PSALM 119:93

A S MUCH AS I ENJOY THE THEOLOGICAL DETAILS of our
discussion about Torahism, the question that matters, in the
end, is "How are we saved?" And on this issue, there seems to
be some disagreement within Torahism. The majority of Torah-keepers
profess the biblical position that salvation comes through faith in Christ
alone, not keeping the Law of Moses.

> For it is by grace you have been saved, through faith—and this
> is not from yourselves, it is the gift of God—not by works, so
> that no one can boast. (Ephesians 2:8-9)

Scripture is clear. We are saved by faith, not works. This was as true
for ancient Israel as it is for the modern Christian. However, Torah-
keepers who acknowledge this are typically quick to add that, once saved,
we must show our love and obedience by keeping the Mosaic
commandments. Jacob's Tent, a Torah-keeping congregation near me,
puts it this way,

> Salvation is a free gift of God and cannot be earned by keeping
> the commandments. However, we believe that holiness and
> obedience to His Torah is God's standard of living for His
> people. We keep the commandments (Torah) because we have
> been redeemed and desire to walk as Yeshua (Jesus) walked. We

don't keep the commandments in order to be saved; we keep the commandments because we are saved and because we love Him.[1]

This statement sounds biblical. After all, Jesus said, "If you love me, you will keep my commandments" (John 14:15). Christ-followers are not free to live life as a law unto themselves. Jesus gave us commandments. And we follow them not to earn His love but *because* we are loved. Where the Jacob's Tent statement veers off course is in its tacit assumption that the commands Yahweh gave to all Christ-followers through Jesus are the exact same commands He gave exclusively to Israel through Moses. And if you've made it this far in this book, you're aware of the many reasons that is not so.

Problems arise, then, in the way Torahists live out this idea of keeping the Mosaic commands. They often adopt an implicit, perhaps even subconscious, view that Torah-keeping indicates one's salvation. Think of a married man claiming to have come to a saving faith in Christ who is unapologetically living out an adulterous lifestyle as if nothing was wrong. And further, he refuses to change his behavior even after being confronted with Scripture on the issue. Such conduct would bring into question the sincerity of that man's faith. This is how many Torah keepers view Christians who do not "keep Torah." Our decision not to eat kosher or keep Shabbat is viewed as unapologetically living in sin and rebelling against God's Law. It brings into question the sincerity of our saving faith as much as if we were living an openly adulterous lifestyle.

I can't tell you the number of times people have shared with me how they have been chastised and looked down on—and in some cases, suffered verbal or emotional abuse—for not keeping Torah. They are labeled "lawless" and accused of living in sin. Despite whatever verbal claims Torah-keepers make about salvation by faith, this kind of divisive, Pharisaical behavior reveals a works-based understanding of salvation. Again, Christianity does not claim to be without laws or commandments. It's just that, because of the work of Christ, the Law of God is fulfilled in a different way under the New Covenant.

For the one who loves another has fulfilled the law . . . Love does no wrong to a neighbor; therefore love is the fulfilling of the law. (Romans 13:8, 10)

---

[1] Bill Cloud, "We Believe" statement, JacobsTent.org.

For the whole law is fulfilled in one word: "You shall love your neighbor as yourself." (Galatians 5:14)

Bear one another's burdens, and so fulfill the law of Christ. (Galatians 6:2)

If you really fulfill the royal law according to the Scripture, "You shall love your neighbor as yourself." (James 2:8)[2]

Salvation Comes from Keeping Torah
While the majority of Torahism agrees that salvation comes through faith in Jesus, there is a faction that has adopted a view of salvation similar to what Judaism teaches today. Helyer explains,

> For Judaism, there is no human failing, with a collective or individual, that requires special divine intervention and that cannot be remedied with the guidance of Torah. Salvation consists of faithful, though not perfect, adherence to the mitzvoth. God in his mercy forgives those whose intentions are upright. The New Testament, however, unambiguously proclaims the finale of Jesus Christ. He is God's last word to sinners (Hebrews 1:1-3), The Word who became flesh, dwelt among us, and reveals the father to sinners (John 1:1-18). By his atoning death on the cross, he draws all people unto himself (John 3:16, 6:35-40, 12:32).[3]

Given that traditional Judaism rejects the New Testament and Jesus as Messiah, it naturally looks to the Torah for a remedy for sin. While Christianity disagrees with their position, at least it is logically coherent. Some Torah-keepers, on the other hand, seem to have both feet firmly planted in midair on this issue. They hold the awkward position of accepting the New Testament as the Word of God yet denying the deity of Christ.

> Can someone explain to me why, when the rich ruler asked, "Yeshua, what must I do to have eternal life?" Yeshua didn't tell him, "Just repeat this prayer after me, 'Dear Jesus, come into my heart and be my savior, Amen?'" Look at Yeshua's answer for

---

[2] See chapter nine "Jesus Kept Torah" for more on this issue.
[3] Larry R. Helyer, "How Does the Bible relate to Judaism?", *Apologetics Study Bible*, ed. Ted Cabal (Holman Bible Publishers, 2007), p. 1758.

what he must do to have eternal life and be prepared to have your Christian doctrine rocked. "Teacher, what good deed must I do to have eternal life?" "Why ask me about what is good?" Jesus replied. "There is only One who is good. But to answer your question—if you want to receive eternal life, keep the commandments." That's right, Yeshua said it. Salvation comes from keeping the commandments. (Rocky S.)

Rocky went on to state that there is a difference between redemption and salvation, claiming that the Christian church preaches them as the same thing when they aren't the same at all. He even provided me with definitions of the two words.

redemption: The action of regaining or gaining possession of something in exchange for payment or clearing a debt.

Redemption, Rocky explained, is something Yeshua did when He died for humanity; He cleared a debt. But that isn't the same thing as salvation.

salvation: Preservation or deliverance from harm, ruin, or loss.

According to Rocky, obeying the Torah will keep us safe and deliver us from harm, ruin, and loss. He summed up his theological theory by explaining that redemption comes through Jesus dying on the cross, while salvation comes through obedience to the Torah. He added, "Once you accept Yeshua as the sacrifice for your redemption, then the Bible talks about working out your soul salvation with fear and trembling."

Analyzing the Argument

Like most Torahist claims I encounter, the first thing I did was consult the Bible and a Dictionary to verify Rocky's statements. I looked up the words *redemption* and *salvation* and discovered that, contrary to what Rocky said, these two words mean the same thing when used in the theological sense. They are synonyms. And further, Matthew's description of Jesus' interaction with the young man in Matthew 19 doesn't stop where Rocky left it. He cited only two verses, making it seem as if Yeshua was teaching that salvation is achieved by keeping the Law of Moses. But that is not the case.

In the verses that follow, the rich young man goes on to ask Yeshua which commandments he needs to keep. Jesus lists six specific commandments from the Mosaic Law, which the rich man says he has kept. Does Yeshua then tell the man he did a great job keeping the commandments and he is now saved? No. Does He instruct the man to follow the other 600-plus commands in the Torah? Nope. Jesus, knowing the rich man's heart, gives him additional commands not found in the Torah. He tells the man to sell everything he owns, give to the poor, and "follow Me" (Matt 19:21). This is too much for the rich man who walks away dejected. Afterward, Yeshua reveals the point of the conversation.

> Then Jesus said to his disciples, "Truly I tell you, it is hard for someone who is rich to enter the kingdom of heaven. Again I tell you, it is easier for a camel to go through the eye of a needle than for someone who is rich to enter the kingdom of God." When the disciples heard this, they were greatly astonished and asked, "Who then can be saved?" Jesus looked at them and said, "With man this is impossible, but with God all things are possible." (Matthew 19:23-26)

Yeshua was showing us that the bar of perfect righteousness is so high that no one can become right with God under their own power. Our only hope comes from God Himself. We can be made righteous only through faith in Jesus. He said, "Follow me," not "follow Moses." The author of Hebrews teaches that "the law made nothing perfect" (Heb 7:18). The apostle Paul wrote, "For by works of the law no human being will be justified in his sight since through the law comes knowledge of sin." (Rom 3:20). The apostle Peter proclaimed that Israel has never been able to keep the law or find salvation in it (Acts 15:10). "No! We believe it is through the grace of our Lord Jesus that we are saved" (Acts 15:11). And Romans 4 teaches how Abraham, who died long before the Torah was given, was saved through faith, not through keeping the commandments. If, as Rocky and other Torah-keepers believe, salvation comes from keeping the Mosaic commandments, then Yeshua's work on the cross was a pointless gesture.

Salvation in The Torah

The idea of salvation through faith, not works, is found in the Torah. There we read that Yahweh set His love and favor upon Israel *before* He gave the law. Israel exhibited no qualities or behaviors that caused God to love her. Schreiner explains,

Observing the Ten Commandments did not constitute the basis upon which Israel would gain life. Israel was rescued by the Lord from Egypt and borne upon eagle's wings (Exodus 19:4). Before the Ten Commandments were given, the Lord declared, "I am the Lord your God, who brought you out of the land of Egypt, out of the house of slavery" (Exodus 20:2). The giving of the law followed the salvation of Israel, and hence such obedience signified Israel's grateful response to the redemption accomplished by the Lord.[4]

In other words, Yahweh took the initiative in choosing and saving His people. Israel's favor in the eyes of the Lord was not due to her obedience. Yahweh loved Israel first and then called upon them to respond with faith. At Mount Sinai, He said to Moses, "Behold, I am coming to you in a thick cloud, that the people may hear when I speak with you and may also believe you forever" (Ex 19:9). His purpose for appearing to Moses on Mount Sinai was so that *the people may believe.*

This pattern is repeated in how Christians find salvation in Jesus. Salvation comes first. "But God demonstrates his own love for us in this: While we were still sinners, Christ died for us" (Rom 5:8). And we receive it by faith, which is then manifest in our obedience.[5] Schreiner adds,

> Believers have been redeemed through the work of Christ, and they respond to his saving mercy with grateful obedience. Such grateful obedience, under both the Mosaic covenant and the new covenant established by Jesus Christ, is not legalistic, for there is no idea that such obedience earns or merits salvation under either the old covenant or the new."[6]

The True Purpose of the Torah

Although God expected Israel's faith as the proper response to His redemption, what actually happened was the opposite. Israel responded in unbelief and disobedience. And God was not surprised by it. In fact, even as the Law of Moses was given, God proclaimed that Israel would

---

[4] Tom Schreiner, *40 Questions About Christians and Biblical Law* (Kregel Publications, 2010), p. 26.

[5] John 14:15, 21, 15:10.

[6] Schreiner, *40 Questions*, p. 26.

disobey that Law, break the covenant, and be driven into exile (Deut 31:16-21).[7] Which raises an interesting question.

If Israel's disobedience and exile were assured, what was the point of the Sinai Covenant? According to both Torahism and rabbinic Judaism, that Covenant is kept by obeying its commands, the Law of Moses. However, when you view the Sinai Covenant within God's entire redemptive story, as it unfolds throughout all of Scripture, its true purpose becomes evident. Its intent was not to lead us to the Law, as Torahism teaches, but rather to ultimately lead us *through* the Law to Yeshua.[8] The New Testament—and Yeshua himself—taught that the Messiah was the end goal and fulfillment of the Torah and the Law.[9] So, to rightly keep the Law today is to place our faith in Jesus (John 5:39-47). Jewish authors Postell, Bar, and Soref expound:

> The apostle Paul writes, "For the law brings wrath, but where there is no law there is no transgression" (Rom. 4:15). In 2 Corinthians 3:6–7, he calls the Sinai covenant a "ministry of death." In Romans 10:3–8, Paul speaks of a righteousness based on the Law, which is opposed to a righteousness based on faith. How could Paul make such statements? The answer is straightforward: by meditating on the Torah.[10]

The Torah's theme is utterly messianic, and it consistently points to Yeshua. From the beginning, it anticipates a disobedient and unbelieving Israel and looks ahead to the blessing that will come through the promised Mashiach.[11] The *Complete Jewish Bible* translation says it this way, "For the goal at which the Torah aims is the Messiah, who offers righteousness to everyone who trusts" (Rom 10:4).

Contrary to what Torahism teaches, true Torah observance today is not keeping the Law of Moses but rather believing in Yeshua, who said, "If you believed Moses, you would believe me, for he wrote about me" (John 5:46). Christians, then, are faithful disciples of Moses in the truest sense; fulfilling the requirements of the Law by loving God and loving people.[12]

---

[7] Also see Deuteronomy 4:25–28; 30:1.

[8] A concept introduced in *Reading Moses, Seeing Jesus* by One For Israel.

[9] John 5:39, 8:56; Luke 24:44-49; Romans 10:4-13.

[10] Postell, Eitan, and Soref, *Reading Moses, Seeing Jesus*, Kindle location 253-257.

[11] Genesis 3:15, 49:1; Numbers 24:14; Deuteronomy 31:29.

[12] Matthew 22:37-40; Mark 12:29-31; Luke 10:25-28, 1 John 3:23.

And he said to him, "You shall love the Lord your God with all
your heart and with all your soul and with all your mind. This is
the great and first commandment. And a second is like it: You
shall love your neighbor as yourself. On these two
commandments depend all the Law and the Prophets. (Matt
22:37-40)

Summary

A minority of Torahists subscribe to the view that salvation is achieved
through the keeping of the Mosaic commands. But both the Old and
New Testaments clearly teach that obeying the Law does not and cannot
save us. The Torah was not given to lead God's people to the Law but
rather to guide them *through* the Law to Yeshua. Salvation comes by
grace through faith in Yeshua alone. We are made right with God by our
faith in what He first did for us. Christians fulfill the requirements of the
Law by loving God and loving people.

21

Conclusion

So if the Son sets you free, you will be free indeed.

JOHN 8:36

C HRISTIANITY AND TORAHISM AGREE on one crucial issue: we accept the same Bible as authoritative Scripture. There is a common source of authority for our discussions. Thus, if corruption exists in the Christian church, it is not to be found in Scripture but rather in the doctrines of men. And when we compare what mainstream Christianity teaches today with the teachings found in Scripture, we find they are highly aligned.

Christian theology is not, as many Torah-keepers assert, grounded in the teachings, writings, or traditions of ancient Rome. You won't hear sermons praising Roman gods or Constantine from the pulpits of Christian churches. No, our theology is based on the teachings of Yeshua and the writings of the whole Christian Bible. The reason Christianity teaches the divinity of Jesus and the reality of the Trinity is not that some early church council said it was true. It is because Scripture says so. Christianity is a faith that is built on—and can be measured against—Scripture itself.

If Torahism wants to rail against the abuses of the Christian Church, I will join them. If they're going to call out Christian teachers whose greed or ignorance causes them to preach a false gospel, they have my full support. Yeshua Himself preached against such things.[1] I even agree with Torahism that in many cases, the modern Church has failed to acknowledge, teach, or perhaps even understand the depth of the

---

[1] See Yeshua's woes to the Pharisees in Matthew 23:1–39; Mark 12:35–40; and Luke 11:37–54, 20:45–47.

Hebraic roots of the faith. We can also agree with many of the historical claims made by Torahism.

Anti-Semitism has existed (and, sadly, still does) in some Christian circles. The Church has at times resorted to violence and oppression. And there are Christian teachers, even in our modern era, who misuse the Word of God in pursuit of fame, fortune, and power. These are abuses and errors that Christians can reject as unbiblical and un-Christlike, and hopefully learn from. At the same time, we recognize these failings do not justify Torahism's theological conclusions. There was ultimately no lasting anti-Jewish theological corruption introduced because of these shortcomings. On the whole, mainstream Christian theology today accords with what was handed down by Jesus and the apostles.

The reason Christians believe the Mosaic Law is no longer in effect is not that we would rather follow what our hearts tell us. And it is not because that is what the church fathers or Rome said. It is because that's what Scripture teaches. And this is where the issue of terminology becomes paramount. Christians are indeed under the authority of all Scripture, including the Torah. But when we examine the Bible as a whole, we find that, while God's Word and His promises are eternal, the Mosaic expression of the Law of God given to Israel was not.

The Law of Moses was holy and righteous and good (Rom 7:12). It served as the "national constitution" of Israel. Its laws were given to guide her from a rag-tag mass of former slaves into an organized and holy nation set apart for Yahweh. But they were a temporary guardian (tutor) intended only to last until Christ (Gal 3:24-25). Consider the significant changes to the Mosaic Law that are taught in the New Testament.

Under the Law of Moses	Under Jesus / New Covenant
Continual animal sacrifices were required to atone for sin (Ex 29:10-14, 35-37, 30:10; Lev 4:1-5:13; Num 6:10-14).	We learn that "it is impossible for the blood of bulls and goats to take away sins" (Heb 10:4), they were only a reminder of sin (10:3). Jesus, however, is our atoning sacrifice (1 John 2:1) "once for all" (Heb 10:10), thus "there is no longer any offering for sin" (10:12).

Under the Law of Moses	Under Jesus / New Covenant
All priests must come from the tribe of Levi (Ex 29:1-8; Deut 18:1-8; Num 18).	Jesus is now our High Priest (Heb 4:14-15), and he came from the tribe of Judah (Heb 7:14), *not* Levi. Further, "when there is a change in the priesthood, there is necessarily a change in the law as well" (Heb 7:12).
The "house of Jacob" and "people of Israel" (aka Jews) are God's chosen people, "a kingdom of priests and a holy nation" (Ex 19:1-6).	All believers in Jesus—whether Jew or Gentile—are "a chosen race, a royal priesthood, a holy nation, a people for his own possession" (1 Peter 2:9).
God's presence dwells among His people in the most holy place of the temple, behind a veil where only the high priest can enter once a year (Exodus 26, 30:10).	The moment Jesus died on the cross, God tore the temple veil, showing we now have direct access to Him (Matt 27:51; Mark 15:38). We, the body of Christ, are now God's temple (1 Cor 3:6:14-20; Eph 2:19-22; 1 Pet 2:5) "Do you not know that you are God's temple and that God's Spirit dwells in you?" (1 Cor 3:16).
Many foods were declared unclean for eating (Leviticus 11).	All food is now permitted (Acts 10:9-16, 15:1-29; Mark 7:1-23; Rom 14:1-15:13; 1 Cor 10:23-33). "Eat whatever is sold in the meat market without raising any question on the ground of conscience. For 'the earth is the Lord's, and the fullness thereof.'" (1 Cor 10:25-26)
Israel was required to circumcise all males at eight days old (Lev 12:3).	"Neither circumcision nor uncircumcision counts for anything, but only faith working through love" (Gal 5:6, 6:15, also see 1 Cor 7:19).
No new commands shall be added to or taken away from the Law of Moses (Deut 4:2, 12:32).	Jesus gave new Commands not found in the Torah (Matt 28:18-20; Mark 16:15; John 13:34, etc.). See chapter six for a deeper discussion.

Under the Law of Moses	Under Jesus / New Covenant
The Law of Moses required seven annual feasts and a weekly Sabbath (Lev 23).	"Therefore let no one pass judgment on you in questions of food and drink, or with regard to a festival or a new moon or a Sabbath. These are a shadow of the things to come, but the substance belongs to Christ." (Col 2:16-17)

Scripture teaches the fulfillment of the Law (Luke 24:44-48) and the end of the Mosaic Covenant (Heb 8:13) upon Yeshua's resurrection. We are no longer obligated to keep the Law of Moses as a legal system. We are free to keep the Mosaic customs as a matter of personal conviction or, in the case of Jewish believers, cultural identify. But they are not a condition of salvation or righteousness. And in the end, we must choose who we will follow. And we cannot follow both Moses and Jesus. The Bible does not give us that option.

A Slippery Slope

We can all admit that finding the right balance between law and grace can be tough. There are ditches on both sides of the road: sinful license on the left and legalism on the right. This is what Romans chapters 6-7 are all about. The mistake made by many Torah-keepers is that of legalism.

> What really is "legalism"? It is the belief that I can become holy and please God by obeying laws. It is measuring spirituality by a list of do's and don'ts. The weakness of legalism is that it sees *sins* (plural) but not *sin* (the root of the trouble). It judges by the outward and not the inward. Furthermore, the legalist fails to understand the real purpose of God's Law and the relationship between Law and grace.[2]

Torahism is a theology that fails to understand the biblical relationship between law and grace and the purpose of the law under the New Covenant. Cassidy notes:

---

[2] Warren W. Wiersbe, *The Bible Exposition Commentary*, vol. 1 (Victor Books, 1996), p. 534.

We have to deal with this choice between two paths of righteousness—one based on our performance and the other based on Christ's life and death. The choice could not be starker—for, as Paul has said, our only boast is the cross of Jesus Christ. In other words, these two potential paths are mutually exclusive. One cannot have righteousness through Christ and one's own performance as well. Jesus's work is perfect, and nothing can be added to it; indeed, the very notion of adding to what God has fully accomplished is not only absurd but offensive, for it is a denial of the sufficiency of what Jesus did on the cross. I can either have him as my savior or try to save myself.[3]

Wanting to explore the Hebrew roots of the Christian faith is a beautiful thing. It is why I study biblical Hebrew, history, archeology, and ancient Near East cultures. The more we understand the context of Jesus and the biblical writers, the more vivid and powerful God's story becomes to us. So I applaud the effort of Torah-keepers to lean into that.

But somewhere along the way, a line is crossed. At some point, Torahism begins to subtly emphasize Moses and deemphasize Jesus. Amazement at finding Christ in the Torah's rituals and feasts leads to a desire to participate in those rituals and feasts. And that desire—which on its own is not a bad thing—evolves into a belief that everyone should be doing so. Which leads to a prideful, legalistic attitude that looks down on Christians who don't keep Saturday Sabbath or eat kosher. Before long, verses in the New Testament that challenge this belief are minimized or dismissed altogether. In extreme cases, entire books or even writers are rejected. When followed to its logical conclusion, Torahism leads away from Christianity and into Judaism.[4]

There is no doubt that the Gospel is a Jewish story. And a proper appreciation for the Hebraic roots of the Christian faith comes from believing and accepting all that the Yeshua HaMashiach taught us about Himself, the purpose of the Torah, and God's reason for walking among us.

And the Word became flesh and dwelt among us, and we have seen his glory, glory as of the only Son from the Father, full of grace and truth . . . For from his fullness we have all received,

---

[3] David P. Cassidy, *Indispensable: The Basics of Christian Belief* (P&R Publishing, 2019), p. 83.
[4] In fact, I personally know of Christians who started with Hebrew Roots and ended up as Jewish converts who rejected Jesus.

grace upon grace. For the law was given through Moses; grace and truth came through Jesus Christ. No one has ever seen God; the only God, who is at the Father's side, he has made him known. (John 1:14, 16-18)

In Closing

In Part One we asked if Torah-keepers should be opposed as false teachers preaching a false Gospel or pulled aside like brothers wandering off the path. Because Torahism is not a monolithic belief system, the answer is often a little of both. There is a diversity of thought on the role the Law ought to play in the life of a Christian, and I believe there is room for honest disagreement.

The Gospel is about repenting of our sin and acknowledging that faith in Christ is the only way to salvation. Torahists who affirm this biblical position can be considered brothers and sisters in Christ. Those who teach anything else are preaching a false Gospel. As Paul warned us, "If anyone is preaching to you a gospel contrary to the one you received, let him be accursed" (Gal 1:9).

We know that a person is not justified by works of the law but through faith in Jesus Christ, so we also have believed in Christ Jesus, in order to be justified by faith in Christ and not by works of the law, because by works of the law no one will be justified. (Galatians 2:16)

When Torahism focuses on how our faith should be lived out, rather than how we are justified or saved, it is a matter between brothers and sisters of the faith. It's a family disagreement on par with disputes about infant baptism versus believers' baptism, or dispensationalism versus covenant theology. These are not unimportant issues. But they are secondary in the sense that there is room for disagreement among believers.

But when Torah-keepers veer off course and begin teaching that keeping the Law makes us even just a tad more righteous, or emphasizing Moses over Christ, they have entered treacherous waters. The line between heresy and a family dispute can quickly get blurry on this issue. This is dangerous ground to travel. Many well-meaning Torah-keepers with genuine faith in Christ have inadvertently crossed into heresy without realizing it.

Any teaching that Christian are required to keep the Law of Moses is unbiblical, so our disagreements are real and important. At the same time, there is much we can learn from our Torahist friends when it comes to appreciating the Jewish roots of our faith and taking Scripture seriously. The typical Torah-keeper is someone who loves God and wants to worship Him in truth. They are just caught up in false teachings. We need to pray for them and interact with them in love. Scripture admonishes us to defend Christian truth claims with gentleness and respect (1 Pet 3:15). As the apostle Paul taught, we should be speaking the truth in love (Eph 4:15) with words full of grace, seasoned with salt (Col 4:6). In an increasingly fractured culture, Christians should be known for showing love and grace to those we disagree with.

It bears repeating: our fight is not with people but with ideas.

Soli Deo Gloria

Name & Subject Index

Glossary Of Hebrew Words & Phrases

Bikkurim	Feast of First Fruits
B'rit Chadashah	New Testament
HaMashiach Yeshua	Jesus the Messiah
Ketuvim	The name of the third section of the Tanakh. The word means "Writings."
Kohanim	Levitical priests
La'Goyim	A Hebrew phrase that means "Light to the Nations."
Lashon shel ze'hurit	Red fabric
Mashiach	Messiah. The word means "anointed one."
Matza	Feast of Unleavened Bread
Mishnah	An authoritative collection of written material embodying the oral tradition of Jewish law and forming the first part of the Talmud. The word literally means "repetition."
Mitzvot	Commandments
Moshe	Moses
Nevi'im	The name of the second section of the Tanakh. The word means "Prophets."
Olam ('olam)	A long duration, antiquity, futurity, forever, perpetual, old, ancient, or world.
Ovlam berit	Perpetual or long-lasting covenant
Pesach	Passover
Rabbi	A Jewish scholar or teacher, especially one who studies or teaches Jewish law.
Rosh Hashanah	Feast of Trumpets; Jewish New Year
Shabbat	Sabbath. The word means both "rest" and the number seven.
Shalom	Peace
Shavuot	Feast of Weeks; Pentecost
Sukkot	Feast of Tabernacles
Talmud	The body of Jewish civil and ceremonial law and legend comprising the Mishnah and the Gemara. The word literally means "learning" or "instruction."
Tanakh	The Hebrew Bible, what Christians call the Old Testament. The word "Tanakh" is an acronym of the first Hebrew letter of each of the Hebrew Bible's three traditional subdivisions: "Ta" for

Torah ("Teaching," also known as the Five Books of Moses), "Na" for Nevi'im (Prophets) and "Kh" for Ketuvim (Writings). It is sometimes written: TaNaKh.

Tisha B'Av An annual fast day in Judaism on which a number of disasters in Jewish history occurred, primarily the destruction of both Solomon's Temple by the Neo-Babylonian Empire and the Second Temple by the Roman Empire in Jerusalem.

Torah The first five books of the Bible: Genesis, Exodus, Leviticus, Numbers and Deuteronomy. Also called the Pentateuch. The Hebrew word literally means "teaching, doctrine, or instruction."

Tu Bishvat A Jewish holiday occurring on the 15th day of the Hebrew month of Shevat. It is also called "Rosh HaShanah La'Ilanot," literally "New Year of the Trees."

Yeshua Jesus

Yeshua haNotzri Jesus of Nazareth

YHWH God. Pronounced Yahweh, Yehovah, or Jehovah. It is the name for God as revealed to Moses as four Hebrew consonants (YHWH) called the tetragrammaton.

Yom Kippur Day of Atonement, a Jewish feast.

From the Author

Thank you for taking the time to read this book! I appreciate your interest in this fascinating topic and I pray something here helped you. If you have questions, thoughts, or feedback I'd love to hear from you. You can reach me on social media or email me directly at rls@rlsolberg.com. I try my best to respond to all correspondence.

Also, if you enjoyed the book, I'd like to ask a quick favor of you. Would you consider submitting a review on Amazon.com? It would mean a lot to me personally, as well as help to spread the truth about heresies like Torahism. Thank you!

Grace & Peace,

R. L. Solberg
RLSolberg.com
Defending the Biblical Roots of Christianity (YouTube)

About the Author

R. L. Solberg is an author, professor, apologist, and theologian based in Nashville, TN, where he lives with his wife of 30 years, Debra. They are stakeholders at the Church of the City, Spring Hill, and have two spectacular daughters, Sami and Maggie, who are out making their mark on the world.

Solberg is a leading Christian apologist concerning *Torahism* (aka Hebrew Roots, Torah-observant Christianity, Pronomianism). He has pursued theology, apologetics, and philosophy formally and informally for more than two decades. He studied at Southern Baptist Theological Seminary and has a Master's Degree in Theological Studies from Williamson College, where he is now an adjunct professor of theology. He also studied Biblical Hebrew at the Hebrew University of Jerusalem. Solberg strives to communicate on complex topics with clarity and grace, bringing a creative perspective to the conversation.

Printed in Great Britain
by Amazon

ac5ea1bc-ae96-446d-9761-b449bbb178f3R01